Mr & Mrs Smith
Hotel Collection

France

A DEUX

The French take serious pride in their style, their sophistication and their expertise on everything from lingerie to gastronomy. Now it's our turn. It is with the greatest pleasure that we unveil our Gallic *invitation au voyage* for Monsieur and Madame Smiths everywhere.

After months of research into France's coastal escapes and country hideaways, we bring you this collection of cool châteaux, contemporary city classics and cosy restaurants with rooms. And you'll find dozens more of our recommended French boutique hotels and haute maisons d'hôte at www.mrandmrssmith.com.

As well as reviews of our favourite hotels and guesthouses in France – from Brittany to Provence and all the prettiest bits in between – you'll find concise Mr & Mrs Smith guides to each of the 12 destinations covered. They offer up-to-date restaurant recommendations, advice on when to visit, where to go and what to pack, as well as insider tips on everything from gourmet delis to festivals and wineries. We'll even enlighten you on the meandering urban art of flânerie.

To glean the nitty-gritty on the best boutique boltholes, we dispatched 31 super-sharp reviewers from either side of the Channel, who visited anonymously and reported back. Experts on fashion (Valérie Abecassis), design (Ilse Crawford), restaurants (Mourad Mazouz, Anthony Demetre) and scent (Linda Pilkington) share their tales, alongside travel writers English and French, every one of them style-savvy and dedicated to footloose Francophilia.

Activate the BlackSmith membership card, which you'll find over the page, and benefit from lovely extra touches when you stay at the hotels, such as a champagne breakfast or a spa treatment on the house. That's not to mention the many fantastic offers on worldwide hotels that Mr & Mrs Smith members are treated to every month – which we hope gives this guidebook an added little *je ne sais quoi*.

Best wishes and, as said in our best French accent, bon voyage!

Smith
Mr & Mrs Smith

(take)

advantage of us

This is your own personal BlackSmith card, which entitles you to six months' free membership. The moment you register it at www.mrandmrssmith.com, you can access the members' area of our website, take advantage of exclusive last-minute offers from our hotels, and get money back on every booking. The card also provides members-only privileges – such as free bottles of champagne on arrival, spa treats, late check-out and more – when you book hotels and self-catering properties through us. Look out for the  icon at the end of each hotel review.

REGISTER NOW

To start getting money back every time you book, hotel offers and exclusive travel benefits, activate your BlackSmith card by registering online at www.mrandmrssmith.com/register-card or by ringing one of the numbers below (it only takes a minute).

ROOM SERVICE

Activate your membership today, and you will also receive our fantastic monthly newsletter *Room Service*. It's packed with news, travel tips, even more offers, and great competitions. We promise not to bombard you with communications, or pass on your details to third parties – this is strictly between you and us.

VAULT VALUE

Depending on your membership level, Mr & Mrs Smith credits up to five per cent of your bookings to a special member's account, which we call the Vault.

AND THERE'S MORE?

If all this isn't enough, you can even get access to VIP airport lounges, automatic room upgrades, flight and car-hire offers, and your own dedicated travel consultant, simply by upgrading your membership to SilverSmith or GoldSmith. Visit www.mrandmrssmith.com for more details.

ON CALL

Thanks to our global Travel Team, Mr & Mrs Smith operates a 24-hour travel service five days a week. Ring any of the numbers below to activate your membership today, and start planning your first Smith adventure.

From the UK, ring 0845 034 0700

From France, ring 0800 906 583

From the US and Canada, call toll-free 1 866 610 3867

From Australia, call 1300 896627

From New Zealand, call 0800 896671

From anywhere in Asia, ring +61 3 8648 8871*

From elsewhere in the world, ring +44 20 8987 4312

* Also check www.mrandmrssmith.com/contact for new free or local call numbers from territories in Asia.

Small print: all offers are dependent on availability and subject to change.

(contents)

Lille

Nord-Pas-de-Calais

Picardy

Rouen

Normandy

Brittany

Rennes

14 16

15   Paris

18 17

Ile-de-France

Reims

Champagne-Ardenne

Lorraine

Strasbourg

Alsace

Pays-de-la-Loire

Nantes

Centre

Burgundy

Bourges

Dijon

Franche-Comté

Poitiers

Poitou-Charentes

20 19

Limousin

Auvergne

28

Lyon

29

27

Rhône-Alpes

Bordeaux

Aquitaine

Midi-Pyrénées

12

23

Provence

Toulouse

10 9   11

24

22

21

7

25

5

8   6

Nice

26

Montpellier

Languedoc-Roussillon

Marseille

31 30

4

2

13

3

1

(at a glance)

BOUTIQUE BED & BREAKFAST

Bastide Saint Mathieu	70
Baudon de Mauny	102
Château de la Couronne	186
Jardins Secrets	120
Hôtel Récamier	166
Le Lodge Kerisper	28
Le Logis de Puygâty	192
La Maison sur la Sorgue	224
Moulin Renaudiots	42
Les Rosées	88

WINE COUNTRY

Château de Bagnols	256
Domaine de Verchant	114
Hôtel Crillon le Brave	218
Moulin Renaudiots	42

GRAND GASTRONOMY

La Bastide de Moustiers	206
Cap d'Antibes Beach Hotel	76
Château de Bagnols	256
Château de Saint Paterne	134
Le Couvent des Minimes Hôtel & Spa	212
Domaine de Verchant	114
La Villa Gallici	236

KIDS WELCOME

Alpaga	250
Château de la Couronne	186
Château de Saint Paterne	134
Le Lodge Kerisper	28

SUPER SPA

Alpaga	250
Cap Estel	82
Cap d'Antibes Beach Hotel	76
Le Couvent d'Hérépian	108
Le Couvent des Minimes Hôtel & Spa	212
Domaine de Verchant	114
Jardins Secrets	120

DESIGN-CONSCIOUS COOL

Arguibel	16
Cap d'Antibes Beach Hotel	76
Château de la Couronne	186
Hôtel Récamier	166
Moulin Renaudiots	42
La Réserve Paris	172

CITY SLICKERS

Baudon de Mauny	102
Hôtel Daniel	148
Hotel Keppler	154
Hôtel Particulier Montmartre	160
Hôtel Récamier	166
Jardins Secrets	120
La Réserve Paris	172

BEACH IN REACH

Arguibel	16
Bastide Saint Mathieu	70
Cap d'Antibes Beach Hotel	76
Cap Estel	82
Hotel Pastis	276
Le Lodge Kerisper	28
La Réserve Ramatuelle	282
Les Rosées	88

GREAT OUTDOORS

Alpaga	250
La Bastide de Moustiers	206
Bastide Saint Mathieu	70
Château de Bagnols	256
Château de la Couronne	186
Chez Odette	56
Le Couvent d'Hérépian	108
Le Couvent des Minimes Hôtel & Spa	212
Hôtel Crillon le Brave	218
Le Logis de Puygâty	192
Le Mas de la Rose	230
Les Servages d'Armelle	262

NATURAL FOR NUPTIALS

La Bastide de Moustiers	206
Bastide Saint Mathieu	70
Cap Estel	82
Château de Bagnols	256
Château de la Couronne	186
Château de Saint Paterne	134
Chez Odette	56
Domaine de Verchant	114
Hôtel Crillon le Brave	218
Le Lodge Kerisper	28
Le Logis de Puygâty	192
Le Mas de la Rose	230
La Réserve Ramatuelle	282
Les Servages d'Armelle	262
La Villa Gallici	236

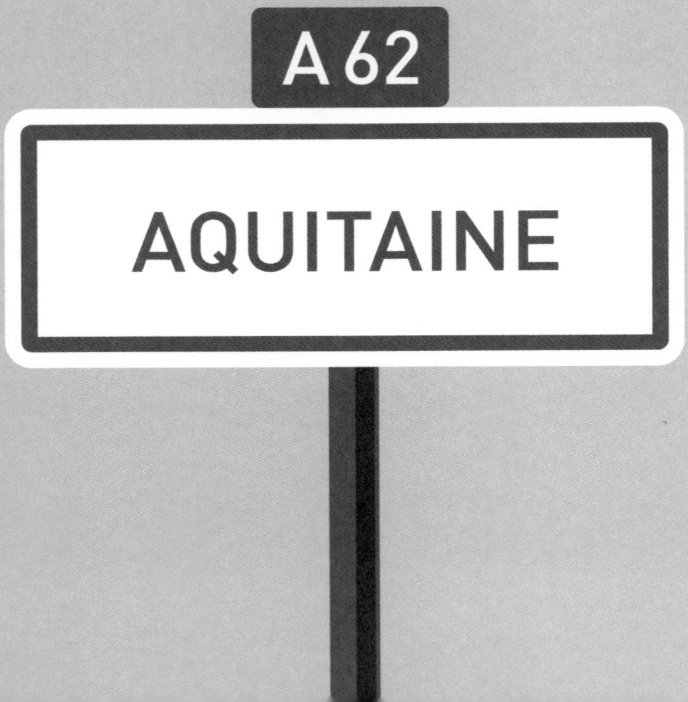
A 62
AQUITAINE

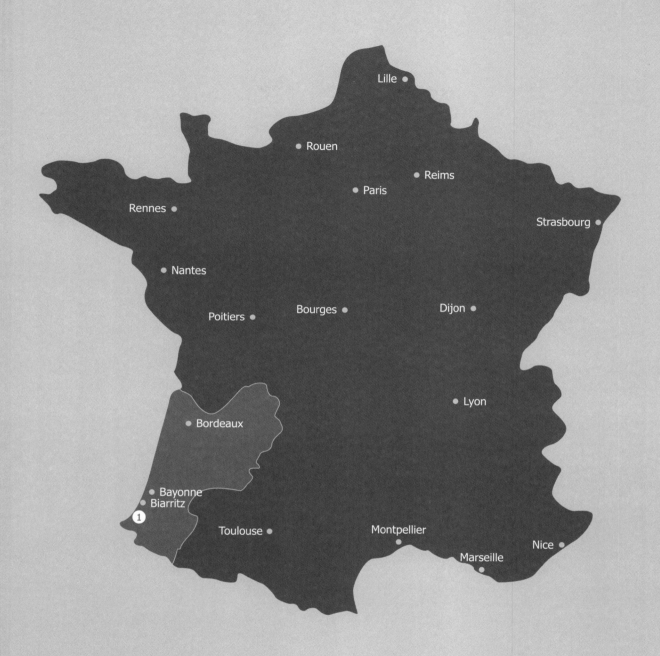

AQUITAINE

1 Arguibel

AQUITAINE

COASTLINE Atlantic shores, Pyrénées peaks
COAST LIFE Basque flavours, surf bathers

Aquitaine is a pea-green pocket of land between the mountains and the coast, with Biarritz and Saint-Jean-de-Luz its seaside jewels. The French-Spanish border means little to locals, who are Basque to the bone, and fly the flag far and wide. You'll see distinctive houses, locals playing *pelote*, sometimes sporting Basque berets, and road signs in Euskara – a language featuring more Xs than a top-shelf title. For cultural contrast, Aquitaine also has a bohemian bent, attracting artists and surfers by the camper-van-load. Getting around is easy, the pace of life easier still. And a cuisine that takes French flavours and applies a tapas twist can only be a recipe for fantastic food.

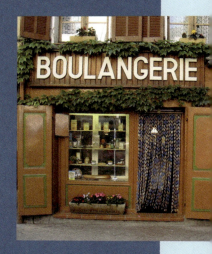

GETTING THERE

Planes EasyJet (www.easyjet.com) and Ryanair (www.ryanair.com) fly from London (Stansted or Gatwick) to Biarritz.
Trains From Gare Montparnasse in Paris, direct trains to Biarritz take just over five hours (www.seat61.com). Once you're down there, there are rail services across the border between Biarritz and San Sebastián via Irun (www.tgv.com).
Automobiles Choose from five car-hire desks at Biarritz Airport, including Hertz (www.hertz.com) and Avis (www.avis.com). It's an easy area to drive around; the E70 coast road caters for most needs. Inland routes around Ahetze can be more twisty-turny, and Guéthary and Bidart are hilly.

LOCAL KNOWLEDGE

Taxis In Biarritz and other biggish towns, there are taxi stands. Out in the sticks, you're best off booking ahead. Around Biarritz, try Atlantic (+33 (0)5 59 03 18 18). Agur (+33 (0)5 59 47 38 38) is good for Saint-Jean-de-Luz.
Siesta and fiesta The Basque siesta is alive and well (but a bit sleepy between 1pm and 5pm). Restaurants run pretty strict lunch and dinner services, so you're unlikely to get served after 2pm or before 6pm. In bigger towns, most shops stay open until 8pm or 9pm. In smaller towns, especially in low season, restaurants often close on Mondays, and shops observe a day of rest on Sundays.
Do go/don't go The landscape doesn't go green on its own: Atlantic fronts bring wind and drizzle throughout the year. July and August are driest, hottest and busiest, so aim for May, June or September – but still make sure you pack a waterproof.
Packing tips Stash your surfboard if you plan to ride the waves, or broken-in hiking boots if you want to yomp the Pyrénées.
Children The Basque people adore children, so they'll guarantee you attention in restaurants, for one thing. Biarritz's Musée de la Mer does everything an aquatic museum should (www.museedelamer.com).
Recommended reads Paddy Woodworth's *The Basque Country: A Cultural History* and *The Basque History of the World* by Mark Kurlansky are essential tomes for amateur anthropologists. Gastronomes should pick up a copy of Kurlansky's companion volume *Cod: A Biography of the Fish That Changed the World*, which, as well as explaining how the Basques discovered America, is also the most entertaining fish book ever.
Local specialities The Atlantic coast means abundant fresh fish and seafood. Try bacalao (salt cod), chipirons (baby squid), and kokotxas (hake throats – a delicacy).

Other regional treats include slightly sparkling txakoli wine, and sagardo, aka Basque cider. Strings of dried red peppers, or piments d'Espelette, are the Basque answer to bunting, and sold as souvenirs.

And... Thalassotherapy, a range of seawater-based body treatments, is widely offered in Pays Basque spas. In Saint-Jean-de-Luz, we recommend the spa at the Helianthal Hotel (www.helianthal.fr).

WORTH GETTING OUT OF BED FOR

Viewpoint On a clear day, take the cog railway from the Col Saint-Ignace to the top of La Rhune (www.rhune.com) for spectacular Pyrenees panoramas. In Biarritz, across from Place Sainte-Eugénie, take the steps to the lookout point for great views of the port.

Arts and culture The city of Bayonne brought chocolate to France, using cocoa beans swiped from the Americas by Columbus. Biarritz's Musée du Chocolat gives you the full story, as well as tasting opportunities (www.planetemuseeduchocolat.com). Traditionally woven to protect cattle from the sun, colourful and stripy Basque fabrics are renowned. The Jean-Vier Basque Eco-Museum in Saint-Jean-de-Luz takes you on a tour of textile traditions, with digressions into Basque culinary and festival heritage (www.jean-vier.com). Biarritz's Musée de la Mer does everything a seaside aquarium should, with added exhibits on Basque ocean-going history (www.museedelamer.com).

Activities Make the most of the Atlantic coast: commune with the waves at Guéthary (+33 (0)6 08 68 88 54) and Saint-Jean-de-Luz (www.ecoledesurfstjeandeluz.com, www.bakunsurf.net), or go scuba diving in Hendaye with Planet Océan (www.planetocean.fr). Based near Saint-Jean-de-Luz, Aqua Balade operates canoeing trips around the region's rivers (+33 (0)6 62 58 09 97; www.aquabalade.com). Aquitaine has around 50 golf courses, many of which are coastal enough to have sea views. The Basque sentier du littoral comprises 25km of signposted paths and lanes along the coast; pick up a map from any tourist office.

Best beach Saint-Jean-de-Luz's bay is an arc of bronze sand, more sheltered than Biarritz, and lined with Belle Epoque buildings that are all faded grandeur. Bidart and Guéthary pride themselves on their wide, flat beaches – ideal for surfing or sunset strolls, but not for swimming.

Daytripper San Sebastián is less than an hour away across the border. Head to the old town for cobbled lanes, countless pastelerías and pintxo bars (A Fuego Negro, at Callea 31 De Agosto, even does pintxo puds). Brave the steep ascent to the town's history museum at La Mota Castle on Mount Urgull (+34 (0)9 43 42 84 17), and enjoy a post-prandial stroll along the sweep of La Concha beach.

Shopping Aquitaine isn't about to creep up on Milan in fashion terms, though there is a smattering of boutiques and surfwear shops in Biarritz and Saint-Jean-de-Luz. Rue Mazagran is Biarritz's Oxford Street: try Boo (+33 (0)5 59 24 61 21) for silver jewellery, and Euskal Linge (+33 (0)5 59 24 76 61) or Helena (+33 (0)5 59 24 06 23) for Basque linen. Côté Lorio (+33 (0)5 59 26 78 38) on Boulevard Thiers in Saint-Jean-de-Luz is an enchanting interiors store, and you can load up on macaroons at Maison Adam on Place Louis XIV (+33 (0)5 59 26 03 54). In Guéthary, Poterie Guéthary at 49 Avenue Harispe (+33 (0)5 59 26 57 14) sells locally made ceramics. There are food markets at Les Halles in Biarritz, Monday to Saturday; the biggest market day in Saint-Jean-de-Luz market is Friday.

Something for nothing Stroll the harbour at Hondarribia, a pretty port on the Spanish side of the River Bidasoa (French Hendaye lies across the water). Three streets back from the harbour, Kalea San Pedro is the hub of Hondarribia's pintxo bars and restaurants.

Don't go home without... a txapela. The classic black wool beret may have strong French associations, but Basque peasants wore 'em first.

ABSOLUTELY AQUITAINE

In most Basque towns you'll find a *frontón*, a paved, walled area dedicated to the region's favourite sport: *pelote*. Played using a woollen ball, and either hands or a scooping wicker racket, the game is distantly related to squash and real tennis and, though its tenure as an Olympic sport ended in 1900, it's still played passionately throughout the Basque Country, in seemingly endless variants. For a chance of catching a match, either check the schedules at www.euskalpilota.com, or look for a man with a swollen hand and follow him to his next game.

DIARY

January Gastro societies gather in San Sebastián to mark the feast of the city's saint, Donostia, with percussion-accompanied parades. May Hendaye hosts a theatre festival, Mai du Théâtre, with a programme of drama from professional, amateur and children's troupes. June Fête de Saint Jean is Saint-Jean-de-Luz's summer-solstice celebration, when locals process in Basque costume, and there's dancing, music and bonfires by the sea. Bidart hosts a two-day music festival, with seaside gigs at Ilbarritz beach to entertain the surf crowd. July The Fête de Thon in Saint-Jean-de-Luz celebrates the mighty tunny fish. Mid-month, Biarritz attracts bods with boards to its annual surf festival. Bayonne hosts the crowd-pulling Fêtes de Bayonne, culminating in a triumph of *sons et lumières*. July–August On a handful of *Nuits de Feux* during the month, fireworks light up the Grande Plage at Biarritz. August During the second week of the month, the residents of Hendaye and Hondarribia join forces for the Fête Basque. Processions, floats and craft fairs mark the occasion. September Biarritz's festival of dance features Basque, flamenco, ballet and contemporary performances, over 10 days in the middle of the month.

Guéthary

Arguibel

STYLE Daring design kaleidoscope
SETTING Between Pyrénées and sea

'The exterior is in keeping with Basque tradition; inside, it's a rainbow gallery of modern design, with a teal-painted lounge at its heart'

A tanned choux bun of a buttock is peeping above a balcony rail, as a damp Enrique Iglesias-alike surfer peels off his wetsuit on the apartment terrace above a Guéthary street. Mr Smith and I haven't even made it to the beach yet but, as views go, it's an encouraging start.

Guéthary, between Saint-Jean-de-Luz and Biarritz on the Atlantic coast, is a hilly village sloping down to the waves, its quiet streets lined with the typical timbered white and red Basque houses that you see throughout the region. One such property is Arguibel, our maroon and white home for the weekend, which looks as though it's just stepped off an Austrian Alp. On the inland side of the village, towards Ahetze, this boutique B&B is separated from Guéthary-on-sea by the main north-south road.

We are greeted by François, a wiry, square-spectacled man with a quiet charm, who co-owns the property with his wife, Mariannick. On closer inspection, Arguibel turns out to be a newbuild, its exterior in keeping with Basque tradition, its setting a carpet of sloping lawn that tapers towards pea-green pastures beyond.

Inside is revealed a rainbow gallery of modern design, with a big teal-painted lounge at its heart. Bokja chairs covered in a kaleidoscopic patchwork of vintage fabrics catch my eye, as do Frida Kahlo-esque collages and sparkly, palette-exhausting paintings by Wilma, a British-born artist who lives in Guéthary.

Arguibel's five rooms, peeling off the lounge and first-floor landing, are flamboyantly themed creations, each a tribute to a character with local ties. Mr Smith's first choice had been the Charlie Chaplin room, an homage in masculine monochrome to the Hollywood star, who holidayed in Guéthary. But Mr Smith didn't make the booking. And I preferred the sound of feathery lamps and currant-coloured silk headboards in chocolate-lime L'Infante on the ground floor, named for the Spanish princess who met Louis XV in the Basque country.

Mr Smith plays cursory attention to the decor, so it's left to me to coo over the details. Light switches. Upholstered switches, no less, in the same praline and gooseberry swirly fabric as the curtains — a real pedant-pleaser. I can tell by the way Mr Smith huffs and puffs around the iPod dock, assuming the manly role of DJ, that he's feeling a tad emasculated by our feminine, frou-frou surrounds. But, as François arrives with glasses of champagne and peanuts for us to enjoy on our private terrace, Mr Smith is soon soothed into holiday mode.

'There's a farm... I found it online... I think it's away from the coast?' These are Mr Smith's vague, stilted clues to François about where we'd thought of heading for dinner. 'La Ferme Ostalapia,' deciphers François, without a flicker of confusion. With equal ease, he secures us 'the last table for tonight' ('I bet he says that to everyone,' speculates Mr Smith ungratefully). The smiley waitress, all confidence and twinkly eyes, brings a mini Kilner jar of rillettes de porc and some baguette toasts with the menus. We're in the white-timbered annexe of the rustic restaurant, packed out with animated locals enjoying Saturday night out. Mr Smith orders cochon de lait rôti — a slab of roast piglet served with moreish frîtes de maison. I work my way through Rossini de canard, served with a tower of ceps and garlicky sauté potatoes. We somehow find room for an almondy, coulis-drizzled tarte aux abricots.

The next morning, from my prone position, I lie looking at the hills — not the green bucolic ones visible through

the arched French doors, but my and Mr Smith's bulging bellies. Not that this holds us back at breakfast. A trolley is wheeled to our table, bearing a choice of steaming, syrupy coffee or loose-leaf tea, brewed in Asian-style clay pots, as well as a basket of pastries and just-baked baguettes, sheep's milk yoghurt, fresh tangerines, apples and redcurrants.

We decide to tour the inland villages by car, through Ahetze to Saint-Pée-sur-Nivelle, where a scan of the main drag delivers the three Bs of the Basque village: bar, bakery, boules. We drive on. Ainhoa, at the top of the Col de Pinodieta, is an emotional and literal high point, the village centred around a high street of shuttered stone houses and cobbled parking bays. We live the French café cliché, sipping grands crèmes and scribbling postcards, only sorry the epicerie opposite isn't open to sell us a string of dried red peppers, as emblematic of Basque identity as the berets and chalets.

The return of the sun lures us to Biarritz the next day, where good weather, bracing beach views and tempting shops are in plentiful supply. Mr Smith is in patient form, only occasionally muttering 'Ryanair' under his breath as I bulk out the luggage allowance with local linens and nuggets of Basque silver jewellery. An evening flight means we have time to catch the sunset at Bidart, Guéthary's beachy neighbour. It's like walking onto the set of *Point Break*, only with fewer masked bank robbers. Surfers dot the sea like croutons in soup, rollers flop onto the raffia-coloured shore, and the amber sun is as big as a boule as it drops over the horizon. Not that it's easy to keep focusing out to sea. Left and right, we are flanked by rippling surfer bods, performing feats of modesty with small towels or zipping up neoprene shorties. As with the light switches, it's left to me to admire the detail. Now, where did my Enrique-alike get to...

Reviewed by Kate Pettifer

NEED TO KNOW
Rooms Five, including two suites.
Rates €110–€270, including tax. Breakfast, €15.
Check-out 12 noon, or later when possible. Earliest check-in, 11am.
Facilities Garden, free WiFi throughout, book, CD and DVD libraries. Flatscreen TV, DVD/CD in the lounge, iPods in lounge and bar. In room: iPod docks, Anne Sémonin products, minibar, bottled water. TV on request.
Children All ages welcome. Cots are free, extra beds €25.
Also The hotel can arrange a taxi from Biarritz train station or airport.

IN THE KNOW
Our favourite rooms Suite Paul-Jean Toulet is a turquoise tour-de-force, with sleek high-design details in bedroom, sitting room and bathroom. Two sets of French doors open onto a balcony with a dining table for four. Of the rooms, No 30 Charlie Chaplin is the biggest, but No 63 Betry Daguerre wins our hearts with its angel-white decor, driftwood bedstead and pebble-shaped pouffe.
Hotel bar Cone chairs and low Verner Panton tables furnish the old-meets-new bar, which has a 1930s-style polished wooden counter and serves fruit juices, wine and champagne, 9am–1pm and 5pm–10pm. At other times, a help-yourself honesty bar operates.
Hotel restaurant No restaurant. Breakfast – taken in the turquoise salon or on the deck – is a French farmers' market in microcosm: fresh fruit, little pots of yoghurt, just-baked brioche, bread and pastries, and wonderful coffee.
Top table On sunny days, the deck – with views over the sloping lawn beyond – is hard to beat.
Room service There isn't any, but you can ask the hotel about takeaway options, which vary according to season.
Dress code Look as though your surfboard's just out back by donning Hawaiian-inspired prints.
Local knowledge If it's the surf you've come for, book into the Quiksilver Surf School in Bidart (+33 (0)5 59 54 78 81; www.ecoledesurf-quiksilver.com).

LOCAL EATING AND DRINKING
Don't be fooled by the name: Le Madrid on Place PJ Toulet in Guéthary serves traditional French fare and has a roomy terrace (+33 (0)5 59 26 52 12; www.lemadrid.com). Michelin-starred Les Frères Ibarboure on Chemin de Ttaliena in Bidart (+33 (0)5 59 54 81 64; www.freresibarboure.com) serves dishes such as lamb sweetbreads and Madeira-laced foie gras in an 18th-century dining room. Try the cod à l'espagnol or veal stew with peppers at La Ferme Ostalapia on Chemin d'Ostalapia in Ahetze (+33 (0)5 59 54 73 79; www.ostalapia.fr), where the terrace has mesmerising mountain views. Bar Basque enjoys a corner spot on Place PJ Toulet, flanked with a pair of terraces (+33 (0)5 59 26 55 00). Bag a deckchair on the grass at Cenitz Ostatua on the Plage de Cenitz in Guéthary for seaside aperitifs (+33 (0)5 59 26 59 16; www.cenitz.fr).

GET A ROOM!
For more information, or to book this hotel, go to www.mrandmrssmith.com. Register your Smith membership card (see pages 4–5) to enjoy exclusive offers and privileges.

 SMITH MEMBER OFFER A drink on the house (wine or champagne); a pass each (worth €30) to the Loreamar Thalasso Spa at Grand Hôtel Saint-Jean-de-Luz; and tickets for the Basque Eco-Museum in Saint-Jean-de-Luz.

Arguibel 1146 chemin de Laharraga, 64210 Guéthary (+33 (0)5 59 41 90 46; www.arguibel.fr)

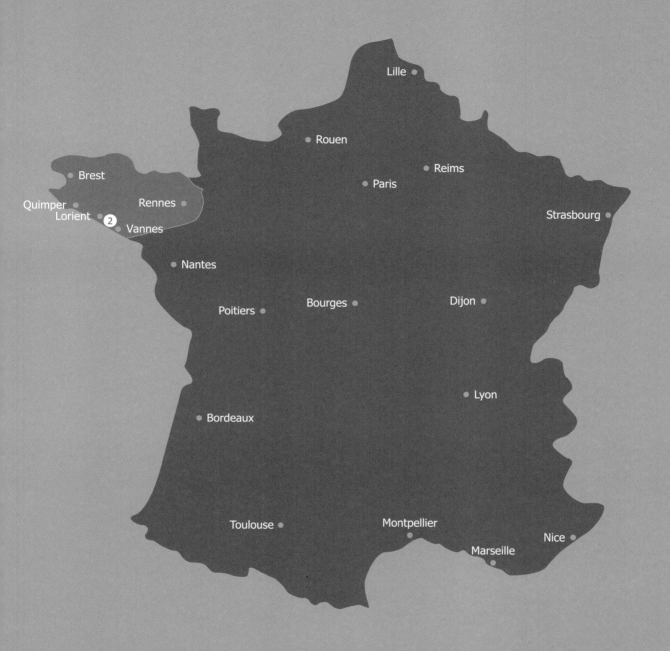

BRITTANY

2 Le Lodge Kerisper

BRITTANY

COASTLINE Craggy cliffs and crêperies
COAST LIFE Naval gazing

Rugged, weatherbeaten, Celtic-tinged Brittany is Cornwall's French twin, and matches its happy-holidays appeal in buckets and spades. This is a place for good old-fashioned fresh air, food and fun, where life is raw-edged and laid-back, with little pretension or polish. Crêpes and cider are rustic specialities; and coastal Brittany is a major European oyster producer, with Cancale and Belon among top spots for magical molluscs. Clifftop villages look out over the Atlantic, whose shorelines are beloved of surfers and seafarers, and dotted with relics, such as the standing stones at Carnac. But it's not all salty sea air: inland from the wonderful beaches, islets and fishing villages are mediaeval castles, mystical lakes and myth-filled forests.

GETTING THERE

Planes Air France (www.airfrance.com) flies from Paris Orly to Lorient and Brest. Ryanair (www.ryanair.com) will convey you to Brittany (Nantes, Brest and Dinard) from Leeds and London airports.
Trains Take the Eurostar (www.eurostar.com) to Paris, then connect to Vannes, Lorient, Quimper or Brest; for Rennes, connect at Lille.
Boats The Breton ports of Saint-Malo and Roscoff are linked to Portsmouth and Plymouth, courtesy of Brittany Ferries (www.brittanyferries.com).
Automobiles There's a lot of territory to cover, so pick up a hire car from one of Europcar's regional outposts, including airports and ports (www.europcar.com), or roll yours onto a ferry.

LOCAL KNOWLEDGE

Taxis You can't flag down taxis, so make sure to book in advance.
Siesta and fiesta Opening hours in seasonal destinations can be erratic; it's best to check ahead so you're not disappointed. Shops usually close for lunch between 12 noon and 2pm.
Do go/don't go Brittany is in full swing between April and October; in winter, many shops, restaurants and cafés will be closed. Give August a miss if you want to skip the hordes – it's prime holidaymaker time.
Packing tips Leave glamorous garments at home. This windy land demands laid-back, lived-in chic. Deck shoes and stripy tops are suitably nautical.
Children In the Gulf of Morbihan, sailing schools will give lessons lasting as long as you choose. Watch 'em wrestle with the sails at Cataschool (www.cataschool.com).
Recommended reads *The Oysters of Locmariaquer* by Eleanor Clark; *Sex, Death and Oysters: A Half-Shell Lover's World Tour* by Robb Walsh.
Local specialities Brittany is the home of the crêpe, which comes filled with all things sweet and savoury. Galettes, the savoury version, are made with buckwheat flour. But seafood is what really brings gastronomes to Brittany: Cancale for oysters, Erquy for scallops, and everywhere in between for fabulous fruits de mer. The sea here even makes a special kind of salt, fleur de sel de Guérande, harvested by hand. The homely meat-and-veg dumpling dish called kig ha farz, also made with buckwheat flour, may be harder to come by, so be sure to order it if you find it. Cakes include le far Breton, often made with prunes, and sugary, buttery kouign amann. Like neighbouring Normandy, Brittany produces cider, served here in dainty ceramic teacups. Or try lambig, a fire-starting spirit that tastes of apples.

And... Brittany's oysters might be its breadwinners, but that fine rustic cuisine likes a bit of butter, too: *doux* is sweet, *demi-sel* is slightly salty; you can even get a green-speckled seaweed variety.

WORTH GETTING OUT OF BED FOR

Viewpoints Head out to the pretty peninsula near the village of Belz and you'll be able to see Saint-Cado, a tiny island scattered with a handful of houses. You can get there via a bridge, but the view is lovelier from the mainland, from which you can see its star turn, a 12th-century chapel.

Arts and culture Quimper is Brittany's history hub. Head there to admire the architecture of the Gothic cathedral, granite bishop's palace and 16th-century mansions, and the old town's cobbled streets and timbered houses. Seaside Carnac has a prehistoric landscape of huge menhirs and ancient burial places. The mediaeval walled town of Concarneau has been attracting artists since the 19th century; follow La Route des Peintres en Cornouaille, an art trail through the southwest quarter. Nearby, Pont Aven is where Paul Gauguin set up his studio. In ducal Vannes, there are museums of fine art and archaeology (La Cohue and Château Gaillard), and the city hosts regular artistic events. Fougères has a literary haunt or two, thanks to eminent former residents Victor Hugo and Gustave Flaubert. The town is packed with ancient structures, including the oldest belfry in Brittany and a mighty example of military defence (the Château de Fougères-sur-Bièvre). Or take a Jules Verne-themed tour in Nantes, the city of his birth.

Activities Brest is one of Brittany's biggest cities, where you can explore the Pont de Recouvrance and castle, then kick back in the bars and cafés of Rue de Siam. The port town of Saint-Malo is a walled city built on a picturesque peninsula. Stop off for some seafood after taking in the Cathedral of Saint Vincent and the maritime castle. Or take a boat trip to Iles des Glénan, a group of islands just south of Concarneau, where there's a fort, sailing school and bird sanctuary. In Vannes, explore the old quarter's cathedral, gardens and gateway port. For cliffs, coastline and crisp, clean air, drive to Quiberon, then walk along the Côte Sauvage. Soak up Arthurian legend on a stroll through Brocéliande forest, also known as Paimpont.

Best beach La Grande Plage in Carnac is the perfect seaside resort, all white sandy shores, gently lapping waves and lots of water-based activities. It's not far from the ancient monoliths, either.

Daytripper Spend a day stalking the streets of Brittany's capital, Rennes. It's the home of Citroën and of Rennes University, founded in 1461. The elegant old centre was rebuilt in the 18th century after a huge fire (the mediaeval main gate, Les Portes Mordelaises, is still standing). Pop into Cathédrale Saint-Pierre to check out its 16th-century Flemish altarpiece, or book a guided tour of the restored Parlement de Bretagne (www.parlement-bretagne.com), which survived the fire in 1720 but didn't get away so lightly during a fishermen's protest in 1994. Finally, if you're Rennes way on a Saturday, don't miss the morning market, one of the biggest in France, selling absolutely everything from croissants to rabbits for the pot.

Shopping Deck yourself out in Breton sweaters and smocks from Armor Lux, with outposts in Quimper, Rennes, Vannes and Brest (www.armorlux.com). In Quimper, you can buy fine Breton lace, as well as local faience pottery with traditional Breton designs (they like yellow and blue borders).

Something for nothing Take in the swampy landscape of the salt flats at Guérande. The square enclosures of marshland are the workplace of skilled *paludiers* (salt panners), who reap the premium *fleur de sel*.

Don't go home without... spotting a woman wearing a *coiffe bigoudène* – a tall hat made from lace, as worn in mediaeval times.

BRILLIANTLY BRITTANY

More than a third of the oysters consumed in France are farmed on the Brittany coast. Head to the northern shores to see tractors at work on the muddy beds in Cancale; afterwards, you'll be able to consume as many freshly picked oysters as you can manage, for a snip of what you'd pay anywhere else.

DIARY

April/May A scallop festival takes place in Saint-Quay-Portrieux on the north coast. Try the Bay of Saint-Brieuc's best while fishing, shopping and listening to Celtic music. May/June Semaine du Golfe Sailing Festival (www.semainedugolfe.asso.fr) on the south coast marks the return of the sailing season, every two years, in the Gulf of Morbihan. July Hennebont in the Morbihan department stages mediaeval-style feasts, tournaments and jousting. In Quimper, Les Fêtes de Cornouaille takes place, a celebration of all things Breton. And there are more Celtic festivities at the end of the month in Lorient (www.festival-interceltique.com). August The Sea Shanty Festival comes round every two years in Paimpol, celebrating maritime music, with the best seafaring songs from Brittany and the rest of the world.

Le Lodge Kerisper

STYLE Collector's cabin
SETTING Portside Brittany

'The walls are adorned with various framed finds, from old-fashioned measuring tapes to fishing paraphernalia, with lamps fashioned from old pop bottles dangling over the bar'

Does anyone know where all the French have gone? During the two and a half hours it takes us to travel from the port of Saint-Malo to southern Brittany, we saw only about 12 other human beings – most of them loitering on the edge of forests with guns, baskets and intent. Reassuring it was, then, when we found ourselves arriving in La Trinité-sur-Mer, a small but bustling sailing town, huddled around a harbour abob with proper-job sailing boats. When you see 100ft catamaran masts, you know you've landed on the planet of serious sea adventurers. You may also know that, wherever sailors go, fun follows and, with any luck, so does a bit of old-fashioned, non-threatening trouble.

For those of us who have spent time in Devon and Cornwall, La Trinité-sur-Mer has a pleasing familiarity. The slate-roofed white houses jut at right angles to one another, perched on gentle slopes looking over the water. Vast mature yew trees peer over the town as if to say: 'Keep calm and carry on, crazy sailors...'

Le Lodge Kerisper stands 100m from the port itself, up a short lane lined with the perfectly manicured gardens of its neighbours. The property is a proudly maintained 19th-century *maison longère* and a cluster of old stone outhouses, centred around a grassed contemporary garden and timber-clad pool area.

As we arrive at the hotel, we are warmly met by Philippe, one half of the owner couple, who immediately offers us a coffee. A shot-in-the-arm espresso is just the ticket: we are travelling as four on this occasion, with Small and Even Smaller Smith along for the ride. And we want it all. We want a hotel that can accommodate our children while also allowing us to behave as though we are here simply to enjoy ourselves.

It's a good start: Le Lodge Kerisper has the kind of atmosphere that many hotels spend years trying to achieve. There's not a shred of pretentiousness – children are greeted by name, and families sit next to couples. We feel instantly at home, as though the place is ours to potter around – whether it's a sneaky visit to the bell jar of pick 'n' mix sweets in the bar, or claiming our own spot in the garden for a read or a snooze.

The interior has it just right. Old grandfather clocks sit alongside photos and paintings of Jim Morrison and Steve McQueen. It's homely and stylish, with a zinc bar, whitewashed panels and linen-upholstered sofas – nothing so uptight that we have to walk around pinning the small folks' arms down. But it is also slick enough for us to feel we are *away*. The walls of the reception/bar/lounge – summery sitting room or cosy cabin, depending on the season – are adorned with various framed finds, from old-fashioned measuring tapes to fishing paraphernalia, with lamps fashioned from old pop bottles dangling over the bar. The old wellies and oilskins give it a somewhat seasidey look, but there's a dash of metropolitan cool in the mix, too.

Le Lodge is restaurantless, but they do serve a cracking breakfast. As a diehard carnivore I am often underwhelmed by the promise of Continental, but this one is varied and super-fresh and a great way to start the day. The lack of in-house dining means getting out and about and, with children, this is no bad thing, so we lunch at the local Le Quai on crab rillettes and moules frites. Then we make our way to the Côte Sauvage, where we promise Small a run on the spectacular surfer's beach and set about collecting as many pebbles and shells as can be stuffed into poncho pockets.

Returning home with suitably rosy faces and tired legs, we retire to our suite for family bathtime. The decor is simple, with white walls, oak floors and old French mirrors, and it has a natty arrangement whereby the bathroom and wardrobe corridor are accessed from both rooms, creating a brilliant sprint circuit for Small and Even Smaller. (Never let it be said that we encourage near-exhaustion in our children to get them to go to bed earlier.)

The other advantage of the circuit is that the wardrobe corridor has sliding doors and accommodates exactly the width of a travel cot. So if, for any reason, you have an Even Smaller in your bedroom but don't want them in your room *all* the time, you can shove their cot in a cupboard and reason that it's a corridor, which isn't quite so bad.

Though there are a handful of easy-going crêperies in the town, and a few restaurant gems further afield, we decided to take up Philippe's offer of having a fruits de mer platter at the hotel. After a somewhat 'Manuel' moment with Yann the barman, who told us we couldn't have our romantic supper in the bar because of *ze selfish odeurr*, we did as we were told, moved to the breakfast room and prepared for an off-the-scale fruits de mer experience.

The only question remaining was what wine should accompany such a feast. We gazed limply at the slender wine menu (just two reds and two whites). Like all the best barmen, Yann detected our hesitation and offered us a generous taster of each; after some showman swilling, we settled on a top-rate creamy Chablis and forgave the list its brevity.

As we cracked our crab claws, wrestled all manner of crustacea from their shells, and sipped wine far superior than any we'd drink at home, we felt visited by our former wit and sparkle. And for a moment there, we felt like we were back in the old days, pre-family, the two of us hanging out and living life just for ourselves. *A la vôtre*, Le Lodge Kerisper.

Reviewed by Oona Bannon

NEED TO KNOW

Rooms 20, including three suites.

Rates €95–€290, not including tax or breakfast, €15.

Check-out 12 noon, but flexible. Earliest check-in, 3pm.

Facilities Outdoor heated pool, spa, DVD and book library, free WiFi throughout, bicycle hire. In rooms: flatscreen TV, CD, bottled water.

Children Extra beds can be added; cots are free. Babysitting with a local nanny costs €8 an hour. The owners like to make children feel at home, so teddies will be waiting on their beds.

Also Pets can come, too. Massage and reflexology can be arranged at the hotel's Wellness Centre.

IN THE KNOW

Our favourite rooms Book a room with a terrace, so you can enjoy the salty sea air and make the most of the outdoor feel of this beach house. Suite 8 has a big south-facing terrace; Room 9 is up in the eaves, so it feels tucked away and cosy. Suite 16 is the perfect pick for families, since it's on the ground floor and opens onto the garden.

Hotel bar Decked out in fairy lights and cute lightshades made from strung-together bottles filled with red liquid, the bar offers 10 malts and a dozen cocktails; the chalkboard wine list is small but well chosen. There's a huge sweet-shop jar of pick 'n' mix jellies to help yourself to.

Hotel restaurant None, but the lodge has a breakfast room where home-made *far Breton* cake is served as part of an ample buffet in the morning. The decor is a mix of old bottles, glass lanterns, wire baskets and balls of twine – all of it nicely weathered.

Top table Choose a table by the window for pool views, or join fellow guests at the long table for chat with your coffee.

Dress code Casual nautical stripes, windproof jackets.

Local knowledge If you're not a sailor already, after a few days in La Trinité-sur-Mer, you'll want to be, especially if you're visiting around the time of the Spi Ouest-France regatta (April). The Société Nautique de la Trinité-sur-Mer (www.snt-voile.org) in the port can organise sailing classes and boat hire.

LOCAL EATING AND DRINKING

Le Chantier on Chemin Passeur in St Philibert has a terrace looking out to sea and serves seafood dishes, including lobster (+33 (0)2 97 55 17 42; closed November to early January). Le Quai on Cours des Quais La Trinité-sur-Mer is popular with locals for its fresh seafood, hearty salads and busy atmosphere (+33 (0)2 97 55 80 26). For something a bit more gastro, try L'Azimut on Rue du Men-Dû (+33 (0)2 97 55 71 88). On Rue du Pô in Carnac, La Calypso is another seafood spot, with pescatorial terrines, gratins and carpaccios (+33 (0)2 97 52 06 14; closed December and January). Seafood and a harbourside terrace beckon at Le Bout du Quai on Quai Benjamin Franklin, St Goustan (+33 (0)42 97 50 87 17).

GET A ROOM!

For more information, or to book this hotel, go to www.mrandmrssmith.com. Register your Smith membership card (see pages 4–5) to enjoy exclusive offers and privileges.

 SMITH MEMBER OFFER A glass of champagne each and a box of Breton salted caramels.

Le Lodge Kerisper 4 rue du Latz, 56470 La Trinité-sur-Mer (+33 (0)2 97 52 88 56; www.lodge-kerisper.com)

HOW TO... TASTE WINE

If you want to pass yourself off as a half-competent wine taster when stopping at a roadside *domaine*, the first thing to get right isn't the tasting at all. It's not even the chat that comes afterwards. Though, if that worries you, here's a tip: any producer will be thrilled if you gaze at your glass and sigh that it was wonderful. To sound more professional, mutter something about 'balance'. A good wine is said to be balanced when its fruit, acidity, oak, alcohol, sweetness (or otherwise), and tannin are in harmony.

No, if you really want to look as though you know what you're doing, the thing to work on is your projection. For whatever reason – social embarrassment, I expect – spitting is the thing that inspires the most nerves among novices. So let me say, right now, that wine tasters always, *always* spit, and they do so quite without self-consciousness. Onto the ground, if outside; into the drain, if in a winery; into a spittoon, if there's one available. A good spitter can stand several feet away from a bucket and project wine from their mouth into it in a neat arc. Lauren Bacall's words in *To Have and Have Not* spring to mind: 'You just put your lips together and blow.' If only it were so simple. My advice for achieving projection? You need to pretend you really want rid of that wine. The bath is the safest place in which to practise this technique.

So what about all that comes beforehand? The first thing to do is tilt the glass so that the meniscus is at an angle, and you can look at the colour of the wine, which will be deeper in the centre (aka the 'core') and lighter towards the rim. As it ages, a wine changes colour, and it begins to show that first at the rim. Whites deepen through straw, gold and amber. Reds fade from livid purple to crimson, garnet and tawny. Colour offers clues about origin, too: a pale rosé is more likely to come from Provence than from the Languedoc.

Next, you need to give the glass a swirl, so that the wine releases its aroma, and take a good sniff. If you're getting a noseful of damp cardboard or drains, the wine may be corked. If not, consider what you're experiencing. A young Loire sauvignon might smell of fresh-mown grass or gunflint. A Saint-Emilion might remind you of fruitcake. A young red Châteauneuf-du-Pape from the southern Rhône might seem fiery and full of red fruit and dried hillside herbs.

After smelling, take a mouthful. Suck in some air at the same time, which will amplify the flavours in your mouth. Swill the wine all around your mouth, consider it... What does it taste of? Does it feel in balance? Or is the oak or even the alcohol drowning the fruit? Is the tannin and acidity giving it structure or does it seem to belly-flop after an initial pleasing impression? And then, finally, spit. You're not done yet. The taste the wine leaves in your mouth (the 'finish') is important, too. A long finish, when the flavour of the wine hangs around, is a good thing. At least, it is as long as you *like* the flavour. And that, when all's said and done, is the most important thing of all.

By Victoria Moore

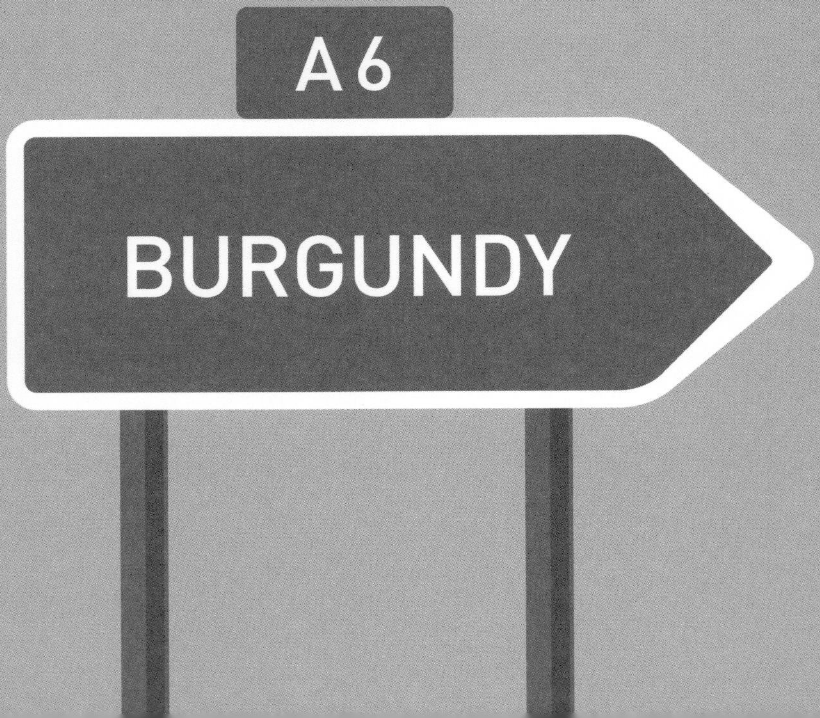
A 6
BURGUNDY

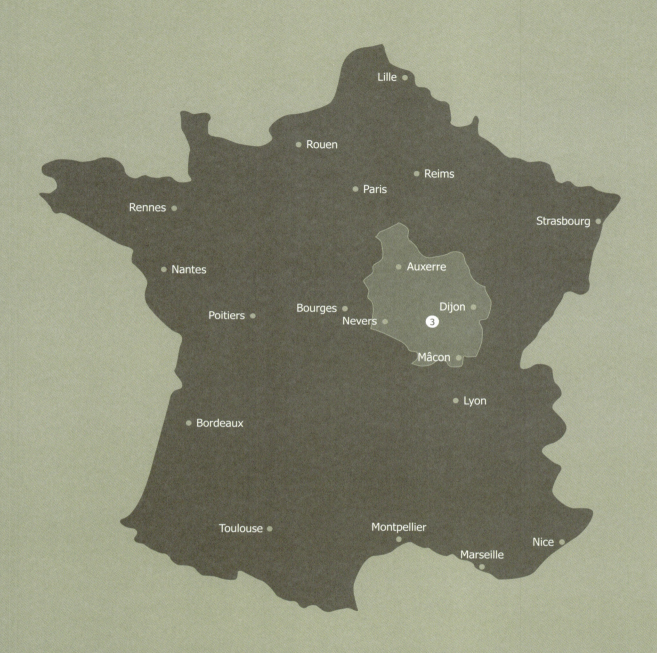

BURGUNDY

③ Moulin Renaudiots

BURGUNDY

COUNTRYSIDE Abbey-crested winelands
COUNTRY LIFE Market shopping, domaine-hopping

Burgundy has unexpected charms to uncork: vineyards, of course, but also tranquil canals and, at its heart, a lake-laden national park. Romanesque churches dot the hills and plains, among them the beautiful Cistercian abbey at Fontenay. And traces of Burgundy's pre-Enlightenment incarnation as a powerful duchy remain, such as the imposing Ducal Palace in the centre of Dijon. Today, it's the region's food and wine that are all-conquering: its rich *gastronomie bourguignonne* and its precious Côte d'Or vintages. Burgundy's towns and rivers – Chablis, Mâcon, Beaune, Pouilly, the Loire and the Saône – make up an oenophile's gazetteer. You don't have to be a wine lover to come on holiday here, but... actually, you do.

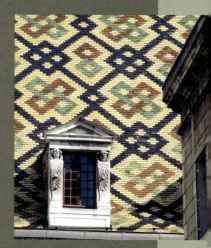

GETTING THERE

Planes British Airways, BMI Baby and EasyJet fly to Lyon Saint-Exupéry from London and some regional UK airports (www.ba.com; www.bmibaby.com; www.easyjet.com). Air France (www.airfrance.com) has flights to Lyon from Orly and Charles de Gaulle airports in Paris.

Trains From the UK, take the Eurostar (www.eurostar.com) from London St Pancras to Lyon via Lille (around six hours), or Paris (slightly quicker, but you connect from a different station). The TGV from Paris Gare de Lyon takes two hours (www.tgv.com).

Automobiles Avis, Europcar, Hertz and National all have desks at Lyon Saint-Exupéry airport (www.lyon.aeroport.fr). Access Burgundy via the A6 from Paris, or the A7 from Marseille.

LOCAL KNOWLEDGE

Taxis In Dijon, there's a taxi rank at the railway station. Otherwise, book one through Taxis Radio Dijon (+33 (0)3 80 41 41 12) or your hotel.

Siesta and fiesta Shops increasingly stay open all day in the bigger cities, but many still take a lunch break, and shut their doors on Sundays. Banks are open Monday to Friday, some on Saturdays. Many restaurants close after 2pm and reopen in the afternoon around 4pm. It's also common for restaurants to shut on Mondays or Tuesdays.

Do go/don't go Summers are hot and sunny; winters are cold and clear. Spring sees more rainfall but fewer crowds in the towns and cities. The oak and maple forests look spectacular in autumn, and the wine harvest takes place in September and October.

Packing tips A corkscrew.

Children Meet the menagerie at Touroparc zoo at Romanèche-Thorins, which has rides and a summertime waterpark (+33 (0)3 85 35 51 53; www.touroparc.com)

Recommended reads *Long Ago in France: The Years in Dijon* by MFK Fisher celebrates the region's cuisine. *The Vintner's Luck* by Elizabeth Knox is a novel set in a small Burgundian village at the time of Napoleon.

Local specialities Burgundy's top restaurants use prized local ingredients, including Charolais beef and Grand Cru wines. Say Dijon, and you think mustard. Grey Poupon, the famous original, is now mass-produced by Kraft; it's worth scouring Dijon's delis for local blends. Celebrated dishes such as boeuf bourguignon and coq au vin are claimed by the region, and it's an excellent place to order escargots. The Morvan area produces wonderful goat's cheese.

And... In Burgundy, DRC stands for Domaine de Romanée-Conti, a small vineyard in the Côte de Nuits that produces some of the world's most expensive wine in tiny quantities. If your budget won't stretch to one of the fabled bottles (reported estimates ricochet between £2,000 and £7,000 a pop), content yourself by reading Richard Olney's *Romanée Conti*.

WORTH GETTING OUT OF BED FOR

Viewpoint Climb the 315 steps of the Philippe Le Bon tower in Dijon for a splendid view over the rooftops of the city's well-preserved mediaeval quarter. The rocky cliffs of Solutré, nearly 500m high, are a prehistoric site where engravings of horses and thousands of equine bones have been discovered. Take the path to its summit and survey the Mâconnais vineyards below, then head to the museum in Solutré-Pouilly for the full history lesson (www.musees-bourgogne.org).

Arts and culture Located in Dijon's magnificent Ducal Palace, the Musée des Beaux-Arts (mba.dijon.fr) has collections both ancient (Egyptian art) and modern (20th century). In Autun on the Rue des Bancs, the Musée Rolin is a cultural archive of the area, housing an impressive restored mosaic of Bellerophon from the 2nd century (www.autun.com). Castles are fairy-tale fabulous in these parts: Château de Commarin in the north has beautiful formal gardens and opulent interiors (www.commarin.com; April to November). Château de Drée, in the south, is all formal gardens and 17th-century finery (+33 (0)3 85 26 84 80; chateau-de-dree.com).

Activities Visit Beaune's Marché aux Vins on Rue Nicolas Rolin, housed in an old church, and sample 15 of the region's wines for €10 (9am–11.30am; 2pm–5.30pm). Get a bird's-eye view of Burgundy's vines from a hot-air balloon with Air Escargot (www.air-escargot.com). The Morvan National Park has over 2,000 square kilometres of countryside to explore, and is popular for cycling and mountain biking (www.parcdumorvan.org). If you don't mind looking daft, it's fun to tour Dijon on a Segway; you can hire the contraptions from the tourist office in Place Darcy (www.dijon-tourism.com; over-12s only).

Perfect picnic Bottle of Burgundy, goat's cheese, baguette – fill your rucksack and make for the town of Volnay, set high on the slopes of the Côte de Beaune. It has magnificent views of the surrounding countryside – the source of those wonderful red wines.

Daytripper Two hours' south of Autun, the city of Lyon rivals Paris for shopping. In the chic area between Place Bellecour and Cordeliers in the Carré d'Or district, browse the boutiques on Rue Emile Zola, Rue Président Edouard

Herriot and Place Kléber. There are great food markets on Quai Saint-Antoine and Croix-Rousse hill. Bring flat shoes for sightseeing in the *traboules* (cobbled alleys) of Vieux Lyon, where you'll notice 18th-century traces of the city's silk industry. Lunch at a *bouchon*, one of Lyon's tiny emblematic bistros: try Le Laurencin on Rue Saint-Jean (+33 (0)4 78 37 97 37) or Café des Fédérations at 8–10 rue Major Martin (+33 (0)4 78 28 26 00).

Shopping The Place de la Mairie in Autun has stalls selling fresh produce, baked treats, saucissons and cheeses every Wednesday and Friday morning. Get your Dijon mustard at La Boutique Maille on Rue de la Liberté, a shrine to the city's favourite condiment. Dijon's Central Market was designed by Gustav Eiffel and is a treasure trove of local specialities. Mâcon, in the south of the Burgundy region, has a fruit, vegetable and flower market every morning (Tuesday to Saturday) in Place aux Herbes, and on Saturday morning on Esplanade Lamartine. The Sunday market in Chablis is also a culinary treat.

Something for nothing Drive 90 minutes west of Dijon to Vézelay, a hill-perched town recognised by Unesco for its significance to pilgrims on their way to Santiago de Compostela. They stop off to pay their respects to Saint Mary Magdalene and her relics at the town's soaring basilica: tours and programmes cost, but it's free to admire the vaulted ceilings and 12th-century stone carvings (+33 (0)3 86 33 39 50).

Don't go home without... a bottle of crème de cassis, the blackcurrant liqueur without which there would be no kir.

BOUNTIFULLY BURGUNDY

Wine, cheese and truffles are all on the menu at Burgundy On A Plate, a British-run company operating guided day tours out of Beaune (+33 (0)3 80 39 09 88; www.burgundyonaplate.com). You can either join a group itinerary or arrange a tailored private tour. The Luxury Wine & Gastronomy tour visits prestigious vineyards in the Côte de Beaune and Côte de Nuits, and invites you to sup on Grand Cru wines and take lunch in a gastronomic restaurant.

DIARY

May Sharpen your leather-patched elbows for the annual antiques fair in Dijon, where dealers and collectors do battle over *brocante* bargains (www.dijon-expocongres.com). In Semur-en-Auxois, all things mediaeval are celebrated during an annual festival. Raise a toast in a themed tavern, enjoy street theatre, and pick up ye olde ornaments in the craft market (www.ville-semur-en-auxois.fr). **June** Blues en Bourgogne takes place in the village of Le Creusot; it's a four-day programme of blues – electric, trad and gospel – featuring performers from France, the UK and the US (www.festival-du-blues.com). **August** Take an empty car boot and a discerning thirst to the Pouilly-sur-Loire Wine Fair – an opportunity to taste the region's finest wines, including Pouilly Fumé, Sancerre and Reuilly. **October** You may have to jog 26.2 miles, but you'll see lovely scenery if you take part in the Grands Crus Marathon, a circuit from/to Maison de Marsannay la Côte (www.marathondesgrandscrus.com). **November** Dijon holds its annual International Food Festival, a major diary date among European food connoisseurs, where you can sample produce and wine from all over the world (www.dijon-expocongres.com). Mid-month, the Hospices de Beaune holds a lively and time-honoured charity wine auction, with some of the best Burgundies up for grabs (www.hospices-de-beaune.com).

Autun

Moulin Renaudiots

STYLE Danish-Dutch designer pad
SETTING Water-edged woodland

'Everything from the artworks to an immense and beautiful collection of glassware has been carefully chosen and perfectly arranged, striking a triumphant balance between old and new'

Moulin Renaudiots, Moulin Renaudiots... I speak French every day of my life but, even so, it's a bit of a mouthful. I can only sympathise with Anglo-Saxon visitors to this countryside chambre d'hôtes, while assuring them that any pronunciation-related jaw-ache will be more than compensated for by the romance of the magnifique Moulin. Elegant, low-key, luxurious: these are the words that enter my head when I try to describe this peaceful place. So who cares how you say its name?

At the bottom of a hill, surrounded by forest, the Moulin sits a few miles outside Autun, a town founded by the Romans back when Augustus wore the laurels. We walk up the tiered front garden, with its stone walls and parterres of herbs and flowers. We reach the few steps that lead to the main door, and the Moulin whispers to us: 'We are not yet another hotel in that tired, camped-up French-countryside style, oh no – we have something special up our stylish sleeve'. Unlike Burgundy's more formal retreats, which feel stuffy at best and, at worst, make you hanker for home and your cherished white walls, this historical hideaway is all about creating a sincere but contemporary experience of France's fine countryside.

It is then that Peter – Danish, tall, smiling – walks down the stairs and welcomes us. He warmly shows us to our room, a vast, high-ceilinged, studio-like boudoir, replete with 1950s furniture and an exceptional mid-century Kai Kristiansen desk. Brightly hued retro glassware provides graphic colour; the only nod towards the country context comes from a stately dark-wood antique wardrobe looming over the bed. We need to concoct a ruse to see all five rooms, so we say we're thinking about booking the whole place. And, once we've seen the oak-beamed ceilings, the limestone fireplaces and the fantastic ensuite sitting rooms, we're contemplating it for real.

In the main living and dining area of the renovated 17th-century water mill, deep greys, beiges and whites complement the natural stone walls, original timber-frame ceiling and polished concrete floor. Furnished with sleek Scandinavian and north-European pieces, the living space is arranged around a fireplace; the dining room aligns neatly, with six square tables and 12 smart chairs.

Everything – from the artworks, which include a series of miniature 'Hopes' (those instantly iconic graffiti odes to a booming Obama), to an immense and beautiful collection of glassware and china – has been carefully chosen and perfectly arranged, striking a triumphant balance between old and new.

Our next encounter is with Jan, who is Dutch, welcoming and soft-spoken. Peter has asked his partner to organise us a reservation at Châteaubriant, a brasserie in Autun, since the table d'hôte isn't on tonight. Peter cooks a few nights a week, generally not on Fridays. We're not sorry to have an excuse to explore, and Peter and Jan, who have lived in the region for years, are brimming with info on what to do (and, crucially, where to avoid).

Crisp-yet-fluffy baguette, croissants and cheese are our perfect Saturday morning breakfast, and we linger in the living room, thumbing our books and succumbing to complete relaxation. Jan joins us, and we ask how they came to acquire the Moulin, eight years ago. The answer summarises four fraught years of construction and refurbishment, a two-year spruce-up of the garden, then the addition of a pool and sprawling deck. As with all perfectionists, they have absolutely not finished, and relish the prospect of further beautification.

For the committed wine lover, few are the pages in the atlas that compete with Burgundy for heady map-reading. We set off on a world-class wine-tasting trek, homing in on Meursault and Pommard (among other legendary producers), and carting back crates of serious reds and whites. After a light lunch in Beaune, where the Hospices de Beaune is an essential architectural/cultural/historic stop, we take our time driving home along the Route des Grands Crus, in order to take in the vine-lined landscape.

When the clock strikes seven, *l'apéro* is served on the terrace (or fireside, when it's unkind outdoors). Here, as the crickets chirp, Mrs Smith sips a crémant de Bourgogne rosé, while I manfully sample the Moulin's signature kir, made with home-crushed crème de cassis. We chat to the other guests: two Belgian couples rejoicing, as we are, in a few precious days' escape. Peter is back on chef duty around eight. We dine on scallops, fennel and truffle vinaigrette, followed by veal filet mignon, then almond and nut tart with pecan caramel. All this is nothing short of divine, and the Côte de Beaune and Côte Chalonnaise aren't bad, either.

Peter and Jan have created a genuine original in the Moulin Renaudiots. Yes, it is beautifully designed and, true, it's beyond welcoming. But what we love most about this boutique guesthouse is its inventive take on the rural retreat. We find a brave new Burgundian world, where the beds are big and comfortable, furniture mid-century iconic, and the bathrooms stylish enough for an interiors shoot. There are strictly no decorative touches depicting scenic châteaux, and definitely no flower-choked curtains that grab you and scream 'Hey city boy! You're in the country now!' No, Moulin Renaudiots is much subtler than that. Everything it utters has substance, and it's all – including the name – conveyed in most seductive tones.

Reviewed by Réda Amalou

NEED TO KNOW
Rooms Five.
Rates €110–€150, including buffet breakfast.
Check-out 11am. Check-in, 4pm.
Facilities Outdoor pool, terraced gardens, library, free WiFi throughout, free parking, Sephora products, fireplaces in some rooms.
Children Cots cost €10; extra beds are €25. The restaurant does a children's menu.
Also Pets are allowed in St André and St Pierre.

IN THE KNOW
Our favourite rooms St André has lots of light, a working fireplace, an Ercol wood-framed settee, concrete floors and direct access to the garden and pool. Pick Arroux if you fancy hardwood floors, lots of space and views of the terraced gardens; it also has an antique armoire and a reading nook upstairs on the loft level. St Andoche has an open bathroom with freestanding bathtub, and the finest views around – of Mont Beuvray and the gardens.
Hotel bars There's no formal bar area, but owners Jan and Peter will bring you drinks in the lounge or on the terrace, any time up until midnight; their speciality *apéro* is a Kir Royale, made with their own crème de cassis. Tea, coffee and soft drinks are free.
Hotel restaurant There's a table d'hôte on Tuesdays, Thursdays, Saturdays and Sundays, when the small black tables in the lounge are pushed together to make a big communal one. Peter does the cooking, a mix of French and Scandinavian, with menus based on what's fresh and what takes his fancy that day. Typical dishes include fried scallops with cauliflower purée, and veal with mushroom risotto, accompanied by wines from the area.
Top table There's only one, but you'll be seated opposite your partner. In summer, guests dine outside on the terrace.
Room service None.
Dress code As comfortable as you'd be in your own (stylish) home.
Local knowledge Make full use of the Morvan forest on your doorstep: hike, fish and canoe your way through the wooded lands and lakes. Base Nautique du Moulin du Vallon in Autun will send you sailing and kayaking (+33 (0)3 85 52 47 09). Wine-tasting country lies an easy drive away.

LOCAL EATING AND DRINKING
Le Chapitre on Place du Terreau in Autun is a relaxed restaurant near Saint-Lazare cathedral in the town's historic quarter (+33 (0)3 85 52 04 01). At 3 rue Jeannin, you'll find Le Chalet Bleu, a dine-in deli with lots of meat and game on the menu (+33 (0)3 85 86 27 30). Down the road at number 14, Le Châteaubriant serves up classic bistro dishes (+33 (0)3 85 52 21 58). Fine dining awaits at Le Charlemagne on Route des Vergelesses, near Beaune (+33 (0)3 80 21 51 45), and at Le Benaton on Faubourg Bretonniere (+33 (0)3 80 22 00 26) in Beaune itself.

GET A ROOM
For more information, or to book this hotel, go to www.mrandmrssmith.com. Register your Smith membership card (see pages 4–5) to enjoy exclusive offers and privileges.

 SMITH MEMBER OFFER A pair of tickets to the Musée Rolin in Autun.

Moulin Renaudiots Chemin du Vieux Moulin, 71400 Autun (+33 (0)3 85 86 97 10; www.moulinrenaudiots.com)

couture

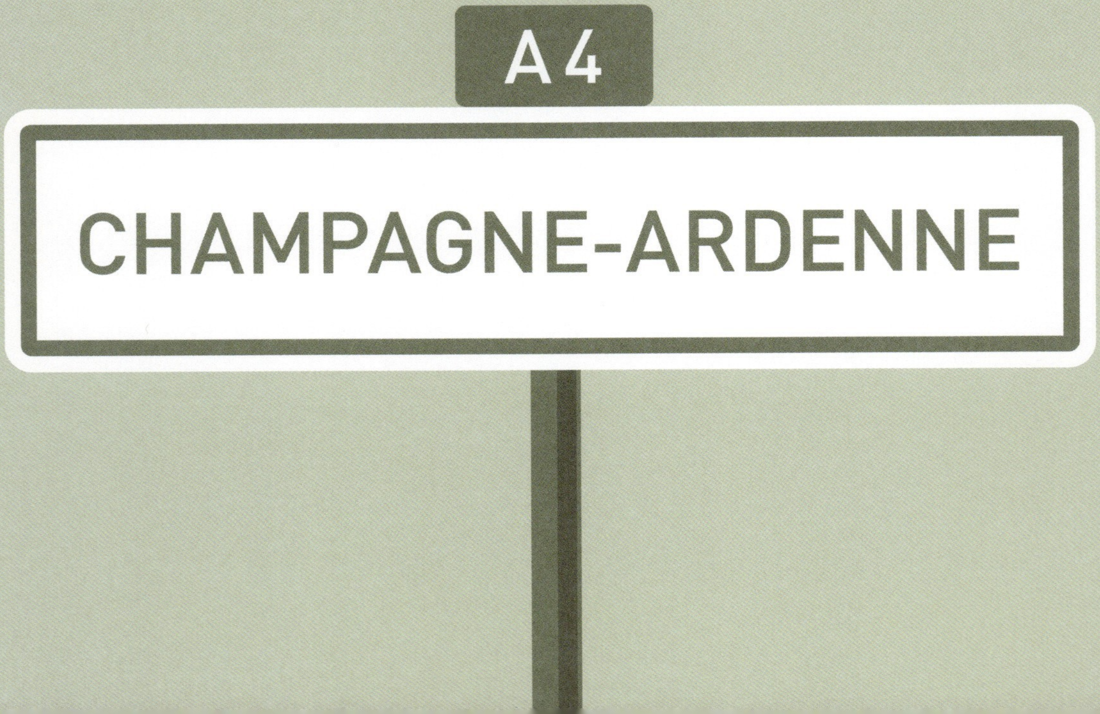
A4
CHAMPAGNE-ARDENNE

CHAMPAGNE-ARDENNE

4 Chez Odette

CHAMPAGNE-ARDENNE

COUNTRYSIDE Forests, farms, fortresses
COUNTRY LIFE Bottled bubbles, bucolic bliss

If only the sheep would quieten down... That's as bumptious as this tranquil corner of France gets. Ardennes is an unspoilt rural *département* in the north-east — not to be confused with its namesake broader region, which extends into Luxembourg and Belgium. The area's World War II past is hard to fathom, so serene is the landscape of farmland and sleepy villages. Local hub Charleville-Mézières is a town of elegant squares, a museum or two, and go-slow cafés and bistros, united by their quiet charm. The Ardennes hills, and rivers Meuse and Semoy are a big draw for outdoorsy peace-seekers, wonderful for walking, fishing, kayaking and climbing. And when aren't you in the mood for a little champagne tasting?

GETTING THERE

Planes Brussels airport is around two hours from the Ardennes by car. That's at least 30 minutes nearer than Paris Charles de Gaulle, with no painful Paris traffic.
Trains Take the TGV from Paris Gare de l'Est to Charleville-Mézières or Sedan (each around two hours).
Automobiles You'll want some wheels to explore the area, if only to get to a carpark from which to hike the forest trails. Hire some at Brussels airport or at the train station in Charleville-Mézières (www.europcar.com).

LOCAL KNOWLEDGE

Taxis You've got more chance of hailing a tractor. Your best bet is to book a cab through your hotel. Sachy Taxi Olivier Philippe, aka STOP, operates out of Florenville (+33 (0)6 83 45 89 70). In Charleville-Mézières, try Allo Taxi (+33 (0)3 24 37 17 17).
Siesta and fiesta Shops in towns such as Sedan and Charleville-Mézières stay open through the day but banks bolt their doors between 12 noon and 2pm. There's 24-hour siesta on Sundays and Mondays.
Do go/don't go You only have to look at the 50-shades-of-green scenery to realise this region gets a lot of rain. Summer months are driest and warmest — any time between May and September — with July and August being peak visitor season.

Packing tips Kayaking kit (ie: stuff you don't mind getting sodden) if you're ready to brave the rapids. And take a picnic rug; why snack indoors when the scenery's this good?
Children Just over the Belgian border, the hi-tech, Crusades-related Archéoscope Godefroid de Bouillon is a great rainy-day standby (www.archeoscopebouillon.be).
Recommended reads *Ordinary Heroes* is Scott Turow's novel set against the backdrop of Ardennes and the Battle of the Bulge. A biography of Rimbaud will provide the lowdown on Charleville-Mézière's most famous son. If the delicious Belgian Ardennes pâté inspires you, Stéphane Reynaud's *Terrine* recipe book is one to pick up post-trip.
Local specialities Ardennes food is a real rustic romp for the tastebuds. There's Ardennes pâté, white pudding and game terrine for unfazed carniphiles; forest mushrooms (if you can find them); and Orval beer brewed by Trappist monks. Dine on pike and trout from the Meuse, and snack sweetly on gâteau mollet (like brioche, only sweeter). The poster product for the region, however, is bubbly. Traditionally drunk to accompany the coronation of French kings in Reims, champagne rules the surrounding landscape, which is striped with chardonnay vines and dotted with more

than 100 champagne houses and around 19,000 smaller growers. Most of the houses offer cellar tours and tastings; try Taittinger (www.taittinger.com), Pommery (www.pommery.com), or Veuve Clicquot (www.veuve-clicquot.com).

And... Try not to crash the hire car – yes, there really is a giant brown pig on the side of the A34 near Charleville-Mézières. When we say pig, really we mean a wild boar called Woinic. And he's smiling. Perhaps because he has the honour of being the 10-metre-tall symbol of the French Ardennes.

WORTH GETTING OUT OF BED FOR

Viewpoint Fairy-tale turrets of purple slate are the icing on the castle at Château Fort de Sedan. Climb the ramparts and peek over a cannon to spy timeless views of the mediaeval town below (www.chateau-fort-sedan.fr).

Arts and culture In Charleville-Mézières, buy a joint ticket for the Musée de l'Ardenne at 31 place Ducale (+33 (0)3 24 32 44 60), packed with military and hunting artefacts, and the Musée Rimbaud, which houses collections of poet-related paraphernalia in a former mill straddling the river, on Quai Arthur Rimbaud (+33 (0)3 24 32 44 65; both closed 12 noon–2pm). L'Institut International de la Marionnette at 7 place Winston Churchill (+33 (0)3 24 33 72 50) has a museum that tells the story of the town's puppetry traditions (see opposite).

Activities In summer, fly like a bird at Aventure Parc Fumay. Their kilometre-long Le Fantasticable cable-slide sends you whizzing head-first across the forest canopy (+33 (0)3 24 57 57 59; www.aventure-parc.fr). Near Florenville, pop over the Belgian border to Bouillon, where you can hire a boat from Semois Kayaks to paddle the river (+32 (0)4 75 24 74 23; www.semois-kayaks.be). Walk the Trans-Ardennes trail – a former towpath that follows the Meuse – from Charleville-Mézières (tourist office: +33 (0)3 24 55 69 90).

Perfect picnic The monks won't mind if you roll up to the beautiful grounds of Orval Abbey near Florenville with a hamper of Ardennes goodies. Your hotel may be able to cater for you, or stock up on cured ham, game pâté, Orval pressed cheese, baguettes from the village bakery and a bottle or two of Orval beer (www.orval.be).

Daytripper You're a little more than an hour away from Luxembourg City, for an urban fix when you're all countrysided out. Its Unesco-listed old town packs a surprising number of museums and restaurants into its narrow streets, and the city ramparts beg to be walked (Chemin de la Corniche has the prettiest panoramas). It would be neglectful not to sample gorgeous gâteaux from one of its many cake shops: try Kaempff-Kohler on Place Guillaume, or Namur on Rue des Capucins. Luxembourg also has the distinction of being the (unofficial) gourmet capital of the world. There are more Michelin-starred restaurants per capita here than in any other country; our pick is Mosconi on Rue Munster, the only two-starred Italian outside of Italy (+352 54 69 94).

Shopping Market days in Charleville-Mézières are Tuesday, Thursday and Saturday. Load up on peaches for your picnic, and gooey cheese for a mid-afternoon graze. In Florenville on Place Albert, Les Chocolats d'Edouard is a cocoa-scented cave of pralines and truffles (+32 (0)61 50 29 72). If you head as far into Belgium as La Roche en Ardennes, pick up one or two stoneware bowls – the town's most famous export. In Sedan, hand-crafted carpets keep the town's textile-industry past alive; find Le Tapis Point de Sedan on Boulevard Gambetta.

Something for nothing In the south of the region, the Argonne forest is a beauty pageant of beech and birch. Head to Olizy-Primat to enjoy a walk in the woods, keeping an eye out for orchids and carnivorous plants along the way.

Don't go home without... experiencing the tastes of the Ardennes, all wrapped up in one dish: cacasse à cul nu, a fricassée of potatoes, bacon and onions. Just what you need after a day's ploughing, herding or sightseeing.

ARDENTLY ARDENNES

Puppets! If you want to pull a few strings, you've come to the right place. On the main square in Charleville-Mézières is the Institute of Marionettes (staffed by humans). Pass by between 10am and 9pm to see characters emerge with Trumptonish charm from its clocktower as the hour strikes. On summer evenings, stooge-led performances provide build-up to September's Marionnettes festival (www.marionnette.com).

DIARY

March Florenville hosts a Fête du Chocolat, when there are tastings, cookery demos and contests themed around choccy (www.feteduchocolat.be). May Sedan launches into tourist season with a Mediaeval Festival, when costumes, parades and jousting take the town back to its past. August Gaume hosts a festival of jazz: big band, blues and contemporary (www.gaume-jazz.be). September The second half of the month brings troupes from across the globe to Charleville-Mézières to perform puppet shows – some 50 a day – in the streets and squares.

Chez Odette

STYLE Character à la carte
SETTING Forested frontier village

'In the bistro, soft candlelight, open fireplaces and huge leather Chesterfield sofas offer the perfect segue between aperitif and supper'

Dead of night in the tiny village of Williers, a few kilometres from the Belgian border, and the mercury reads minus six. It feels as if we're entering a land that time forgot: winding, snow-covered roads, forested either side for miles. We strain to make out a handful of turn-of-the-century cottages. A clearing finally reveals two charming farmhouses, emanating warm, inviting light from both sides of the road. Ah, Chez Odette!

The supremely affable Jorge comes running out of nowhere to greet us on this breathtakingly cold night. Ushered into the seductive, candlelit entrance, we pad across a black furry rug and up some tiny stairs to room No 9. The lack of formality is refreshing. A brief explanation reveals we are residing in the newly renovated nine-roomed farmhouse on the opposite side to Odette's original bistro. We've arrived at our very own private bolthole in the countryside.

Being the metrosexual man I am, I've allowed Mrs Smith to whisk me away for a pre-Valentine's winter break in this unique enclave on the eastern edge of France. Since I've broken my foot on a recent trip to Thailand, doing anything energetic is not an option. (Hopping, incidentally, really does nothing for one's masculine prowess.) So I am relieved to see that this looks the kind of place I can kick back — well, without actually kicking — relax and savour the simplicity of life.

A log-filled fireplace in our room is beckoning to be lit with the smart faux-leather fire igniter — the kind of bizarrely expensive item you might seek in Asprey for the man who has everything. This extraordinarily designed room is most unexpected in this rural part of the Ardennes. It's pure luxury, unadulterated yet understated.

United by the chocolate theme throughout, there's a multiplicity of mahogany hues; a sumptuous fur bedspread enhances the air of decadence. Logs are piled from floor to ceiling in one corner, and individual tables and lamps designed by the notable Marcel Wanders add modernist precision. As for the enormous bath tub, it is so deep that when it's filled Mrs Smith is immersed neck-deep in water. When I hit the walk-in tiled shower, it's like standing under Niagara Falls. Your average guesthouse this isn't.

Downstairs, a small, deliciously cosy living room and library is decked out with classic coffee-table books and board games. Mrs Smith challenges me to a game of chess by another fireplace glowing merrily away. Next door, we find a miniscule but well-stocked honesty bar. Depending on your thirst, being honest can be expensive. Luckily, I learned to make cocktails in Ibiza, and you know how generous those Spanish barmen are with their measures…

Across the way is the lovingly restored bistro, where the hotel's namesake Odette originally held court. She died in 1999, but left the village's main hub as her legacy. Soft candlelight, open fireplaces, a small bar and huge leather Chesterfield sofas offer the perfect segue between aperitif and supper. Old Odette-era photographs adorn the walls; a flatscreen TV shows Charlie Chaplin films; unobtrusive downbeat tunes play in the background — it is old and new blended perfectly. We sink into the deep leather sofa to try out the much-revered local ale, brewed by the Trappist monks at the Orval monastery.

'It's just 5km away,' Jorge informs us, trying to convince us we should take a brisk walk there in the morning. Hmm… snow, aforementioned injury — perhaps not. But a quick drive is an option, as it's indeed a trip worth making. Built in the 1100s, the monastery, with its cheese factory and brewery, is steeped in history. Had I been able, a hike through the dense forest would have been my choice of travel; it'd be the perfect walk for a balmy day. Perhaps when I'm feeling more bipedal. One can only imagine how this sleepy spot must spring to life in the full glory of summer. Kayaking, horse riding, hiking through forests; and the fairy-tale city of Luxembourg is just a short hop on the train from the small town of Florenville — there's so much to partake in.

Sipping our rich, deep golden brew from the traditional goblet-style glass, we make our menu selections before being seated in the neatly arranged, original-beamed restaurant. Here, Miguel Giltaire presides over beautifully presented food. Gastronomic? Yes. Overtly elaborate or

pretentious? No. Plumping for the pan-roasted steak, I decide not to insult the French too much, and I order it *à point*, as opposed to my usual (incinerated). Although tempted by the monkfish, shellfish and lobster spaghetti, Mrs Smith has succulent braised pigeon accompanied by puréed sweet potato. A triumvirate of crème brûlées (brown-sugar baked apple, hazelnut praline and tangy-tart citrus) rounds off our meal perfectly. Wanting for nothing, we trot off to bed in our very private residence, just across the way.

The overriding feeling you get here is that the presence and character of Odette lives on. She has been lovingly immortalised by the hotel's new owner, a close friend of hers. He has painstakingly maintained original features and balanced them with contemporary design to rival that of any boutique hotel. Odette herself never left the village in her entire life. Hearing of future plans to open an Odette by the sea, and maybe one in London, I for one look forward to greeting her wherever she may appear.

Reviewed by Barry Ashworth

NEED TO KNOW

Rooms Nine, including two suites, spread between a pair of buildings.
Rates €170–€260, including tax. Breakfast, €19.
Check-out 12 noon, but may be flexible. Earliest check-in, 2pm.
Facilities Book/DVD library, free WiFi throughout, bikes for hire. In rooms: flatscreen TV, DVD/CD, iPod dock, bottled water.
Children Chez Odette is happy to provide baby beds (€25) and highchairs.
Also Pets are welcome, and there's plenty of dog-walking acreage in the surrounding woodland.

IN THE KNOW

Our favourite rooms No 9 has everything going for it: peaceful privacy, far from any bustle, dark-wood walls, a working open fireplace, deep-set bath with separate shower, and wonderful views of the village and fields beyond. No 5 has exposed beams and a spacious, barn-like feel. No 1 is ideal for families – huge, with bay windows.
Hotel bar Attached to a snug sitting room with cosy cushioned sofas and board games aplenty, Odette's bar-bistro is the place to sample the local Trappist brew, Orval, accompanied by the customary tot of Picon bitters. Guests generally only have to pay for bottled drinks.
Hotel restaurant The hotel's poised and polished eatery is a picture of romance, with black-wood furniture, lamplight and inventive seasonal cuisine. (Closed from Sunday evening to Tuesday afternoon.)
Top table On the terrace, at a table twinkling with tea lights.
Room service Anything on the restaurant or bistro menu can be brought to your room before 8pm.
Dress code Mr Smith should aim for country-gent casual; demure summer dress for Madame.
Local knowledge Ask nicely, and Odette's staff will whisk you 5km down the road to L'Abbaye d'Orval in Belgium, where you can experience the twin pleasures of rambling around abbey ruins and taste-testing Trappist brews (www.orval.be).

LOCAL EATING AND DRINKING

With just 38 residents, Williers is the third smallest town in France, so local demand for gourmet eating is more than met by Chez Odette. Fortunately, the Belgian border is minutes away, allowing you to sample another nation's food style. The dishes at La Roseraie in Lacuisine, Florenville, are reliably delicious (+32 (0)6 131 1039; www.laroseraie-lacuisine.net; closed Tuesdays and Wednesdays). Brasserie Albert 1er in the centre of Florenville is recommended for an alfresco tasting tour of Belgian beer, with good fresh fish and salads (+32 (0)6 131 1091). Opposite the Abbey in Orval, La Nouvelle Hostellerie d'Orval offers hearty rustic lunches, with plenty of monk-made beer and cheese (+32 (0)6 131 4365).

GET A ROOM!

For more information, or to book this hotel, go to www.mrandmrssmith.com. Register your Smith membership card (see pages 4–5) to enjoy exclusive offers and privileges.

 SMITH MEMBER OFFER A bottle of champagne.

Chez Odette 18 rue Principale, 08110 Williers (+33 (0)3 24 55 49 55; www.chez-odette.com)

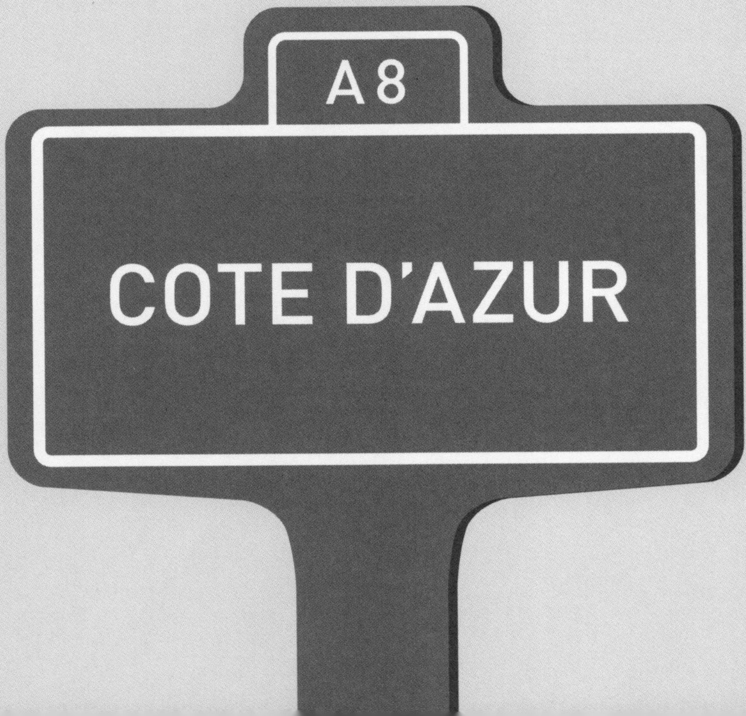
A8
COTE D'AZUR

COTE D'AZUR

5 Bastide Saint Mathieu

6 Cap d'Antibes Beach Hotel

7 Cap Estel

8 Les Rosées

COTE D'AZUR

COASTLINE Pines, palms and pools
COAST LIFE Portside posing, artwork ogling

This is where rustic glamour was invented: a balmy playground, equally endowed with show-off glitz and craggy, pine-clad coastline. Beautiful beaches stretch east from Hyères towards the Italian border; the celebrated hot spots – Cannes, Nice and Monte Carlo – are synonymous with unashamed ostentation, and have Italianate architecture and rock-star villas to match. When the boats and Bulgari get too much, you can retreat to the region's mediaeval villages. Èze, Mougins and Saint-Paul-de-Vence crown the cypress-dotted hills, all quaint cobbled alleys, casual cafés and ruined ramparts. The one thing you can't escape is the Mediterranean, its blue brilliance a timeless lure, whether you're Pablo Picasso or Paris Hilton.

GETTING THERE

Planes British Airways, BMI Baby, EasyJet and Air France cover the regional airports of Nice (in the east) and Marseille (in the west) between them (www.ba.com; www.bmibaby.com; www.easyjet.com; www.airfrance.com).
Trains From London, take the train via Lille to Marseille; from Paris, board the TGV. The coast-hugging track from Marseille to Menton – stopping at Toulon, Saint-Raphaël, Cannes, Antibes, Nice and Monaco – is spectacular, in some spots putting you closer to the Med than a beachfront sunlounger (www.tgv.com).
Automobiles Driving to the south coast can be a cross-country epic. Instead, put your car on the train in Paris, courtesy of Autotrain, board a separate passenger train, and take to the road in Avignon, Fréjus or Nice (ring Rail Europe on 0844 848 4050).

LOCAL KNOWLEDGE

Taxis Towns such as Nice, Cannes and Monte Carlo have taxi ranks, but you'll have no luck hailing. For middle-of-nowhere fares, ask your hotel to book a cab.
Siesta and fiesta Most shops are open 9am–12pm, then from 2pm or 3pm until 7pm. Banks open Tuesday to Friday, 8am–12pm and 1pm–5pm.
Do go/don't go To make the most of the coast, go May to September, but check the social calendar to avoid the road-clogging traffic that accompanies events such as the Monaco Grand Prix and Cannes Film Festival.
Packing tips Merrell walking shoes for rambling in the hills; budgie-smugglers or your least substantial bikini for the beach at Cannes.
Children Head 15km out of Grasse and take the tykes underground at Saint-Cézaire caves, where some of the limestone 'tites are at least 150,000 years old (www.lesgrottesdesaintcezaire.com).
Recommended reads Super-Cannes by JG Ballard; Tender is the Night by F Scott Fitzgerald; To Catch a Thief by David Dodge.
Local specialities Light, pale rosé wine from Provence. Langoustines, goat's cheese and Cavaillon melons are among the region's big-flavour, low-food-miles favourites. Expect plenty of grilled fish, bouillabaisse and authentic salade niçoise.
And... The working port (and resort) of La Ciotat stakes its claim on cinematic history, as the home of movie pioneers the Lumière brothers, and as the set of their 1895 motion picture (among the first ever to be shown in public) The Entrance of the Train into La Ciotat Station. Their story is recorded at the Ciotaden Museum on Quai Ganteaume (+33 (0)4 42 71 40 99; closed Tuesdays).

WORTH GETTING OUT OF BED FOR

Viewpoint There are many reasons to visit the perched mediaeval village of Èze: castle ruins, the picturesque Jardin Exotique and, not least, the bird's-eye views of Cap Ferrat from the restaurant terrace at swish Château Eza (+33 (0)4 93 41 12 24). In Cannes, walk up to Notre-Dame de l'Espérance, atop Suquet hill, for views east over the Vieux Port and the bay, and west towards La Corniche de l'Estérel coast road, as it wends its winding way along the craggy coast to Saint-Raphaël.

Arts and culture An impressive roll-call of artists have fallen for the Côte d'Azur: Van Gogh, Monet, Matisse, Picasso, Chagall, Cocteau and co, inspiring less-garlanded painters and sculptors (and art lovers) to flock here. Saint-Paul-de-Vence is a hilltop village crammed with galleries and arty residents; you can dine among incredible canvases at Picasso's old haunt, the legendary La Colombe d'Or (+33 (0)4 93 32 80 02). In Nice, head to the starkly striking Musée d'Art Moderne et d'Art Contemporain on the Promenade des Arts, to explore the American Pop and New Realist art collections (+33 (0)4 97 13 42 01; www.mamac-nice.org). The home of the Cannes Film Festival, the Palais des Festivals on La Croisette has a walk of fame outside, with stars' handprints pressed into the paving stones (+33 (0)4 93 39 01 01; www.palaisdesfestivals.com).

Activities The Verdon Gorge is a winner for rafting and canyoning (www.aboard-rafting.com). Walk the Martel trail, along and above the river – a hardy 14km hike that gives stunning views of the canyons and cliffs (www.lapaludsurverdon.com). Or walk by the coast through the Calanques, between Cassis and Marseille, a riverine landscape of cliffs and coves with 40 marked trails (www.marseille-tourisme.com). Charter a yacht to explore the coast (www.aquacruise.com). In winter, it's possible to ski at Isola 2000, two hours from Nice; or try ice-karting or ice-driving if you dare (www.sportsloisirs.net). Thanks to clear waters and colourful corals, the Côte d'Azur makes for divine diving. For Padi-certified clubs along the coast, check out www.divazur.com; local sub-aqua treasure include ruined submerged villages, sunken statues and World War II wrecks. (Remember always to leave a day between diving and flying.)

Best beach East of Nice, the coast curves round towards the headland of Saint-Jean-Cap-Ferrat, holding an enticing patchwork of navy and azure waters in its rocky embrace. Families can splash around at Plage de Passable or the villa-fringed Plage de Paloma, where Coco Chanel once bathed.

Daytripper For a peaceful beach picnic with a pine-forest backdrop, take the boat out from Cannes to the Iles des Lérins. The biggest, Ile Sainte-Marguerite, has quiet sandy coves and a fortress. There's also a boat service to smaller Saint-Honorat, with its 19th-century abbey buildings; it's worth venturing to the cliffs behind the cloisters, to find the mediaeval fortress (www.abbayedelerins.com).

Shopping Monte Carlo's fancy retail is found around the Boulevard des Moulins and in the Metropole mall. Cannes is well stocked with labels, jewels, art and Rolls-Royces (you'll have to head to Antibes to buy your yacht). La Croisette, Rue d'Antibes and the streets between them are the credit-card-flexing centre, where you'll find Hermès, Chanel et al. Get up early in Marseille and enjoy the spectacle of fish and seafood traded daily at the *marché aux poissons* at the Vieux Port. Cours Saleya market in Nice is a foodie paradise, except on Mondays, when it's all antiques.

Something for nothing Grasse perfumery Fragonard treats visitors to free guided tours of its premises, either at the original HQ in the town centre, or at the flower factory on the outskirts (www.fragonard.com).

Don't go home without... strolling along the strand in Cannes – aka La Croisette – as the sun goes down, and stopping at art deco Martinez Hotel for pre-dinner pastis.

COMPLETELY COTE D'AZUR

Millionaires, established or aspiring, can hire a Bentley – have it delivered to your hotel – and tour the Grande Corniche, a classic driving route along the highest of the coast roads from Nice to Menton (www.platinium-ca.com). What started life as a mule track along which Napoleon and the boys could invade Italy is now a smoothly Tarmacked regular on car ads, its sweeping bends making light work of the coastal contours. You may not make it as far as Menton, but try to get to Turbie, a hilltop hamlet with a Roman monument, La Trophée des Alpes (www.ville-la-turbie.fr; closed Mondays). It's one of many excuses to stop the car and admire the jaw-dropping views.

DIARY

February Monte Carlo's glamorous Primo Cup sailing competition fills the marina (www.yacht-club-monaco.mc).
May The Cannes Film Festival lures industry luminaries and gong-hopeful A-listers to town, for premieres, parties and paparazzi opps (www.festival-cannes.fr). It's followed by the F1 Monaco Grand Prix (www.monte-carlo.mc/formule1).
July The Nice Jazz Festival takes place, largely in the ruins of the Roman amphitheatre (www.nicejazzfestival.fr).
September Les Etoiles de Mougins brings chefs from across the Continent to the mediaeval village for demonstrations, tastings and general gastro celebrations (www.lesetoilesdemougins.com).

Bastide Saint Mathieu

STYLE Regally rustic villa
SETTING Green, green Grasse

'Mr Smith is drawn to the huge canopied four-poster bed, while I peer through each of the French doors, with their views to rolling misty hills bare of any other buildings'

It might seem unwise for a retailer to jump ship a few days before Christmas, leaving behind a hectic workload, breathless staff and hordes of festive shoppers. But since you can't beat the bliss of finding yourself surrounded by palm trees within two hours of leaving a sub-zero London, Mr Smith and I let ourselves surrender to the allure of the South of France. That's the great thing about flying into Nice: your holiday begins immediately, with the romance of the Riviera on the airport's doorstep.

As a perfumer, I visit Grasse several times a year. My journey always begins with the same swerving climb from sea level up into the foothills of the Alpes-Maritimes. However, on this occasion, my destination is not a fragrance house but the pine-scented Bastide Saint Mathieu, a luxury guesthouse occupying an 18th-century property 10 minutes from the town centre.

Magically, unmanned, the wrought-iron gates fling themselves open, and our car slowly crunches up the long gravel driveway. We pass groves of ancient olive trees and the kind of flawless rustic French landscape that inspires people to move here permanently. The first thing that strikes us about this pristinely restored country residence, is La Bastide's perfectly proportioned grand façade, and the calming creamy colour of the weathered stonework.

Our host, William Howard, an English gentleman with a kind and welcoming manner, whisks away our bags and leads us to a big warm-toned room on the first floor. Having deliberately not peeked online beforehand, we don't know what to expect from our boudoir. (Mr Smith and I rather enjoy that moment of apprehension as we check into hotels, however upscale.) And the Cole Porter Room proves exactly the right kind of surprise. Not only is it the size of a small apartment, but the log fire is also blazing beautifully, and there's a fine Georgian table laden with bowls of clementines, nuts and chocolate, as well as bottles of wine and water, crystal glasses and pots of orchids.

Antique furnishings (including cabinets stuffed with the family silver), big cosy chairs and wonderfully comfortable sofas still leave enough space for guests to do a couple of cartwheels – which is what you feel like doing as you take in such splendour. Mr Smith is magnetically drawn to the huge canopied four-poster bed, while I peer through each of the many French doors, with their views to rolling misty hills bare of any other buildings. Mayfair shoppers are a million miles away from my thoughts and, instead, I'm dreaming that I actually live in this amber-hued suite. It is quite remarkable for well-seasoned luxury travellers not to be able to find a *single* fault in a hotel room.

The lavish proportions extend to the marble ensuite with original latch door. The size of a modest living room, the bathroom is beautiful, clean and welcoming. There's a pillow for your head in the bath, books on an Indian wooden table, vases of fresh roses and charming shuttered windows. Everything about this splendid hotel is beyond superlative so, to make sure we aren't

dreaming, Mr Smith and I settle down to take stock in front of the fire – promptly nodding off.

Bastide Saint Mathieu is comprised of six good-sized, carefully restored rooms, all of which I sneak a look into. Each has been decorated differently, but all are steeped in the Howards' special blend of English country-house comfort, featuring big stone fireplaces, and pieces from their impressive and eclectic collection of antiques. If you were a privacy-seeking extended family wanting to avoid the usual Riviera haunts, this seven-star villa would be perfect to rent in its entirety.

Following our stealthily executed site inspection, we're ready to head out for dinner. Tilly Howard isn't merely full of recommendations – she takes the time to really listen to what we want, rather than deliver a stock list. There is no shortage of restaurants to choose from in and around Grasse, from fancy affairs to the bistros serving humble but delicious Provençal fare in Place des Aires, the energetic and charming square in the old town.

Mr Smith decides on the special-occasion option, slightly further away, and so our taxi leads us to Plascassier and La Bastide Saint Antoine, a very elegant restaurant with stunning views.

I'm all for fine dining, but my bugbear is bonsai-scaled portions; it seems to be an unwritten rule that the more refined the restaurant, the less substantial the morsels of food. My starter is so tiny that I temporarily lose sight of the lobster against the floral plate. At least we know that we have plenty of goodies waiting in our room if we get peckish later.

When we wake from an idyllic night's sleep, a scrumptious breakfast is awaiting us in the dining room – no nouvelle cuisine servings here. Fresh, sweet clementine juice, crisp baguettes, bircher muesli, organic yoghurt and eggs any style beckon us to the long wooden table hearthside, seating 14 and overlooking the courtyard. It's a blissful alternative to the pre-Christmas frenzy we're missing out on back in London, not to mention a genius way to prepare for the imminent festive onslaught.

Thanks to owners who keep on getting everything just right, it's impossible not to feel sublimely relaxed during every moment of your stay at the Bastide. If you insist on existing a little more energetically, there is plenty to do, with badminton, golf, tennis and sailing within the realms of possibility, as well as a very inviting swimming pool in the garden. Secretly, I'm rather happy we're visiting in winter: we have every excuse just to put our feet up by the fire.

Reviewed by Linda Pilkington

NEED TO KNOW

Rooms Six: one suite, four junior suites and a double.

Rates €250–€380, including breakfast but not tax.

Check-out 12 noon, but flexible, depending on availability. Earliest check-in, 2pm.

Facilities Outdoor pool with pergola, spa, gardens, boules piste, book and DVD library, free WiFi throughout. In rooms: TV, DVD on request, bottled water.

Children Youngsters are welcome, with cots provided for €20, extra beds at €40, and babysitting at around €15 an hour.

Also Bastide Saint Mathieu is a sociable sort of place, hosting pétanque matches and occasional opera events. Pets are welcome, and there's a relaxed policy towards smoking: outside is best, but inside won't be frowned on. Rooms are wheelchair-accessible, and there's a handy helipad.

IN THE KNOW

Our favourite rooms The Cole Porter Junior Suite is a sprawling, luxurious expanse on the top floor, with beautiful views of the gardens from the private terrace; its warm palette of peach, gold and terracotta offsets antique furniture in heavy, dark wood. The sitting area has a big Provençal stone fireplace, and the marble bathroom has his-and-hers basins, so you won't have to queue to clean your teeth. The James Baldwin Room, with stone walls and muted hues, has two double beds.

Hotel bar There's no bar, but if you ask the accommodating owners nicely, you'll get whatever you fancy.

Hotel restaurant In spite of Bastide Saint Mathieu's B&B status, private dinners can be arranged on request, to be served in the small dining room.

Top table If it's a balmy night, sit out on the terrace or in the pretty *cuisine d'été*, beside the gardens: a patio with a roof supported by wooden beams.

Room service There's no room service as such, but if you want a snack or a drink, speak and ye shall receive.

Dress code Relaxed and floaty, with short sleeves and flirty hemlines so you can bask in the sun.

Local knowledge Visit Grasse's perfumery museums: there's Fragonard (www.fragonard.com), Molinard (www.molinard.com) and Galimard (www.galimard.com) to choose from. If you prefer the smell of sea salt and sun lotion, set up camp on one of the dazzling beaches at Antibes, Cannes or Nice, all a short drive away.

LOCAL EATING AND DRINKING

For huge bowls of bouillabaisse, head to beachside Tétou on Avenue des Frères Roustan, Golfe-Juan (+33 (0)4 93 63 71 16). No cards, so come armed with euro. Lou Fassum at 381 route de Plascassier in Grasse (+33 (0)4 93 60 14 44) serves up gastronomic French fare, with enticing views of the Cannes coast. The Willy Wonka of the truffle world, Clément Bruno, has a wonderful restaurant in Lorgues, which uses the fabulous fungi in starters, mains and puddings: a tiny roadside sign points the way to Restaurant Bruno, set amid picturesque scenery at Campagne Mariette, Route des Arcs (+33 (0)4 94 85 93 93). If you're celebrating a special occasion, work your way through La Bastide Saint Antoine's exciting, expensive menu, at 48 avenue Henri-Dunant, Grasse (+33 (0)4 93 70 94 94). There are many seafood brasseries on Rue d'Antibes in Cannes.

GET A ROOM!

For more information, or to book this hotel, go to www.mrandmrssmith.com. Register your Smith membership card (see pages 4–5) to enjoy exclusive offers and privileges.

 SMITH MEMBER OFFER A bottle of Valcolombe Cuvée Baroque or champagne. Stay three to four days and make your own fragrance at Galimard perfumery in Grasse. For bookings of five days or more, you'll also be treated to dinner (not including wine) at a local gastronomic restaurant.

Bastide Saint Mathieu 35 chemin de Blumenthal, 06130 Saint Mathieu, Grasse
(+33 (0)4 97 01 10 00; www.bastidestmathieu.com)

Cap d'Antibes Beach Hotel

STYLE Minimalism for maximalists
SETTING Cream of the Côte

'A palette of mushroom, white and sand is picked out with glimmery metallic accents, such as golden velvet pillows and a delicately sequinned throw on the bed'

On a balmy evening just out of season, fetching up late on an exclusive promontory of the Côte d'Azur is confusing. It's dark and eerily quiet. We can see inky Mediterranean waves, inches from the coastal road, and the glitter of lights from discreet villas on one side and ultra-expensive yachts on the other.

Rusty French combined with a first-gen SatNav sees us swing past Cap d'Antibes Beach Hotel twice before we hit the bull's-eye. Yet once we arrive we wonder how we could ever have missed it; the entrance is chic, brutalist-modernist, low-slung and bright white. Positioned on the littoral road – literally and conceptually between the Cap's two Significant Other places to stay, the *grande dame* Belles Rives and the ostentatiously glitzy Hotel du Cap Eden Roc – our destination is unusually contemporary for this well-developed Medside playground.

Owing to a warm welcome from kind young staff, who ply us with champagne and smiles, our journey woes quickly melt away. Dinner timings are strict, as we've come to

fear in La Belle France, and we've missed the last service. Not to worry: a plate of local cheeses and glorious cured ham, and a chilled Provençal rosé arrive swiftly on our private terrace. We're protected by rustling palms and lulled by the sound of boats bobbing nearby.

Built on the hallowed ground of a beach club that attracted Hollywood royalty such as Cary Grant and Sophia Loren at the height of their fling, this wedge of land between two bijou marinas has been intelligently transformed into a stylish mini-resort. Cleverly crammed onto a relatively small footprint, Cap d'Antibes Beach Hotel has 27 rooms, two restaurants, a bar, spa, garden, pool and beach.

Our quarters are faultlessly designed, with smart divisions: the bedroom zone is separated from the bathroom by the three-quarter height, tiger-striped wenge-wood bedhead, providing a feeling of spaciousness. The headboard also incorporates a panel of frosted glass looking into the ensuite, for some sexy peeping. The bathroom is perfectly planned, with a double sink, bath for two, walk-in wet room with rain shower, piles of plump white towels and locally produced L'Occitane unguents. There are moments of invention, too. The iridescent purple mosaic tiling reminds us of the pearly insides of mussel shells.

Neutral floor tiling in smooth stone, textured cement on the ceiling, and electric roller doors on the full-length windows out to the terrace may make our room sound like a glamorous garage, but it's far from coldly minimal. A palette of mushroom, white and sand is picked out with glimmery metallic accents, such as golden velvet pillows and a delicately sequinned throw on the bed. I especially love the Italian-designed desk chair, covered in silvery techno fibre, and a low, comfortable chair that integrates a table into its armrest – it looks as though it's been built of plaited rope, covered in glue and left to harden. To top it all, each room has a wall-sized digital artwork, celebrating the secrets of the sea. Ours has the electrified outline of a mammoth stingray on a moody background of copper, chocolate brown and amber. It's time for bed,

and the last lights to be turned off are the glittering LEDs that are built into the bedhead, like stars.

Waking to a view of incredible coastline, you're reminded of just what a desirable bit of real estate this is. Once the garage doors are up, and we're no longer hermetically sealed in our cooled room, we hear the lively shore, abuzz with the sounds of motorbikes, speedboats, yacht bells and other visitors. The energy is infectious, and we're anxious to join the throng – after breakfast, of course.

Peerless pastries and *oeufs en cocotte* are served on a peaceful back terrace. Looking out across the waves and yachts to the Iles de Lérins, we decide to dedicate our morning to all-action watersports. Waterskiing from Belles Rives hotel is easily organised and, in no time, we're skiing straight off the private jetty. I wish I had got some practice in beforehand to emulate the nonchalance of the old hand ahead of me, who casually slips onto the water, glides between million-pound yachts and returns, after 30 minutes, barely wet at all.

We get our scuba fix with a single dive from the Cap (seeing mostly seaweed and costly hulls – the Med ain't the Maldives), and finish our odyssey with an afternoon trip to the wild and wooded Ile Sainte-Marguerite, one of the two Lérins islands we spied earlier. Surprised by hidden rocky beaches backed by scented pines and eucalyptus, we sip Orangina in the shade of the fortress that once held the Man in the Iron Mask. On the way back, we stop off at ritzy Juan-les-Pins, where tarnished blondes in mini minis and every speck of land are dedicated to sunning or posing. It's a lot of fun.

Two of the greediest people on the planet, we've had our pulses speeding up steadily about dinner at Les Pêcheurs. Designed like an ocean liner, with full-length windows facing the port on one side, and an extended terrace overlooking the blue sea on the other, Les Pêcheurs is modern and streamlined. The hotel's marine theming reaches its logical peak here, with all manner of fresh fish and just-caught crustacea given the star treatment. All the ingredients that aren't plucked from beneath the waves are sourced from the coastal hills of the Côte d'Azur and the Italian Riviera; pungent French thyme, salty little olives from Taggia, Genoese basil, and sweet, tart Provençal tomatoes play supporting roles. The dishes are all zhuzhed up with a dash of orientalism, creative presentation skills and a set of very sharp knives.

Afterwards, we eddy off for a last digestif aboard our deck – sorry, I mean on our terrace. As the noises of the day are replaced by a soundtrack of swishing palms and swaying masts, we're lulled, finally, into a sea of tranquillity.

Reviewed by Mr & Mrs Smith

NEED TO KNOW

Rooms 27, including five suites.
Rates €390–€2,100, not including breakfast, from €29, or tax.
Check-out 12 noon. Earliest check-in, 3pm.
Facilities Private beach, outdoor 'vitality' pool, spa, gardens, book and DVD library, free broadband. In rooms:
flatscreen TV, minibar, bottled water, L'Occitane products.
Children Little Smiths of six or older are welcome. The restaurant has a children's menu; cots are free for babies, and
babysitting with a local nanny can be organised (book a day in advance). The pool is for over-16s only.
Also Pets can come too, for €25 a day. Secure parking costs €25 a day.

IN THE KNOW

Our favourite rooms Deluxe Room 208 comes with dazzling views, but Room 210 has the best fish mural (every room
has one), covering an entire wall. You can sea-gaze from Suite 201, which also has a cosy sitting area and a well-sized
bathroom with a shower and free-standing tub. Suite 105 has its own private garden.
Hotel bar In a minimalist space by the lobby, with white walls and aubergine-coloured murals, the glossy red bar is
surrounded by egg-shaped tables and chairs. A wall of slanted bookshelves divides bar from restaurant.
Hotel restaurant There are two restaurants: Les Pêcheurs, a stylish eatery with gastronomic gravitas; and the more
casual beach restaurant, Le Cap. Food at Les Pêcheurs is a sensory surprise, with dishes such as veal served with
celeriac, mango and vanilla-flower salt. Le Cap serves up pasta, fish and Provençal dishes.
Top table Sit by the window at Les Pêcheurs, or close to the waves at Le Cap.
Room service Snacks and dishes from Le Cap's menu can be ordered 24 hours a day.
Dress code Don your most dazzling dinner attire for Les Pêcheurs (jackets required for men). A polo shirt or sarong will
stand you in good stead at Le Cap.
Local knowledge Hop on a boat to pine- and eucalyptus-covered Ile Sainte-Marguerite; boats leave from Cannes, or the
hotel can arrange a private charter from its beach. Tour the island's nature reserve and the old fortress prison, then
top up your tan on the peaceful shores.

LOCAL EATING AND DRINKING

Built into the ramparts and directly overlooking the sea, the fine-dining restaurant Les Vieux Murs, at 25 promenade
Amiral de Grasse, is decorated with Murano chandeliers and Italian art (+33 (0)4 93 34 06 73). For a romantic tryst, try
for a table in the shade of Le Figuier de Saint-Esprit's 40-year-old fig tree, at 14 rue de Saint-Esprit (+33 (0)4 93 34 50 12).
Restaurant de Bacon, on Boulevard Bacon, started as a simple seafood joint and is now renowned as a sophisticated
establishment (+33 (0)4 93 61 50 02). Cocktails and great Italian food are on offer at L'Enoteca, 6 rue Aubernon (+33
(0)4 93 34 03 90). Kitted out with velvety baroque furniture, Mamalu is a less formal setting for excellent pasta, at 11
cours Masséna (+33 (0)4 93 34 40 07). The hotel can arrange for you to have a beachside lunch, and even book your
sun loungers at La Plage Keller (+33 (0)4 93 61 28 23), at Cap La Garoupe, one of the area's most beautiful bays.

GET A ROOM

For more information, or to book this hotel, go to www.mrandmrssmith.com. Register your Smith membership card
(see pages 4–5) to enjoy exclusive offers and privileges.

 SMITH MEMBER OFFER A bottle of rosé and a 30-minute Omnisens massage.

Cap d'Antibes Beach Hotel 10 boulevard Maréchal Juin, 06160 Cap d'Antibes
(+33 (0)4 92 93 13 30; www.ca-beachhotel.com)

Eze

Cap Estel

STYLE Glamorous Med mansion
SETTING Lavishly landscaped clifftop

'I take a little wander into the gorgeous garden, where an infinity pool leads to the private beach and a promenade with an exquisite view'

Reviewing is new to me: as a restaurateur, I'm usually on the other side of the game. However, relishing the prospect of embarking on an espionage mission with Mrs Smith, I morph swiftly into a suave spy as we touch down in the South of France. And I take my role seriously. When we arrive at Nice, the only car on offer at Terminal 1 is a Skoda. Now, to go unnoticed in a five-star hotel, we're going to need something a little more luxurious, so we go the extra distance (on a bus, to Terminal 2) and find ourselves a nice Mercedes.

It's just a half-hour drive until we reach the winding road we are looking for, where a very small sign indicates that the legendary hotel is nearby. Faintly, in the night, we can see Cap Estel, built as a summer home in 1898, converted into a hotel in 1950, and lavishly renovated between 2001 and 2004. Once we're through the gates, we swing along another kilometre of bends, amid beautiful Mediterranean gardens. The modernist-style stone and stucco hotel looks like a private residence,

perhaps the second home of a big Hollywood producer; it presides over its own mature balustraded gardens, with glossy fig, pine and palm trees, which stop where the sea starts. We park our now-suitable car in front of the palatial entrance and step into the vast lobby.

It's not long before we're shown to our room where, once the door shuts, we pull on our detective gloves, adopt low, discreet voices, and inspect every corner, every drawer, every bar of premium soap. We admire the luxurious proportions, and are especially taken with a dressing room big enough to host Mrs Smith's entire summer wardrobe; it even has room to spare for a few sarongs for me. The bathroom has underfloor heating, a shower that packs a punch, and ample cupboard and drawer space – not always a given in luxury hotels.

The modern-classic decor is soothing and reassuringly expensive-looking, with nothing to jar the senses, though we wouldn't have minded a design quirk or two; 'understated chic' can fly rather close to unadventurous beige. We continue our special-agent duties, entering deep cover, as we do the things couples usually do in hotel rooms. I undertake to judge the comfort of the bed, the smoothness of the Frette sheets and the positioning of the giant flatscreen TV, while Mrs Smith tests the plumbing by running a fuming hot bath. She asks me to join her, to verify the size of the tub. I usually steer clear of such experiences but, as a committed gatherer of intelligence, I get in. I can report that it is indeed comfortable, deep and wide enough for two adults.

Hey, it's 9pm! We're expected downstairs at the restaurant. We leap into our clothes and into the lift, which takes us to garden level and La Table du Cap Estel. Perhaps because I own a few restaurants myself, I'm hard to please. And perhaps because I know what it's like to be savaged by critics, I don't want to be too rough. The Mediterranean cuisine is light and refined, though hardly at the vanguard of contemporary cooking. We're duly impressed by the locally sourced vegetables, which are freshly plucked from Cap Estel's own gardens.

It seems appropriate, at this point, to return to our room for a long night's sleep. Call us risqué, but we've brought along an eight-hour history documentary – the kind you never have time to watch at home. After a few hours of grainy footage, I'm moved to give Mrs Smith a goodnight kiss. Our bed seems to be made of two brand-new mattresses that are rather out of sync, so I have to climb up my side of the mountain with an ice axe and ski down hers. We nonetheless manage to sleep like angels.

After an extravagant, breakfast-missing lie-in, we open our shutters to a magnificent view of palm trees and cliffs. Strolling, sleepy-eyed, onto the roomy terrace, we see the sea and its divine bays, and the salt air reminds us we have appetites. We head to the bar for a coffee and a club sandwich, gaze directed towards the floor-to-ceiling bay windows of the Empire-style salon. While Mrs Smith returns to the scene of the lie-in for yet more horizontality, I take a little wander into the gorgeous garden, where an infinity pool leads to the private beach and a promenade with an exquisite view.

Later on, I find the state-of-the-art spa and submit to an expert massage. The sound of the waves and the wind against the cliff give me the impression I'm drifting on a boat, far away from land. It's very relaxing, and I'm lost to the world.

Strolling back through the dusk, I cross the garden again, admiring the beautifully restored building. It's time to take Mrs Smith into Nice for home-style dinner at La Petite Maison. Then we drive back along the coast for a little nightlife at Le Bar Américain in the Hôtel de Paris in Monaco. (It is only possible to do this with ease out of season – when it's thronged, the traffic's a dampener on such gallivanting.) The Hôtel de Paris is a grand old place on the same square as the legendary Casino de Monte-Carlo. As we walk into the bar, a dapper bartender seats us at a small table. To the right, the singer and her band; in front, through a door into the main lobby, the end of a party taking place in the extraordinary Galerie Empire. Glittering in long dresses and tuxedos, guests waltz into the bar, full of energy. It's perfect, like theatre – over a 1962 armagnac.

We return to Cap Estel feeling we've had a true Riviera night; on the drive back, we gossip about Greta Garbo, Gina Lollobrigida, David Niven and Rudolf Nureyev, in whose glamorous footsteps we are following by making Cap Estel our hideaway for a few days off-duty and undisturbed. Our mission as spies for Mr & Mrs Smith accomplished, we spend the rest of our stay investigating nothing more than the possibility of getting up in time for a croissant.

Reviewed by Mourad Mazouz

NEED TO KNOW

Rooms 18, including 14 suites.

Rates €430–€12,900, not including city tax of €1.50 a person a night. Breakfast, from €28.

Check-out 12 noon, but late check-out may be available for a charge. Earliest check-in, 4pm.

Facilities Cinema, spa, gym, library with DVDs and CDs. In rooms: flatscreen TV, DVD/CD, free WiFi, minibar and bottled water.

Children If you're prepared to share, bring the mini-Smiths. Extra beds are free for under-12s, babysitting is available from €16 an hour, and the restaurant does a children's menu.

Also Beneath the terraced gardens is Cap Estel's own secluded stony beach, kitted out with sunloungers.

IN THE KNOW

Our favourite rooms The property is in four parts: Le Cap is the original building; La Corniche is an Italian-style pavilion; La Mer and Le Parc are both positioned at the edge of the peninsula. Suite 210, Le Cap, is a palatial expanse with cream and oatmeal decor, high ceilings, a living room with splashes of crayon-bright colour, a vast terrace and two bedrooms and bathrooms. Suite 410, also in the main building, could double up as a company HQ, with its office space, big lounge area, kitchen and terrace – but the ruby accents and African artefacts mean it's far from corporate. La Mer's white and airy rooms, perched above the water, are more modest in size, but they have views of the pretty beach.

Hotel bar The traditionally styled bar, with chandeliers, cream leather bar stools and glossy, toffee-toned wooden surfaces, serves cocktails until 11pm. There is also a pool bar in summer.

Hotel restaurant La Table du Cap Estel's neutral decor, low leather chairs, and black-and-white tiled floor provide a sophisticated backdrop to the culinary offerings, which include foie gras with mashed asparagus and rhubarb sorbet.

Top table Request a table outside, so you can bay-watch as you eat.

Room service Cold snacks (sandwiches, salads, cheeseboards) are available 7.30am–10pm.

Dress code Côte d'Azur allure: a coral or chartreuse dress, a crisp linen shirt.

Local knowledge Seek out floral blooms and scents at the Jardin Exotique (www.eze-riviera.com) and continue the fragrant theme at Grasse perfumeries Galimard and Fragonard, which both have shops in Eze village.

LOCAL EATING AND DRINKING

The impressive cooking at Auberge de Troubadour, 4 rue du Brec, Eze (+33 (0)4 93 41 19 03) belies its diminutive size. For gastronomic tasting menus and deep-blue Riviera views, eat at Château Eza, on Rue de la Pise (+33 (0)4 93 41 12 24). Le Cactus on La Placette (+33 (0)4 93 41 19 02) is great for snacks and treats, including crêpes, salads, sandwiches and ice-cream. Eza Café at 197 avenue de Verdun (+33 (0)4 93 41 12 79) is another enticing light-bitery, offering fresh pasta and sushi, along with traditional French fare.

GET A ROOM!

For more information, or to book this hotel, go to www.mrandmrssmith.com. Register your Smith membership card (see pages 4–5) to enjoy exclusive offers and privileges.

 SMITH MEMBER OFFER A bottle of champagne and, if your stay is three nights or longer, a 30-minute massage each.

Cap Estel 1312 avenue Raymond Poincaré, 06360 Eze-Bord-de-mer (+33 (0)4 93 76 29 29; www.capestel.com)

Mougins

Les Rosées

STYLE Hearts and flowers
SETTING Super Cannes

'It's a lovingly restored country house, sitting in the same flower-filled garden where it has snoozed peacefully for more than 400 years'

We are, it turns out, the only non-honeymooners at Les Rosées, and it isn't hard to see why — it just doesn't get much more romantic than this. As pretty as its name, it's a lovingly restored, traditional Provençal country house, sitting in the same flower-filled garden where it has snoozed peacefully for more than 400 years. The village of Mougins, only a 20-minute drive from the glitz of Cannes, is to be our gloriously tranquil base for exploring the most glittering stretch of the French Riviera.

Arriving late and weary, we don't fancy venturing out for dinner, but a little life-saver of ham and cheese with a glass of wine in our room is rustled up, no problem. We are in the Isadora suite (a favourite of Liza Minnelli, apparently), whose big bedroom opens onto a turreted lounge. After our long car journey, the bed, with its clouds of crisp linen, is heavenly.

The flagstoned rooms have a rustic feel, yet they're stylish and restrained, decorated in warm, earthy tones,

à la French country chic. I'm quite happy making like Minnelli in my turret, but there's another low-key lounge downstairs, full of magazines and books, and with a grand piano. Homely touches betray the influence of the owner's Canadian wife: all-organic breakfast is a treat of croissants, home-made jams and cold meats, served on white tablecloths in the idyllic garden. The pool is a good size and, if we weren't on the doorstep of so many of Europe's A-list towns, we could easily spend a blissful day reading in the shade of the trees.

I convince Mr Smith that we have to visit the famous Fragonard factory in nearby Grasse, the perfume capital of the world. After the olfactory excesses of the city described in Patrick Süskind's novel *Perfume*, I am a little disappointed by how clinical it all is today. A guide explains the whole process, from distillation to bottling. Did you know that to extract one kilo of rose essence you must distil 3,000 kilos of roses? The tour is free but ends, predictably, in the factory shop, with a fairly heavy sell. Mr Smith grumbles, but agrees to treat me to a tiny bottle (only, I suspect, because our attractive and fragrant guide recommends it so warmly). The products at Les Rosées are Fragonard, so I've already had a chance to sample them in the luxury of our pretty, Provençal-style bathroom.

Wanting to clear our heads, we decide to head to Cannes for a spot of sea air. I work on the culture desk of a newspaper, and I've always found myself more than a little envious when the film critics set off to the famous festival every year (though, as books editor, I do get to sit in a rainy tent in Hay-on-Wye). So I am very much looking forward to finally promenading the Croisette, even if it isn't red-carpet season. Some enticing smells along the front remind us that it's lunchtime; after much indecision over the choice of rather intimidating beachside restaurants, we settle down for lunch and some serious people-watching. No wonder everyone

tends to wear giant sunglasses – all that bling can be rather blinding.

Daring to join the rows of oil-slicked bodies, laid out like so many king prawns, takes more than a little courage. Once we've taken out a small mortgage on two sunloungers, we join everybody in pretending not to be ogling everyone else. We have only been enjoying this for half an hour or so before the sun is eclipsed by the arrival of a scary-looking DJ and a boombox so large it can surely be heard in Monaco. We wander off to the marina for a tour of the yachts.

After the glare of Cannes, coming back to mediaeval Mougins is rather like taking a languid, flower-filled bath. All winding bougainvillea-bedecked streets of artisan shops, fountains and restaurants, it is exactly how you would imagine a picturesque village on the French Riviera to be – only *more* picturesque.

And it's always nice to follow where Jean Cocteau, Man Ray, Christian Dior, Catherine Deneuve, Edith Piaf and Jacques Brel have led. Most famously, Pablo Picasso spent the last 15 years of his life in Mougins, high on a clifftop overlooking the Côte d'Azur, after he married Jacqueline Roque. The village's Musée de la Photographie has a wonderful collection of portraits of him and other 20th-century icons.

It is early evening by the time we get back to base, and Mougins' townspeople and tourists — all elegantly turned out — are beginning to emerge for drinks in the square before dinner. There are so many lovely-looking restaurants that it's almost impossible to choose one, but in the end we plump for Le Petit Fouet, liking the sound of its name. Thank goodness we did, or else I might never have discovered strawberry soup. The 'Little Whip' is also a foodie emporium, and I buy several pots of posh jam for a fraction of the price they're sold at in the French delicatessen near my London office.

The highlight of the trip for Mr Smith is undoubtedly driving along the heart-stopping coastal roads. For me, it has been the complete tranquillity of Les Rosées, a soothing contrast to our high-rolling, scent-inhaling, beachwear-clad excursions to Grasse and Cannes. I probably stand as much chance of persuading the film critics to let me tag along for the film festival next year as I do of ousting Nicole Kidman out of a leading role. Still, that doesn't mean Les Rosées won't play a star part in the sequel to our séjour in Provence — coming soon.

Reviewed by Lisa Allardice

NEED TO KNOW

Rooms Five, including four suites.

Rates €250–€450, including Continental breakfast and tax.

Check-out Noon, but flexible, subject to availability. Check-in, from 3pm. The doors are locked at 10.30pm, so ring ahead if it looks as though you'll arrive later.

Facilities Outdoor swimming pool, gardens, library, treatment room for massages. In rooms: free WiFi, CD, iPod dock, minibar and Fragonard products.

Children Cots are available at €20, extra beds at €40; babysitting with a local nanny can be arranged for €10 an hour, booked a day in advance.

Also Pets can come too, free. There are no TVs in rooms, but there's a flatscreen to borrow if you're desperate.

IN THE KNOW

Our favourite rooms With honey-hued walls, a tower-shaped reading room full of natural light, separate dressing space and marble bathroom in shell pink, Isadora is the most romantic suite. Taking up the whole top floor, spacious and contemporary Serguey is coloured with cool neutrals, and has a working fireplace and a slate wet room. For a quirky stay, book the restored and re-upholstered Romany caravan, which has a little terrace. The garden-level suites St Honorat and St Marguerite both have space for an extra bed in the sitting room, so they're good options for families.

Hotel bar No bar, but you can sample the hotel's stash of robust reds and medal-winning local whites (plus home-made orange or nut wines) beneath the olive trees, in your boudoir, or nestling on velvet cushions in the salon.

Hotel restaurant Only breakfast is served, an offering of organic, fair-trade local produce, plus sweet, flaky sultana pastries and jam from the hotel's kitchen.

Top table Plump for a breakfast table in the shadow of the tower, by the outdoor sofa.

Room service A selection of drinks and snacks is on offer from 8.30am until 10.30pm.

Dress code Chic and comfy: cool linens and espadrilles.

Local knowledge The Fragonard perfumery in Grasse, at 20 boulevard Fragonard (+33 (0)4 92 42 34 34), provides the hotel's products – and will create a bespoke scent for you, too. The sweet-toothed should head to Confiserie Florian at Le Pont du Loup, Tourrettes-sur-Loup (+33 (0)4 93 59 32 91), a 35-minute drive from Les Rosées: a bonbon factory offering free tours and tastings. While you're there, stop and let your sugar rush subside at nearby Gourdon, a mediaeval village near the Gorges du Loup. Back in Mougins, the Musée de la Photographie has a permanent exhibition of portraits of Picasso, and works by Robert Doisneau and Lucien Clergue (+33 (0)4 93 75 85 67).

LOCAL EATING AND DRINKING

Book a table at Le Petit Fouet at 12 place du Village (+33 (0)4 92 92 11 70), replete with beams, chandeliers, barmen crooning along to old French songs – and a parrot that peers down at you while you eat. The walls are lined with irresistible *confitures*, candles and loose-leaf teas to take home, and tables spill out onto a terrace. Head next door to sample the foie gras at Resto des Arts on Rue du Maréchal Foch (+33 (0)4 93 75 60 03), open from 7pm until late (closed Sundays and Mondays). Pop along for lunch at Le Bistrot de Mougins, by the fountain in Place du Village (+33 (0)4 93 75 78 34). Bagsy a seat under the umbrellas outside; for supper, nip down the steps into the cellar.

GET A ROOM!

For more information, or to book this hotel, go to www.mrandmrssmith.com. Register your Smith membership card (see pages 4–5) to enjoy exclusive offers and privileges.

SMITH MEMBER OFFER A bottle of champagne on arrival.

Les Rosées 238 chemin de Font Neuve, 06250 Mougins (+33 (0)4 92 92 29 64; www.lesrosees.com)

HOW TO... BE A FLANEUR

In 1863, poet Charles Baudelaire described the flâneur – a city rambler, more or less – as a passionate spectator, for whom it is 'an immense joy to set up house in the heart of the multitude, amid the ebb and flow of movement'. Decadent, cynical, unabashedly metropolitan, Baudelaire was the founding father of flânerie, and its executor par excellence. Like his disciple Walter Benjamin, he was a 'botanist on asphalt,' an ambling, shambling, half-cut stroller with an eye so finely tuned to the urban drama that he will forever be the Copernicus of the crowded street.

For those keen to emulate Baudelaire and other great flâneurs of the past, Paris is the perfect place to 'walk the city in order to experience it'. Small enough to stroll at your leisure, big enough to teem with the street life that stimulates the senses of the urban anthropologist, the City of Lights is the spiritual home of the discriminating pedestrian, and a good starting point for flâneur ingénues.

There are no rules to flânerie (flâneurs don't do rules), but there are ways of heightening your awareness of the near-at-hand, and first-timers would be well-advised to bear them in mind when they set out to explore the city:
• Leave your watch and map at the hotel. The flâneur is always in the right place at the right time. She can never be late and never be lost. For the flâneur, the journey is the destination.
• Resist the temptation to photograph everything. There was a time in the middle of the century when, as Susan Sontag noted, the camera was an essential component of flânerie. Today, though, the camera is so ubiquitous that, instead of enhancing perception, it impedes it. Rather than looking at things through the reductive prism of their mega-pixelled mobile phones, today's flâneurs are advised to carry a notepad and pen. Like their antecedents, they should take notes, scratch down fragments, recreate the city in words. (Don't even *think* about taking a camcorder.)
• Take your lover. True, the solitude of the true flâneur sharpens the senses, but how could we recommend anything but flânerie à deux? As well as being an extra pair of eyes, a co-flâneur can help improvise routes and double the chances of uncovering the essence of a city.
• Avoid the preconceived. Guided walks and open-top buses are anathema to the flâneur, who is an observer of the overlooked, an aficionado of the odd. While the tourist is herded from gift shop to gift shop, the flâneur probes in the opposite direction. In Paris, she'll often end up in the out-of-the-way arrondissements – the 19th, the 20th – the parts of the city beyond the postcard clichés, where the urban inferno still bubbles.
• Lastly, don't timetable. Flânerie is not an activity you can squeeze in between elevenses and lunch if there's too long a queue at the Louvre. It's about more than just avoiding the tourist traps – it's a new way of seeing, a whole mode of being.

By David Annand

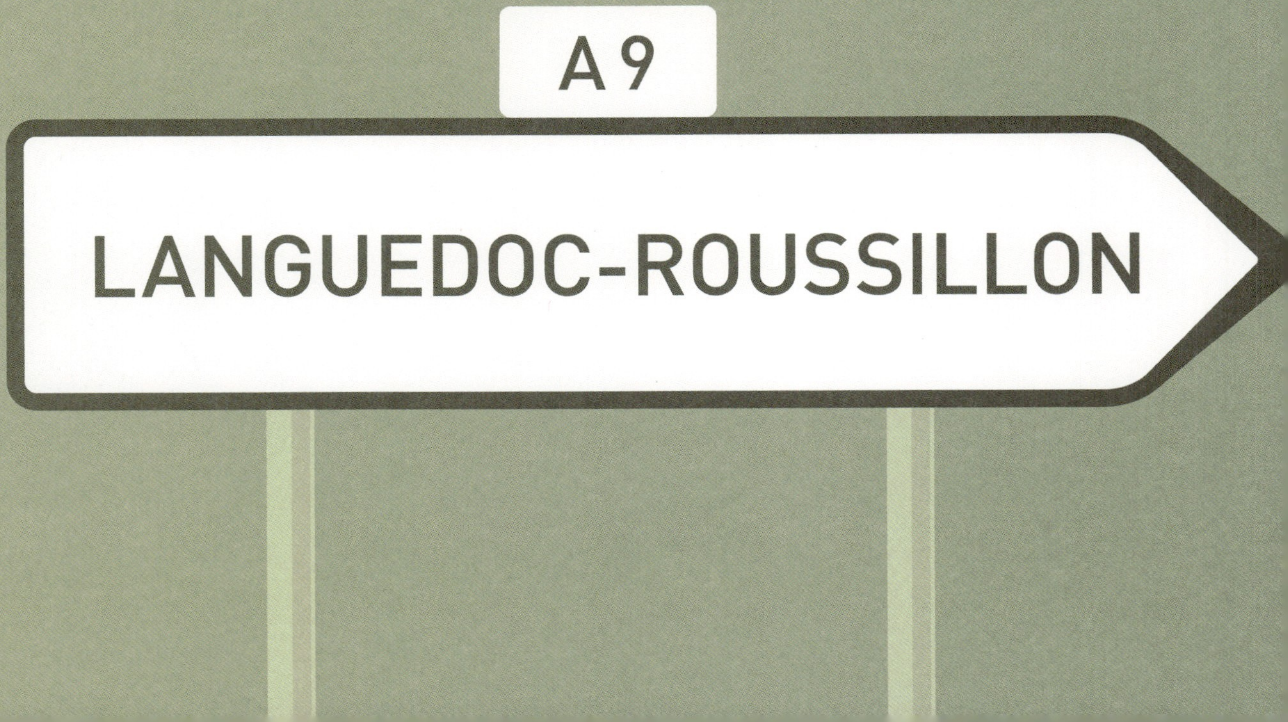
A 9
LANGUEDOC-ROUSSILLON

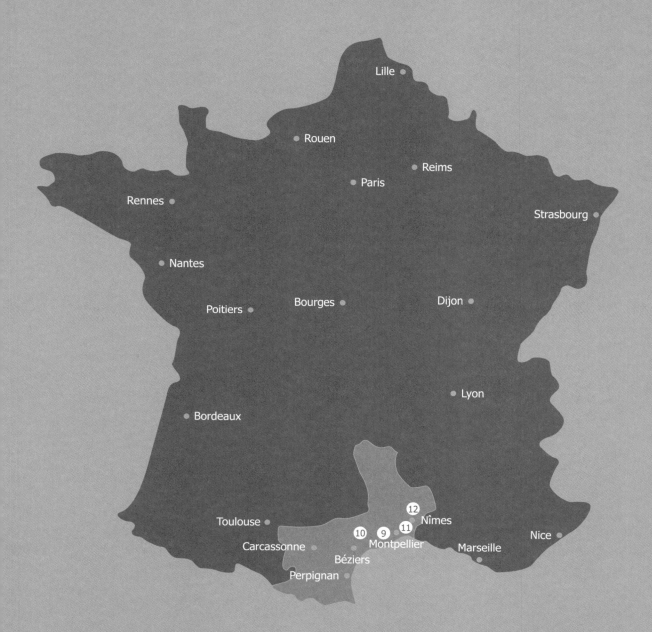

Lille

Rouen

Reims

Paris

Rennes

Strasbourg

Nantes

Bourges

Dijon

Poitiers

Lyon

Bordeaux

Toulouse

12 Nîmes

11

10 9

Montpellier

Marseille

Nice

Carcassonne

Béziers

Perpignan

LANGUEDOC-ROUSSILLON

9 Baudon de Mauny

10 Le Couvent d'Hérépian

11 Domaine de Verchant

12 Jardins Secrets

LANGUEDOC-ROUSSILLON

COUNTRYSIDE Historical hills, Roman relics
COUNTRY LIFE Bric-à-brac, strolling and sunshine

Sprawling from the chestnut-dotted Cévennes mountains to a flamingo-festooned Mediterranean coast, by way of magnificent ancient cities and rolling winelands, this region has reason to puff out its chest when declaring its rural and metropolitan offerings. Not only does Languedoc-Roussillon offer lovely sun-soaked landscape and world-class eating and drinking, but each slice of this neighbour to Provence also has its own distinct flavour. Soak up the vineyards of the Uzège, ogle the awe-inspiring Pont du Gard, and take in superb Roman antiquities in Nîmes. In summer, pleasure is a given wherever you roam, but Uzès and Montpellier yield cultural treasures – ancient and modern – all year round.

GETTING THERE

Planes From the UK, Ryanair flies from Bristol and London Stansted to Montpellier (www.ryanair.com); EasyJet flies in from London Gatwick (www.easyjet.com). You can access the west of the region via Carcassonne from Bournemouth, London, Leeds, Liverpool, Edinburgh and East Midlands with Ryanair. Air France flies from Paris Orly to Montpellier (www.airfrance.com).

Trains The TGV goes from Paris Gare de Lyon to Perpignan via Nîmes, Montpellier, Béziers and Narbonne (www.tgv.com). UK passengers should take the Eurostar from London St Pancras to Lille and change (www.eurostar.com).

Automobiles The A9 motorway runs through, with exits to Narbonne, Béziers, Montpellier and Nîmes. If you're travelling from the north, connect via the A7. Montpellier is seven hours from Paris and three hours from Lyon. Pick up a hire car at Montpellier or Carcassonne airports, Nîmes or Montpellier train stations (www.avis.com; www.hertz.com; www.europcar.com). Your train will need to arrive before 7pm, though, and only Europcar has a desk at the station in Montpellier.

LOCAL KNOWLEDGE

Taxis You're unlikely to need a cab in the smaller cities, since the streets were made for strolling; in Montpellier there's a shiny tramway linking the station, Place de la Comédie and Eighties-built quartier Antigone. If you do want one, you'll need to ring; if it's a 'late-night return to the sticks' scenario, book through your hotel.

Siesta and fiesta Most shops open 9am–12pm and 3pm–7pm, and close on Sundays. Banks share the same morning hours, then open 1.30pm–5.30pm. Lunch service often ends at 1.30pm. People usually go out to eat around 8pm. There are few nightclubs to speak of.

Do go/don't go High season (July, August and early September) is the busiest tourist time, but it's buzzy rather than crowded. Late September is quiet but not too quiet.

Packing tips Cobble-friendly sandals, proper sunglasses; extra bag for all the cool old pastis bottles, glassware and mid-century lamps you'll find in the brocantes.

Children See the sea-life at the Aquarium Mare Nostrum in Montpellier (+33 (0)4 67 13 05 50; www.aquariummarenostrum.fr).

Recommended reads The poems of Sète-born Paul Valéry, sometime Surrealist and namesake of Montpellier's university of arts and literature. The Incomplete Husband by Ben Faccini.

Local specialities Look out for bourride de Sète, a local seafood speciality. Rich, bean-laden cassoulets feature on most menus. The area is also well known for three foods: a zingy goat's cheese called Pélardon, garlic and olive oil. Expect a combination on most menus, if not most dishes. Wash down with the region's plentiful supply of syrah and cinsault reds and rosemary-tinged whites. And... Purveyors of pocket-money treats Haribo are based in Nîmes. And they have a museum dedicated to sweeties, the Musée du Bonbon, on Pont des Charettes (+33 (0)4 66 22 74 39; www.haribo.com).

WORTH GETTING OUT OF BED FOR

Viewpoint Gaze on the green Cévennes mountains from the Parc du Duché gardens in Uzès, which lies in the foothills, technically.

Arts and culture If you'd like to be astonished by some ancient sites, visit the 20,000-seat Roman amphitheatre in Nîmes, which doubles as a bullring and theatre venue. Then check out the Maison Carrée temple, occupying the site of the old Roman forum. In Montpellier, Musée Fabre, housed in the old Jesuit college, has impressive collections, including works by Rubens, Monet and Delacroix, as well as rarities by Frédéric Bazille and Pierre Soulages (+33 (0)4 67 14 83 00; museefabre. montpellier-agglo.com).

Activities Go hot-air ballooning with Les Montgolfières du Sud (+33 (0)4 66 37 28 02; www.sudmontgolfiere. com). Paragliding is offered at the nearby village of Seynes (+33 (0)4 86 87 0440; www.parapentesud.com). Canoe along the jaw-dropping Gardon from Collias to the Pont du Gard with Kayak Vert (+33 (0)4 66 22 80 76; www.canoe-france.com/gardon; March to October). Sample fine vintages at Mas de Daumac Gassac vineyard outside Aniane, where tours and tastings take place 10am–12pm, then 2pm–6pm, and all day in July and August (+33 (0)4 67 57 88 45; www.daumas-gassac.com).

Perfect picnic The Jardins de la Fontaine in Nîmes were once hailed as the grandest in Europe. In Uzès, the gardens of the Parc du Duché are comparably beautiful; or there's a small cave, La Grotte de la Baume, half an hour's walk away, towards Pont Saint-Nicolas.

Daytripper Pont du Gard (www.pontdugard.fr), the famed triple-decker aqueduct built by the Romans to deliver drinking water from Uzès through the hills of the Uzège to Nîmes is a feat of engineering to be marvelled at. There's an excellent visitor centre, and plenty of hiking trails. Bring some change to pay for parking.

Shopping Pick up local produce on market days. Uzès has a busy Saturday market selling home-made goodies, from honey to linen quilts; bric-à-brac and antiques can be found around Place aux Herbes. Rue de la Madeleine in Nîmes is great for window-shopping. For labels, head to Rue Saint-Firmin and marble-paved Rue de l'Ancien-Courrier in Montpellier; other upmarket boutiques can be found among the high-street names around Rue de la Loge and Place de la Comédie. Montpellier's Polygone centre houses Zara, Sephora and a few fashion brands, plus a supermarket. Regional edible treats can be found on Rue de l'Argenterie (we like the sweets at Pinto, number 14), and at Les Arceaux market. For second-hand French literature, try the Rue de l'Université.

Something for nothing In the west of the region, the ramparts and turrets of the fairy-tale mediaeval city at Carcassonne are a tourist magnet for good reason. On the Unesco World Heritage list, the old city is open free to visitors, who swarm to see its three kilometres of battlements, double-walled construction and dozens of towers. Strip away the souvenir shops, packed cafés and crowds, and it lives up to the step-back-in-time cliché.

Don't go home without... a trip to the beach. One of the best is just south of Montpellier at La Grande Motte; the city's summer playground of Palavas-les-Flots is another option, with good bus links. Cap d'Agde is the region's water-sports capital, and the sandy peninsula of Vias is popular with families. Hidden treasure Beauduc is near Porte de St Louis du Rhône in the Camargue. If you can find the right path, a 20-minute walk will win you a sandy strip all to yourself.

LUSTROUSLY LANGUEDOC-ROUSSILLON

Occitania is a label loosely defining the sweep of southerly French areas where the Occitan tongue is still spoken. Closest to Catalan, this Romance language evolved from Latin, and is spoken as far west as the Val d'Aran in Spain, and in Italy's Piedmont and Liguria to the east. For evidence of it around Montpellier, look out for the city's Occitan name, Montpelhièr, or scour the *tabacs* for a copy of weekly Occitan newspaper *La Setmana*, and read all about it (or it least gaze at its mysterious, heavily accented lexicon).

DIARY

May In Nîmes, it's all about the bullfighting at the Féria de Pentecôte, which lasts for five days around Whitsun. June Printemps des Comédiens (www.printempsdescomediens.com) brings global theatre and circus performance to Montpellier. International artists and choreographers throng to the south for the Modern Dance Festival in Uzès (www.uzesdanse.fr) and Festival Internationale Montpellier Danse (www.montpellierdanse.com). July Nîmes Festival is a colourful celebration of culture contemporary and classical (www.festivaldenimes.com). Later in the month, there's also a Classical Music Festival (www.nuitsmusicalesuzes.org). October The Montpellier Mediterranean Film Festival is an important date on the global-cinema calendar (www.cinemed.tm.fr). November The Festival d'Abrivado – a Camarguais bull race at Saintes-Maries-de-la-Mer – sees dozens of kamikaze cowboys charging across the beach.

Montpellier

Baudon de Mauny

STYLE Château in the city
SETTING Narrow mediaeval streets

'Here-and-now touches don't diffuse the
way-back-when feel; it's like stepping
into the past, but without surrendering any
modern-day sybaritic requirements'

Saturday morning has never been so peaceful. Though a blazing sun is doing its best to bore its way through the window-masking muslin, our vast bedchamber is cool, calm and airy. All around us is white. The walls and lofty ceiling, decorated with frescoes of frolicking fauna, are the colour of milk; and everything, from the huge bed in which we are lying, to the curtains that ripple gently in the breeze of a Montpellier morning, is Arctic-pale. I feel as though I'm in John Lennon's 'Imagine' video. All we're missing is a white baby grand.

My Yoko is just starting to stir. Mrs Smith extricates herself from the soft cotton sheets in which she's spent the night, and begins her journey across several feet of cool flagstones towards the bathroom. I turn over and allow myself to fall back into the sort of blissful half-sleep you can only achieve when you know you've got nothing remotely pressing to do.

As Mrs Smith takes full advantage of the luxurious toiletries in the ensuite, where antique charm meets contemporary cool, I look around the room through barely open eyes. Peacock-feather lamps stand next to a vase of lilies on a sinuous darkwood table, several small white circular rugs dot the floor, and a pair of scarlet Scandinavian-style chairs add a striking splash of colour to one end of the chamber. Such here-and-now touches somehow don't diffuse the way-back-when feel; it's like being able to step into the past, but without surrendering any modern-day sybaritic requirements. It's amazing how laid-back and utterly at home I feel. If that loud rendition of a Belinda Carlisle song I can hear over the pitter-patter of the shower is anything to go by, I'd say Mrs Smith feels the same way.

'Did last night really happen?' she asks, emerging from the *salle de bain* draped in a huge, white fluffy towel. It seems unbelievable, now we're ensconced in such tranquil surroundings but, yes, alas, last night did happen. Somewhere between checking ourselves into this beautiful 18th-century townhouse in Montpellier's ancient centre, and returning to our chambre d'hôte around midnight, we'd ended up in a slanging match with a furious chef out in the Place du Marché aux Fleurs. On paper, our choice of restaurant was perfect – alfresco tables, a supposedly new take on French cuisine, a quasi-celebrity chef – but an unsolicited side order of aggression left a none-too-sweet taste in our mouths.

Thank goodness, then, for Baudon de Mauny, just a short walk away from the Place du Marché aux Fleurs. Just to walk through its heavy, centuries-old wooden front door into the silent cobbled courtyard that leads to its grand stone staircase is – if you'll permit me another Lennon moment – an instant calmer. And by the time we'd reclined awhile on the antique scarlet sofa in the first-floor salon, glasses of velvety Faugères red in hand, our anger had completely disappeared.

The next morning, after a late breakfast of pastries, fresh bread and fruit, we leave the hotel behind and

head once more into the beautiful streets of the old town. Bathed in sunlight, its elegantly crumbling mediaeval buildings glow nobly, while its corkscrew alleyways provide all the shade a freckle-cheeked closet ginger such as me requires. Although Mrs Smith, with enough Italian genes in her lineage to withstand the Mediterranean glare, is all for joining the locals and stretching out in the Jardin du Champ de Mars, I manage to lure her into the excellent – and air-conditioned – Musée Fabre to see an exhibition of surprisingly gynaecological 19th-century paintings.

By dusk, we're drinking champagne cocktails outside a parkside bar off Rue Foch, watching leather-faced old men smoke on benches while their wives drag four-legged pompoms up and down the paths. Then we wander into the cobblestoned heart of the old town and secure an outside table at Le Grillardin where, on first inspection at least, no one seems to be demanding their money back or

threatening to inflict GBH on the chef. Our meal – which includes a wonderfully sticky and salty salad of pig's trotters, and garlicky, herb-infused cuttlefish – is superb. And, despite the presence of a roaming band of reggae-murdering trustafarians in the Place de la Chapelle Neuve, the experience is 100 times finer than the disaster of 24 hours ago.

Back in our soothing, all-white chamber at Baudon de Mauny, I lounge on the bed and flick through an hilariously translated local-history book – 'Saint Roch of Montpellier went alone in a wood and could have died if a dog had not brought him bread every day with a friend hand' – while Mrs Smith takes full advantage of the free WiFi to email a picture or two of this fair city to her friends. There are guests in Baudon de Mauny's other four rooms – it's just that, thanks to the hotel's laid-back ambience, we never see them. Everyone's getting up when they want, lounging in the salon when the mood takes them and generally being as relaxed about everything as we are. Like John and Yoko, we only have to imagine all the people.

Reviewed by Rufus Purdy

NEED TO KNOW

Rooms Five: two suites, two junior suites and a superior double.
Rates €160–€250, including tax. Breakfast, €15.
Check-out 12 noon, but flexible, depending on bookings. Earliest check-in, 4pm (earlier by arrangement).
Facilities Library, free WiFi throughout. In rooms: flatscreen TV, DVD, iPod docks, bottled water.
Children Welcome in ground-floor suites Les Papillons and Les Pavôts. Babies can stay free in cots; extra beds are €40 for children up to 15. Babysitting can be arranged a week in advance for €15 an hour.
Also Non-smoking throughout. Two-night minimum stay (one-night stays are possible, but incur an extra €50 charge).

IN THE KNOW

Our favourite rooms Junior suite Les Gypseries has a mammoth-tubbed bathroom, floor-to-ceiling windows and walk-in wardrobe; a hand-carved bucolic scene and faux-fur bedspread may sound rustic, but it's all swag-free and minimal. The two suites on the ground floor, Les Papillons and Les Pavôts, are ideal for long stays or family visits, since they share a full kitchen. Look out for Cole & Son wallpaper that inspired the rooms' names, for example: the flamingoes in superior double Les Flamants Roses.
Hotel bar Soft drinks are provided free, and there's an honesty bar in the main lounge.
Hotel restaurant There's no restaurant, but group dining (for a minimum of six) can be arranged at weekends: Provençal or French, according to your whim.
Top table In the main room, the red sofas in front of the stone fireplace are ideal for savouring an aperitif.
Room service None as such: the selection of beers and regional wines in the honesty bar are your in-room drinks, and you can ask for snacks such as crisps or peanuts.
Dress code Comfortable cashmere loungewear, in which to sprawl, wineglass in hand.
Local knowledge Make time for the facelifted Musée Fabre. It may not be the place for Picassos or Monets, but is well endowed with art gems from the 1600s to the 1900s. The Halles Castellane, on the corner of Rue Saint-Guilhem and Rue de la Loge, is a covered food market, selling fresh fruit, flowers and, crucially, bread and saucisson. Montpellier is eminently flâneur-friendly: once you've explored the Ecusson (the lovely old centre), stroll further afield to grittier Cours Gambetta, the neoclassical housing estates of Antigone or studenty Rue de l'Université.

LOCAL EATING AND DRINKING

At 2 rue de la Carbonnerie, L'Heure Bleue is a trifold temptation, rolling a tearoom, art gallery and antiques shop into one (+33 (0)4 67 66 41 05). Carnivores and/or oenophiles should head to Le Comptoir de l'Arc at 2 rue Hôtel de Ville, which serves an exquisite steak tartare au pesto (+33 (0)4 67 60 30 79). Close to the Musée Fabre at 39 boulevard Bonne Nouvelle, Insense is famed for its foie gras crème brûlée (+33 (0)4 67 58 97 78). Make sure you book in plenty of time if you want to go gastro at La Maison de la Lozère at 27 rue de l'Aiguillerie; it's one of the finest restaurants in town, and accordingly popular (+33 (0)4 67 66 46 36).

GET A ROOM!

For more information, or to book this hotel, go to www.mrandmrssmith.com. Register your Smith membership card (see pages 4–5) to enjoy exclusive offers and privileges.

 SMITH MEMBER OFFER A bottle of local wine.

Baudon de Mauny 1 rue de la Carbonnerie, 34000 Montpellier (+33 (0)4 67 02 21 77; www.baudondemauny.com)

Le Couvent d'Hérépian

STYLE Vaulted mod-convent
SETTING Pastoral Languedoc

'Half an hour of gentle, expert kneading
in the mini-spa leaves me with barely
the will to pour my apricotty, almondy bulk
into the small blue-tiled pool'

It's a hellish scene. The sweat glistens on the red, bullish neck of our tattooed host, as he plunges his shovel once more into the fiery depths of the oven. Tension electrifies the over-heated air, and snarled curses send terrorised staff running from the kitchen. The shovel emerges, bearing a pizza of the kind known as Sergio. It shares its name with the restaurant and, presumably, also with the demonic cook, who cackles heartily as he flings the dish towards one of his nervous customers.

In Hérépian, a charming 1980s timewarp of a village in the Languedoc-Roussillon region, this mozzarella-topped manifestation of fire and fury appears to be the main Friday night attraction. Mrs Smith and I wolf down the remainder of our food and knock back the rest of a bottle of rosé, before we scuttle, giggling like naughty nuns, back to our convent.

It's the second time we've gone from hell to heaven in a single day. It is perhaps when you arrive in less-than-rosy circumstances that a hotel has a chance to show its true colours, and I feel we can reliably vouch for Le Couvent d'Hérépian. After a sweat-soaked, infuriating few hours spent beside a broken-down hire car, and an afternoon of golden sunshine wasted in trilingual negotiations at a garage, our final resting place needed to be pretty special if our moods were to be lifted.

Our first impressions of Le Couvent were delightful, the austere 17th-century façade giving way to an interior that more than lives up to the fantasy of a fairy-tale castle, filled with chandeliers and candlelit stone staircases, and the whole building somehow enveloped in a delicious chocolatey fragrance. The bar, lounge and suites are stylishly and comfortably kitted out, and the pre-stocked, in-room iPods are a great touch. I particularly appreciated the honesty bar when, following our day of automotive tribulation, I was able to storm in silently and dilute my frustration with alcohol without feeling the need to make small talk with bar staff or sit around looking pleadingly at passing waiters.

The hotel's staff are extremely considerate, treating us with an unfailing kindness and sensitivity. When Mrs Smith clumsily smashes to smithereens one of the soap dispensers in our meticulously coordinated bathroom, the manager, Fabrice, says it is *pas grave* and immediately inquires whether anyone has been hurt. When our breakdown forces us to cancel a spa appointment at short notice, the masseuse sympathises and sweetly offers to squeeze us in the next day. When we arrive back from an ill-fated trip to the coast – involving 5km traffic jams and erratic air-conditioning – we are greeted with charcuterie and sympathy, followed swiftly by a delicious fideuà (a noodly version of paella) and a glass or three of local red.

On Sunday we are woken by the peal of bells from the village church, but even the splendid sun-washed mountain view that fills our open window takes its time in outmatching the softness of our mattress. In the patchwork of gardens below, the neighbours busily tend their vines. This encourages us to get active or, at least,

to stumble sleep-drunk down to the garden terrace, where we eat a breakfast of perfect crisp croissants, local hams and cheeses, and home-made fig jam. After this feast, I sit back and await my massage, watching swallows criss-cross a moon that's outstaying its welcome in the deep-blue sky.

I feel a twinge of guilt about the levels of our weekend indulgence when I think of Le Couvent d'Hérépian's earlier inhabitants. The nuns who lived in the sturdy stone structure back in the 1600s would have been unlikely, I reflect, to have spent many of their days attempting to consume their own body weight in red wine, or eating quantities of dairy produce that would make the Milky Bar Kid worry about gallstones. But the genius of Le Couvent is that its owners have managed to sustain the aura of a religious retreat, while packing in all manner of epicurean delights.

Nearby spa town Lamalou-les-Bains doesn't stand much of a chance with us, not when we have de-stressing

sessions booked here, in Le Couvent's own mini-spa, where massage and calm are dispensed in a treatment room and a diminutive hydrotherapy pool, housed in stone vaults and looking out over the garden towards the mountains.

I head to the the spa after breakfast, allowing a little time to elapse and requesting moderate handling. The half-hour of gentle, expert kneading that ensues leaves me with barely the will to pour my apricotty, almondy bulk into the small blue-tiled pool. Afterwards, aware that there are only a few hours to go before we have to leave, I step out into the garden in my fluffy white robe to take one last breath of it all, catching a waft of scent from the blooms cascading out of giant pots on the lawn. Like those nuns, I'm finding it all rather heavenly. The trials of the day before, along with the crowds and noise of our life at home in London, seem four centuries away.

Reviewed by Ian Griffiths

NEED TO KNOW
Rooms 13 suites.
Rates Low season: €120–€265. High season: €180–€370. Buffet breakfast, €15.
Check-out 11am. Earliest check-in, 3pm.
Facilities Indoor and outdoor pools, spa, library with CDs and DVDs, free WiFi throughout. In rooms: kitchenette with hob, microwave, coffee-maker and fridge, flatscreen TV, DVD/CD, preloaded iPod and dock, L'Occitane bath products.
Children Although it's more of an adults' escape, the hotel can provide extra beds for €30 a night, and babysitting by arrangement.
Also The spa products are freshly prepared, organic and use locally sourced ingredients: camomile, olive, lavender, honey, thyme and grapeseed.

IN THE KNOW
Our favourite rooms The four south-facing suites on the upper floors each have private balconies looking out over the village of Hérépian and the Monts d'Orb. The ground-floor suites have dinky terraces, but without the grand panoramas of the suites above. The split-level Garden Suite comes with toasty underfloor heating.
Hotel bar The honesty bar is down in a vaulted limestone cellar, where you can sink into chunky contemporary chairs with a glass of local wine; it can be plundered all night long. Aperitifs are served every evening in the bar, salon or gardens.
Hotel restaurant Le Couvent d'Hérépian offers a table d'hôte, given a day's notice. Chef and charcutier Michel Aninat, noted for his *saucisse* by Rick Stein, prepares tapas and hearty dishes such as lamb confit and coq au vin.
Top table You can perch anywhere you like for wine and nibbles. Make a beeline for the main terrace on a balmy evening; when it's chillier, the fireplace in the salon has a cluster of cosy armchairs.
Room service Breakfast can be brought to you, and there's a tapas menu served until 7.30pm.
Dress code Low-key and loungey.
Local knowledge The village of Lamalou-les-Bains is a short drive from the hotel, and offers both a nine-hole golf course with gorgeous views (+33 (0)4 67 95 08 47), and mineral springs where you can indulge in thermal treatments and therapies.

LOCAL EATING AND DRINKING
Sample Hérépian's celebrated black turnips at L'Ocre Rouge (+33 (0)4 67 95 06 93; www.locrerouge.fr). It's one of the region's best eateries and is particularly recommended for its wine-matching prowess. L'Auberge de l'Abbaye in Villemagne serves fresh regional cuisine for around €50 a head, wine included (+33 (0)4 67 95 34 84). There are just two choices for each course on the menu at L'Atelier at 22 rue les Puits in Bédarieux, where limited variety is amply compensated for by culinary invention (+33 (0)4 67 23 86 02). Named after the stone-walled building's former incarnation, La Forge in Bédarieux, at 22 avenue Abbé-Tarroux, serves very good fish and game dishes, with menus starting at €15 (+33 (0)4 67 95 13 13).

GET A ROOM!
For more information, or to book this hotel, go to www.mrandmrssmith.com. Register your Smith membership card (see pages 4–5) to enjoy exclusive offers and privileges.

 SMITH MEMBER OFFER A bottle of Château de Raissac.

Le Couvent d'Hérépian 2 rue du Couvent, 34600 Hérépian (+33 (0)4 67 23 36 30; www.couventherepian.com)

Domaine de Verchant

STYLE Revamped mansion
SETTING Manicured vineyard

'Not only do we have a bathroom about
the size of Montpellier airport, but there's also
a wraparound balcony that overlooks
the lagoon-like pool and the majestic grassy
sweep down to the vines'

Ooooh!' say Mrs Smith and I, simultaneously, involuntarily and somewhat ridiculously, as our cab crunches up Domaine de Verchant's serpentine drive. Some 17 hectares of vine-striped fields, now looking rusty and golden in the weak autumn sun, with a cluster of sandy-stoned farm buildings in the lawned and leafy centre – it looks like the perfect setting for a weekend of wine-splashed rural escapism. Which is handy, because that's what we have planned.

Verchant has been here since 1582, when a dying bishop handed the estate to a Montpellier family (the date of the transaction has lent a name to the domaine's wines), but it took another 420 years before owners Pierre and Chantal arrived on the scene and turned the working winery into a working winery with a deluxe hotel and spa in the middle. Upgraded to a terrace room, we not only have a bathroom the approximate size of Montpellier airport, but there's also a wraparound balcony that overlooks the lagoon-like pool and the majestic grassy sweep down to the vines.

Mrs Smith clocks the aesthetics (bright white with scarlet pops, floor-to-ceiling windows, gigantic snaking desk lamp, creamy stone arches) while I conduct the functionality overview: how the shower works (middle knob for temperature, top for intensity); what channels on TV (BBC World, French soft porn). A *Star Trek* button panel has me a little stumped beyond light-dimming and blind-closing. I'm sure with more application I could have got it to summon an android chambermaid.

We follow stairs down to the courtyard, past buildings and barns and men carrying ladders purposefully. This doesn't feel like a boutique hotel – it's more like a farm stay, only with incredibly luxurious bedrooms and some of the sharpest decor in the South of France. Not an environment in which you'd expect to find one of Montpellier's most celebrated spas, but there it is, looking out through glass walls, over row upon row of grapevines. While my wife is plastered with various Anne Sémonin unguents, I head straight to what has been intriguingly dubbed the 'experience shower', ie: disco-lighting equipment attached to the ceiling, and three curiously labelled buttons attached to the wall. Hmm. Now, am I in the mood for Cool Fog, Atlantic Ocean or African Storm? I opt for all three in turn. First, a blue spotlight, a chilly trickle and a puff of minty air. It's like being trapped inside a damp packet of Polos. Atlantic Ocean ups the trickle to a torrent, glows red, then cues up a soundtrack of squawking seagulls. African Storm is green, warm and, yes, minty, but the seagulls are still here (or possibly they're parrots, it's hard to tell).

'How was the experience-shower experience?' asks a newly radiant Mrs Smith. 'Like a foggy Atlantic storm off the coast of Guinea-Bissau. With added spearmint.' Mrs Smith leads me to the sauna and hammam, where we steam and bake ourselves before being ushered to the sink full of ice and the bucket on a rope. 'What happens if I pull the rope?' I ask. 'You're transported to a magical land of fairies and unicorns.' Turns out she was lying. Now, *that's*

an experience shower. Once the screaming stops, I realise that a gallon of icy water to the face is actually quite refreshing. Our appetites are suitably worked up for the hotel's other boast: fine dining.

Verchant's restaurant is run by the Pourcel twins, possibly the best chef team to ever share womb-space. Laurent and Jacques are the brains behind the much-fêted Le Jardin des Sens, so by the time we're seated in the little eatery, glugging on the hotel's own glorious red, we're quietly confident that the food won't disappoint. A *bien-être* menu caters to the detox crowd – normally something I'd avoid like a busy gym, but the brine-boiled guinea fowl and asparagus (thank you, pocket dictionary, for deciphering that one) proves too tempting, especially when paired with a starter of three types of foie gras from the less health-orientated menu. The waiter arrives to tell us that if we want the hot chocolate biscuit, we need to order

it soon, since it takes a while to prepare. We're sold. It's a steamy, thick, liquidy paradise of a dessert, which Mrs Smith declares 'better than sex'. I could feel offended, but in this instance, she's right.

The next day, we take the 15-minute trip into Montpellier old town, and spend the afternoon strolling along stately boulevards and narrow side streets, cursing the fact that we've chosen to turn up on a Monday, when the art-stuffed Museé Fabre is closed, berating the fact that I forgot to pack socks and speculating as to why Montpellier needs quite so many photocopying shops per capita, yet has so few sock outlets. Eventually, *chaussettes* sorted, we bar-hop through the twilight, before settling at surely the best bistro ever. We find Bistrot d'Alco entirely by accident, but this is one we'll be raving about until we've no friends left to listen. A three-course meal for less than you'd pay for a cocktail. A lady in the middle of the restaurant manning a stove exclusively for crêpes suzette. Duck breast carpaccio as tender as jelly, and a perfect hunk of beef served with curried chickpeas and a jacket potato. Everything about the place is excellent (although someone could tell them they don't need topless women on their business cards).

Satisfied and sluggish with all that we've eaten and drunk, we take a cab back to Verchant for our final night (I only hope the ever-polite waiting staff didn't notice Mrs Smith launching head-first into the plate-glass door). The hotel has been a fabulous opportunity to relax in a beautiful landscape immersed in fine wine and wonder. And, like the mint-spraying shower, it's been entirely refreshing.

Reviewed by Mr & Mrs Smith

NEED TO KNOW

Rooms 22, including four suites.

Rates Low season, €230–€550; high season, €300–€800. Rates include tax but not breakfast, €25.

Check-out 12 noon. Earliest check-in, 3pm.

Facilities Spa with heated hydrotherapy pool and five treatment cabins, sauna, hammam, Jacuzzi and gym, outdoor swimming pool, wine-tasting *caveau*, gardens, free WiFi throughout, valet parking. In rooms: flatscreen TV, DVD, Anne Sémonin or Hermès products. Some rooms have PCs and printers, and some suites have Bose sound systems and iPod docks.

Children Cots are provided free; extra beds are €18. The restaurant has a children's menu, and breakfast is included for under-12s. A local babysitter can be arranged.

Also Pets can come too, for €20 a day.

IN THE KNOW

Our favourite rooms In the Neige d'Avril honeymoon suite, there's a round bed with sheer white curtains, a dressing room and sitting area and an enormous hydro-massage tub. The suite also has a private terrace. We love the pool-facing Chinoise Suite, the Marie Charlotte Room for its hand-carved antique Indian door, and the Nur Mahal Room, which has access to the garden from its own terrace. La Forge apartment is great for families. It has lots of space and an upstairs lounge with views over the vineyards.

Hotel bar A bright space with mosaic flooring, square grey tables and egg-shaped swivel chairs in olive-green leather, the bar is the perfect place to test-taste Verchant's own wines, as well as sampling the fine single-malt selection.

Hotel restaurant The Pourcel twins are behind the elegant but unfussy gourmet restaurant. There's a bien-être menu of grilled fish and so on, providing gastronomic back-up for the good work done in the hotel spa, but those on a more gluttonous track needn't worry – there's an à la carte offering of delicious Mediterranean cuisine.

Top table In warm weather, sit outside by the pool. Indoors, ask for a table by the arched glass door so you can gaze out at your luxuriantly landscaped surroundings.

Room service There's a 24-hour menu of light bites and drinks.

Dress code Effortless sleek chic, but note the gravel paths aren't heel-friendly.

Local knowledge Pack your visors, sweaters and slacks. There are several golf courses in the area, including Domaine de Massane and Golf de la Grande Motte.

LOCAL EATING AND DRINKING

The HQ of the Pourcel twins is Le Jardin des Sens at 11 avenue St-Lazare in Montpellier (+33 (0)4 99 58 38 38), a showcase for their much-fêted Mediterranean flavours. Effet Mer (+33 (0)4 67 56 02 14) on the beach is one Montpellier's swishest social spots, with live DJ sets and super-sleek sunloungers. In the old town, Comptoir de l'Arc on Rue Hôtel de Ville (+33 (0)4 67 60 30 79) is a corner brasserie on a pretty square, and a great place for lunch and people-watching. L'Heure Bleue (+33 (0)4 67 66 41 05) on Rue de la Carbonnerie is a tearoom, art gallery and antiques shop in one. For the best steak tartare in town, try Bistrot d'Alco on Rue Bonnier d'Alco (+33 (0)4 67 63 12 89).

GET A ROOM!

For more information, or to book this hotel, go to www.mrandmrssmith.com. Register your Smith membership card (see pages 4–5) to enjoy exclusive offers and privileges.

 SMITH MEMBER OFFER A bottle of red or white from the hotel vineyard, and a 10 per cent discount on spa treatments and massages.

Domaine de Verchant 1 boulevard Philippe Lamour, 34170 Castelnau-le-Lez (+33 4 67 07 26 00; www.domainedeverchant.com)

Nîmes

Jardins Secrets

STYLE Toile de Jouy, tant de joie
SETTING Hidden in the old city

'It's a storehouse of diversions and pleasures, a maze of objects offering a thousand and one places for lovers to disappear together'

If, God forbid, it transpired that a raging bull, hellbent on vengeance, were to break out of a bullfight taking place in Nîmes' mighty arena, it would be here, at Jardins Secrets, that I'd come to seek refuge. Even if the runaway beast were to knock down the door, charge past the swimming pool and career into the salon, stamping his hooves, I'd be quite sure to escape without having to pole-vault out of the window. Try as he might to find his footing on the waxed floorboards, my pursuer would only succeed in skidding on a kilim, goring the hangings, sticking his horns through paintings and silk cushions, and getting in a rare tangle with the chandeliers.

The sheer weight of the collectibles gathered at Jardins Secrets would bow a crazed bull's head more effectively than any number of jabs from a picador's spear. The communal areas of this charming bourgeois villa reveal a veritable little 18th-century museum – a private one, of course.

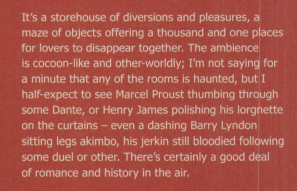

It's a storehouse of diversions and pleasures, a maze of objects offering a thousand and one places for lovers to disappear together. The ambience is cocoon-like and other-worldly; I'm not saying for a minute that any of the rooms is haunted, but I half-expect to see Marcel Proust thumbing through some Dante, or Henry James polishing his lorgnette on the curtains – even a dashing Barry Lyndon sitting legs akimbo, his jerkin still bloodied following some duel or other. There's certainly a good deal of romance and history in the air.

Back to the beginning of our tale: Jardins Secrets is hidden, naturally enough, on a discreet city-centre street. A simple copper sign – the sort you'd never notice if you weren't looking for it – announces the hotel entrance. You find it, you ring, the door opens and you enter a miniature garden of Eden, with banana plants, olive trees, deckchairs and a pool. In the heart of Nîmes, it's a wonderful surprise.

Annabelle Valentin and her husband Christophe perfected their ultra-chic antique-laden boutique hotel five years ago. I say 'perfected', but the work is never finished: last year they added a new wing to the original building, an old coaching inn where horse-drawn carriages used to stop, with great picture windows and thick walls. The operatically designed annexe, built in the style of an Andalusian cloister, with columns and capitals, gave them several extra bedrooms, putting the running total at 14. With names such as Grisailles, Suite de Madame, Suite de l'Orangerie, Lolita and Madone, all are different, though all are marked by the same penumbral elegance. Some are so suffused with their pre-revolutionary past that I feel like striking a Marat-like pose in the bath.

The interiors are far from conventionally Mediterranean, rather opulent with brocade and leather armchairs and overstuffed sofas, which go down well with a largely Anglo-Saxon clientele. Jardins Secrets has a definite appeal not only for trysting lovers, but also for whisky drinkers, cricket men, Dickens readers, and anyone partial to a mantelpiece stacked with atlases and art books. We come and go, during our stay, between the bar, hung with handpainted scenes of Hindustan, the red salon, the music room and the lobby, dominated by a Holy Virgin. Other rooms lead on from these, and all lend themselves to relaxing, dozing or, during Féria, relating tales of the day's thrills. In the morning, each group of guests occupies its own salon, where breakfast is served by waitresses in Proustian black dresses and white aprons. Canaries chirrup softly from within their architecturally impressive cages. And by night, when it's candlelit, intimacy, secrecy and seduction seem second nature.

Whereas Annabelle continues to scour the region's *brocantes* for antiques, orientalist paintings, Chinese porcelain, pretty tea services — all of which is displayed without seeming to gather a single grain of dust — Christophe is the green-fingered one, the head gardener. (His home-made jams, served at breakfast, are faintingly good, some containing rose or

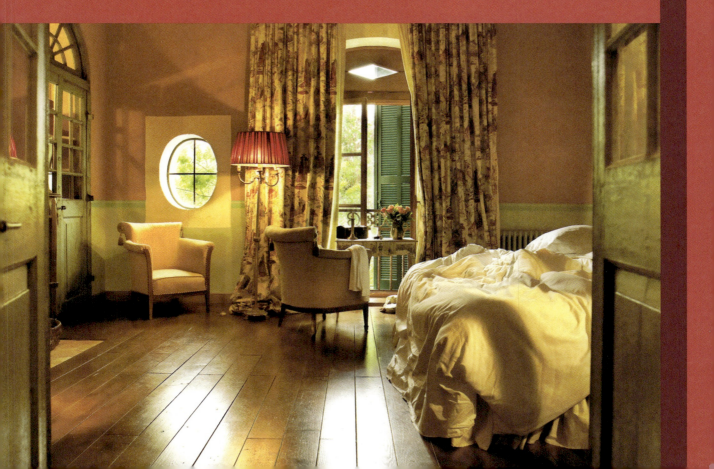

violet petals.) A globetrotting former photographer, he learned his trade in Africa, where he was director of a hotel group in Sierra Leone. Before having to flee from rebellion and civil war, he tells me, he found himself face to face with a green mamba, that legend among poisonous snakes, which he coolly dispatched. Aha, so an escaped bull would be a doddle. Knowing we're in safe hands, I sit back in my armchair and stretch out my legs – my well-tended, expertly massaged, scented legs, fresh from the superb spa and hammam concealed beneath the cloisters.

In spite of my torpor, and our protected, charmed environment, I jump a little. Is that the sound of far-off thunder? I imagine the mistral wind rising and hurling itself at the ancient stone monuments of Roman Nîmes, sheets of steely-grey rain descending... But the sky is cloudless, ideal, azure. Nope, it was nothing but a passing TGV, rumbling along metallically somewhere in the neighbourhood. In these mysterious secret gardens, even the alarming beasts aren't always quite what you expect.

Reviewed by Philippe Trétiack

NEED TO KNOW

Rooms 14, including seven suites.

Rates €195–€410, not including breakfast, €25.

Check-out 12 noon. Earliest check-in, 2pm.

Facilities Outdoor heated pool, spa with hammam, gardens, free WiFi throughout. In rooms: flatscreen TV, bottled water.

Children Cots can be supplied for €40, extra beds for €80. You'll have to bring your own babysitter, though, and remind youngsters to be respectful of the many delicate objets d'arts and pindrop-peaceful gardens.

Also For €40, you can pack your pet. As though the hotel weren't relaxing enough, the diminutive but magnificent Source des Secrets spa offers Chinese, Japanese and ayurvedic massages by the plunge pool.

IN THE KNOW

Our favourite rooms With its green and purple colour scheme, stained-glass window by the bath and over-the-top chandeliers, the bold decor of Alick sets our hearts aflutter. Jannette feels lighter and brighter, with eggshell and black tones, and musical notation adorning the lampshades and long curtains. Both look out over the cloister. Double deluxe Grisailles (named for its 18th-century chiaroscuro painting) and junior suite L'Orangerie have garden views.

Hotel bar Beers, wines, spirits and soft drinks can be brought to you by staff in the antique-filled, trompe-l'oeil salon, until 2am.

Hotel restaurant The only official meal here is the first of the day – but, goodness, does their cake-baking, *confiture*-conjuring kitchen go to town. Breakfast can be served in any of the hotel's salons, or outside.

Top table Secure a spot on the terrace in the walled garden, among the birdcages and bougainvillea.

Room service You can request drinks in your room, as well as cheese or charcuterie platters.

Dress code Refined, relaxed and a little bit dashing.

Local knowledge Classicists and Roman architecture enthusiasts will be in their element. Nîmes is littered with relics and ruins from the empire's glory days, such as the amphitheatre, the Maison Carrée temple, and the awe-evoking Pont du Gard, a drive out of town. Fashion boffins will already know that the city's signature fabric, *serge de Nîmes*, gave its name to a certain workwear fabric.

LOCAL EATING AND DRINKING

The courtyard restaurant of **Bar Le 9** on Rue de L'Etoile has a romantic and relaxed atmosphere, and serves excellent fish dishes (+33 (0)4 66 21 80 77). **Le Lisita**, on Boulevard des Arènes, is the city's restaurant du jour (+33 (0)4 66 67 29 15), but the enchantingly named **Le Darling** on Rue Madeleine (+33 (0)4 66 67 04 99) is hot on its heels, serving inventive amuse-bouches and artistically jus'd main dishes. **Aux Plaisirs des Halles** on Rue Littré serves delicious Provençal cooking on a beautiful terrace (+33 (0)4 66 36 01 02; closed Sundays and Mondays). The bistro-style **Jardin d'Hadrien**, on Rue Enclos Rey, has a shaded garden and works miracles with local beef and lamb (+33 (0)4 66 21 86 65). Slinky **L'Exaequo** on Rue Bigot is perfect for late-night mojitos and flamenco (+33 (0)4 66 21 71 96).

GET A ROOM!

For more information, or to book this hotel, go to www.mrandmrssmith.com. Register your Smith membership card (see pages 4–5) to enjoy exclusive offers and privileges.

 SMITH MEMBER OFFER A bottle of rosé.

Jardins Secrets 3 rue Gaston Maruejols, 30000 Nîmes (+33 (0)4 66 84 82 64; www.jardinssecrets.net)

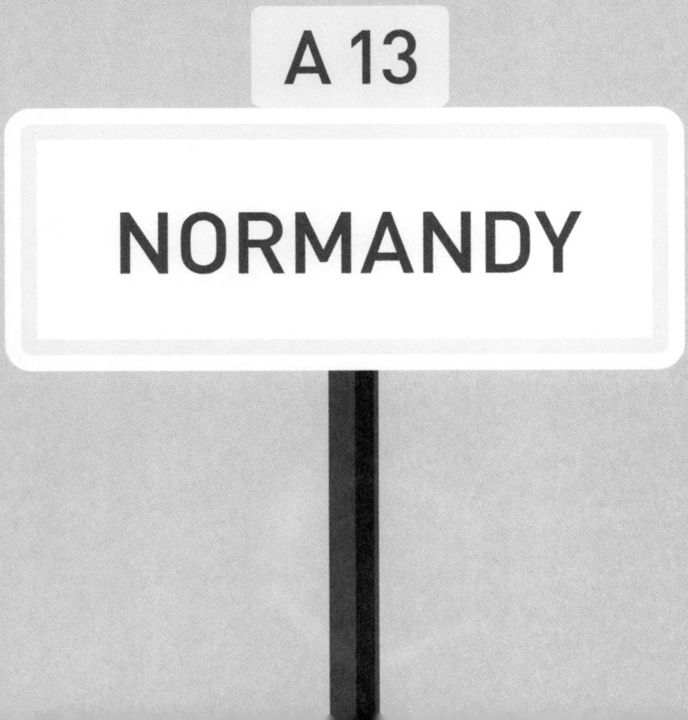
A 13
NORMANDY

Lille

Dieppe

Le Havre

Rouen

Caen Honfleur

⑬

Rennes

Reims

Paris

Strasbourg

Nantes

Poitiers Bourges Dijon

Lyon

Bordeaux

Toulouse Montpellier Nice

Marseille

NORMANDY

⑬ Château de Saint Paterne

NORMANDY

COUNTRYSIDE Fecund farmland-on-sea
COUNTRY LIFE Beachcombing, rustic roaming

Normandy's miles of fertile field and orchard are its heart and soul; Channel-side, sandy strands and chalky cliffs are punctuated by ports great and small, as well as elegant seaside resorts such as Deauville and Trouville. It is weightily historic, the place where William the Conqueror was born, Joan of Arc perished at the stake, and Allied forces invaded and liberated Europe during World War II; you'll find rich pickings among castles, cathedrals and museums. Gastronomically, Normandy is celebrated for Camembert, oysters, forestfuls of fungi, and all things appley, from sugar candy to Calvados. And don't fret about food miles – in a fat-of-the-land destination like this one, your lunch will have travelled no more than yards.

GETTING THERE

Planes Catch a domestic flight from Lyon to Rouen (www.airfrance.com) if you're coming from the Midi. Paris Charles de Gaulle is the nearest access point for passengers from the UK and elsewhere.
Trains From Paris, it's a swift two hours between the Gare Saint-Lazare and central Caen (www.sncf.com). For Lower Normandy, take the TGV from Paris Montparnasse to Le Mans (one hour). Marseille to Rennes is a six-hour schlep (www.tgv.com).
Boats Channel-side Normandy is served by a glut of ports providing easy access by ferry from the UK. For Honfleur, Le Havre is nearest, though Dieppe will do nicely (www.ldlines.com). Alençon is a two-hour drive from Le Havre.
Automobiles From Paris, the A13 and A11 motorways take you to the north and south of the region respectively. Rouen is a two-hour drive from Calais, 90 minutes from Paris, or one hour from Le Havre.

LOCAL KNOWLEDGE

Taxis There are few Norman towns big enough to warrant cabbing it. In Rouen, you'll find taxi stands on both sides of the river. Caen's pick-up points include the train station. In remoter areas, ask your hotel to book a car for you.
Siesta and fiesta In bigger towns, shops are open 9am–7pm, banks 9am–5pm. Banks close on Saturday afternoons, and most businesses have a two-day weekend on Sundays and Mondays. In small towns and villages, shops generally shut 12pm–2pm.
Do go/don't go As you'd expect of a northwesterly, coastal area, Normandy can be wet and windy. July and August are the sunniest months, June and September quieter. Whenever you go, take rainy-day gear.
Packing tips A sturdy, airtight Tupperware box, into which you can seal your homebound Camembert, leaving your luggage unperfumed.
Children Visit the fan-shaped Naturoscope complex in Honfleur, which houses a swirling kaleidoscope of butterflies (+33 (0)2 31 81 77 00; www.naturoscope.com).
Recommended reads Madame Bovary in particular, of Rouen-born Gustave Flaubert's novels. Short stories by Guy de Maupassant (we love Boule de Suif). Jane Webster's Normandy-themed book of photographs, stories and recipes, At My French Table.
Local specialities Typically, Norman food is steeped in country tradition. There's cider from Pays d'Auge, Calvados from its namesake département, and a thousand creamy cheeses, including Camembert, Livarot and Pont-l'Evêque. Normandy also has its own version of dulce de leche, called confiture de lait.

And… Calvados – apple brandy – is Normandy's answer to sorbet. A shot of the regional liqueur, called a *trou Normand*, is often served between courses at dinner as a palate-cleanser.

WORTH GETTING OUT OF BED FOR

Viewpoint In Honfleur, the frieze of pastel-coloured buildings around the port, reflected in the water – disturbed only by boats bobbing on their moorings – is pure painterly inspiration.

Arts and culture Rouen's Notre-Dame Cathedral is gargantuan and Gothic (tourist office: +33 (0)2 32 08 32 40). A trove of paintings and sculptures, with lots from the 17th (Caravaggio, Rubens, Velázquez) and 19th centuries (Moreau, Monet, Degas, Delacroix), awaits at the Museum of Fine Art on Esplanade Marcel-Duchamp (+33 (0)2 35 71 28 40). In Honfleur, the Eugène Boudin Museum on Place Erik Satie features works not only by its namesake painter, but also by Dubourg, Monet and more (+33 (0)2 31 89 54 00).

Activities Canter along the sands, west of Trouville, with Domaine Equestre de Grangues (+33 (0)2 31 28 04 28; www.cabourg-equitation.com). Learn to surf in Trouville with the North Shore Surf School, attached to the surf shop at 21 rue Victor Hugo (+33 (0)2 31 88 99 94). Kayak down tranquil tree-lined rivers in the Perche Regional Park from Nogent-le-Rotrou with Club Canoë-Kayak Percheron (+33 (0)2 37 52 78 82). For a walk in the woods, head to Bellême, a fortified town in southerly Orne that lends its name to the surrounding forest. In Higher Normandy, the Seine wends its way westwards from Rouen through the glades of Roumare and Brotonne; you can cycle or walk the wooded paths.

Best beach Chalk cliffs and limestone-clouded seas stretch along the coastline of the Seine-Maritime north of Honfleur, sometimes called the Alabaster Coast. Head to Etretat, where a sweeping shingle beach is guarded at either end by a dramatic stone needle jutting out of the sea, and eroding chalk arches. Admire these sea sculptures from the pebbled shore or clifftop footpaths above.

Daytripper Le Mont Saint-Michel is one of France's most iconic attractions. Around a two-hour drive from Alençon or Honfleur, in the far south-west of the region, it's a rocky island whose rampart-guarded mediaeval town is crowned by a majestic abbey, with restaurants and museums inside its walls. At the ramparts' edge, Auberge Saint-Pierre on Grande Rue (+33 (0)2 33 60 14 03) is the place to roll up your sleeves for a seafood platter.

Shopping Thursday is market day in Alençon. Pick up saucisson, cider and aromatic cheeses on Place de la Magdeleine, Place de la Paix and Place du Point du Jour. In Honfleur, there's a fruit and veg fest on Saturdays in Place Sainte-Catherine, as well as flower and fashion stalls on the other side of the old harbour. Gribouille at 16 rue de l'Homme de Bois looks touristy but offers a mouthwatering array of well-sourced produce: ciders, pommeau (a lighter kind of Calvados), liqueurs, terrines and preserves. If you're venturing to the Cherbourg peninsula, epicerie Maison Gosselin at 27 rue de Verrüe in Saint-Vaast-la-Hougue is a gourmet's dream: the rose- and verbena-flavoured rice puddings stand out (+33 (0)2 33 54 40 06; www.maison-gosselin.fr).

Something for nothing A trip to the Bayeux War Cemetery makes for a sombre and moving experience. On the D5 bypass around the town, it is the site of more than 4,500 graves of fallen World War II soldiers. While you're there, cross the road to read the long list of names on the Bayeux Memorial (www.cwgc.org).

Don't go home without… seeing the Bayeux tapestry, 70 metres wide and 1,000 years old, a crazily detailed chronicle in cloth. Starring Edward the Confessor, William the Conqueror and the unlucky Harold, it's a pictorial account of William's rise to the throne of England, and its immediacy affords a true frisson. See it at the museum in central Bayeux on Rue de Nesmond (+33 (0)2 31 51 25 50; www.tapisserie-bayeux.fr).

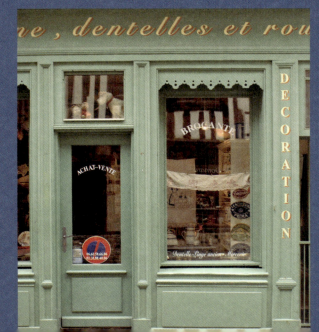

NOTICEABLY NORMANDY

Apples. Fresh from the orchard or fortified into Calvados brandy, this humble fruit is the bedrock of Norman cuisine. Find them filling tarts, fermented into cider, pickled into chutney, and flavouring mussel dishes. Pommeau is particularly lovely, an aged blend of Calvados and apple juice and, mercifully, half the strength of apple brandy. Uncork it with a creamy blue cheese for company.

DIARY

May The boats of Honfleur get their glad rags on – bunting and streamers – to coincide with Pentecost for the yearly Sailors' Pilgrimage. Watch the spectacle and witness a colourful parade through the streets (www.ot-honfleur.fr). June Pull on a Breton top and join the hundreds of yachties hanging out harbourside for Deauville International Week regatta (www.deauville-week.fr). Down the coast from Trouville, kites flying off the beach at Houlgate make a pretty spectacle at the start of the month (www.plein-vent.fr). *Chitty Chitty Bang Bang* meets *Cannonball Run* as a procession of vintage cars tours the region; if your wheels are old enough, you can register to join in (www.tourdenormandie.com). July Mackerel is the excuse for a maritime festival in Trouville (www.trouvillesurmer.org); and the season of night walks at Mont Saint-Michel begins, continuing through August (www.monuments-nationaux.fr). September Gongs and gowns come to Deauville for the annual American Film Festival. You can buy a daily pass to see any of the 100 screenings (www.festival-deauville.com). Septembre Musical brings classical concerts across the county of Orne (www.septembre-musical.com). October Mid-month, the Fête du Ventre et de la Gastronomie Normande is held in Rouen, and stalls selling cider, cheese, mushrooms, apples and the rest line the streets for one magnificent market.

Château de Saint Paterne

STYLE Fine food, fresh heir
SETTING Cusp of the Loire

'It is identifiably a grand family home, one to which you've been invited for a long weekend of sumptuous meals and good hosting'

Outside it's raining hard, and all we can see of northern France are *autoroute* reflectors glowing green under the glare of our headlights as we speed towards Le Mans. We're tired, crotchety, cursing this country's passion for rail strikes, and fantasising wildly about the bread, cheese and carafe of wine we've been promised on arrival. I'm confident it won't consist of a plastic-wrapped slice of supermarket cheddar. 'Do you think there'll be Pont L'Eveque?' I ask Mr Smith. 'And gooey Camembert?' he counters. 'And something radioactively whiffy, with proper French bread to squash it on...'

By the time we reach the village of Saint-Paterne in the Perche region, we're almost delirious with hunger. We pass the church and peer into inky blackness through sprays of water to make out the bulk of a small turreted château dating back to the 15th century, and take a sharp right turn into its rewardingly crunchy gravel driveway.

It's 10.30pm and we haven't so much as packed up the SatNav when the front door swings open and proprietor Ségolène de Valbray appears to greet us. She shows us into a series of communal salons furnished with parquet floors, faded rugs and antiques, promising us not just cheese, but a tray in our room with a plate of something warm. 'We haven't really put away dinner yet,' she says.

This is the beauty of Château de Saint Paterne. There are 10 rooms and suites, each spacious and with its own distinctive character. Yet, though guests' privacy is never compromised, this maison d'hôte retains the sense of being a grand family home (which it is: the de Valbrays have lived here for centuries) to which you're invited for a long weekend of sumptuous meals and good hosting.

A reassuring smell of wood smoke emanates from the open fire in the drawing-room grate, and we're tempted to curl up in a salon – perhaps the one with velvety, wine-coloured walls, comfortable armchairs and bold display of tall church candles. But Ségolène is already throwing open a back door and marching us outside, over more gravel, past a wet lawn, towards a high-ceilinged garden building whose high windows are illuminated by the warm light glowing inside.

This is the Orangerie, an airy space that must be suffused with sunshine in summer yet is still, at the less sympathetic end of October, surprisingly cosy. It feels like an extension of the outdoors: a painted garden picture hangs like wallpaper along one entire, long wall; the enormous bed is built out of great big hunks and chunks of naked wood; and the semi-open-plan bathroom is painted a sprightly lime green. Even the chandelier seems to be made of branches. My ragged senses are still being soothed by decadent details – a pair of champagne flutes beside the bath, the oversized sink piled with L'Occitane toiletries, terracotta tiles with underfloor heating – when there's a knock at the door.

The tray – no, two trays – arrive, crammed with dishes. This is a four-course feast, not a supper. We feel regally pampered. Spiced mussel soup might

not have been my first choice so late (it's now 11pm) but it's so good I finish it. Next comes a meltingly tender lamb tagine studded with medjool dates, made by the Moroccan housekeeper. I'm too tired to tackle the plump, glistening strawberry tart, or make a hole in the cheese, which comes on a plate of dressed lettuce leaves – and I start to wonder how much this might all be costing. (€30 each, it turns out, which is extraordinary considering the quality.) No fan of clever-clever foams wrung out of a daringly unappetising set of ingredients, or over-worked edible sculptures on ridiculously shaped plates, I'm relieved to find the food at Château de Saint Paterne is pitched at the level of home cooking, if you could actually cook that well.

As we discover the following night, the way dinner usually goes is that guests gather for a convivial fireside aperitif at 8pm (in my case, an unholily strong G&T). Then, at about 8.30pm, everyone moves on to the dining room to eat a set menu

by candelight at their own tables. In the kitchen in his pinny most evenings is Charles-Henry de Valbray himself. Where did he learn such skills, I ask, sighing over a beautifully light asparagus mousseline, and magret de canard cooked with honey and crispy little potatoes. Charles-Henry shrugs. 'Just at home, in the family kitchen.'

The wine list is short, just a handful of reds and whites. Like the British aristocracy, it takes refuge in well-bred clarets. It'd be nice to see a few more exciting bottles, though what's here is good. I love that it's sold by the bottle, but when we ask for a glass of Pouilly-Fumé each, Ségolène says that's fine – she will drink the rest herself.

Much of our time is spent dreaming of whiling away a few days here in warmer weather; the outdoor pool is open until the end of September, and we'd have the run of the 25-acre grounds. The lawn is dotted with chairs and tables begging for you to sit with a book, sipping a local drop. As for its Smith credentials, there's a fairy-tale quality, and it's romantic, too. King Henry IV apparently stole away here for trysts with his lovers. More prosaically, the motoring museum at nearby Le Mans is said to be excellent. I am drawn to the glittering Loire, about an hour and a half's drive away, where there are wine producers galore, so you can drop in for a tasting without making an appointment.

Our greatest temptation? To keep coming back, staying in a different room each time: we love Chambre Henri IV, whose antique wardrobe is carved with faces that Charles-Henry admits terrified him as a child; and Chambre du Parc with its attic bathroom. A secret door in a room downstairs opens onto a stone spiral staircase that takes you to another suite, the more modern Mystères. Consider them all earmarked.

Reviewed by Victoria Moore

NEED TO KNOW

Rooms 10, including six suites.

Rates €135–€240, including tax but not breakfast, €13.

Check-out 12 noon, but flexible according to availability. Earliest check-in, 2.30pm.

Facilities Outdoor pool, tennis courts, CD, DVD and book libraries, in-room massage, free WiFi throughout. In rooms: flatscreen TV, DVD/CD, iPod dock, L'Occitane products.

Children Extra beds can be added to all rooms, except Maréchal, for €15 a night (free if you book a family room). Cots for babies cost nothing. Baby monitors can be borrowed. Children's dinner is served at 7.15pm.

Also Pets can stay for €10 a night.

IN THE KNOW

Our favourite rooms L'Orangerie is set apart from the château, a huge, self-contained suite with an open bathroom, vast wooden bed and one wall made from a 19th-century backdrop found in a Barcelona theatre. The château's most modern room is the Chambre des Mystères, romantically secluded up two narrow flights of winding stairs. It's chocolate-coloured, with bold red accents. For a stay that's steeped in history, go for the Chambre d'Henri IV, where France's first Bourbon king kipped.

Hotel bar There's an honesty bar in the salon, a grand space in which to nurse a nightcap and pretend you own the château, to the sounds of jazz, lounge and classical.

Hotel restaurant Owner Charles-Henry de Valbray is a self-taught chef who prepares a terrific set dinner, served around 8pm each evening. Typical dishes include beetroot and caper gazpacho with cucumber sorbet, veal tagine with dried fruits, and apricot puffs with rosemary ice-cream.

Top table Take your pick from the drawing room or dining room, out on the terrace if the sun is shining, or in the Moroccan-inspired games room, which can be decorated romantically if you're planning to propose.

Dress code Bohemian and chic, to match owners Ségolène and Charles-Henry.

Local knowledge Head to Alençon to see the reassuringly expensive *point d'Alençon* embroidery being made. Only a dozen or so lacemakers have the closely guarded skills required.

LOCAL EATING AND DRINKING

The château's owners have a gastronomic side project: Rive Droite, a collection of dining rooms set in the town's 18th-century former lace museum on Rue du Pont Neuf in Alençon, where you can enjoy seasonal food either indoors or on a pretty riverside terrace. Saint-Céneri le Gérei is often voted as one of France's most beautiful villages, and its other boast is painters' school turned rustic bistro L'Auberge des Peintres (+33 (0)2 33 26 49 18), where dishes such as seafood cassoulet and a very good black pudding exemplify simple French food done well. In La Perrière, La Maison d'Horbée on the Grande Place (+33 (0)2 33 73 18 41) is a tearoom, gallery and antique shop in one, for browsing *brocante* with your coffee and brioche. In Neufchâtel-en-Saosnois, Le Relais des Etangs de Guibert (+33 (0)2 43 97 15 38), overlooking a woodland-fringed lake, serves specialities such as carpaccio of foie gras and lobster.

GET A ROOM!

For more information, or to book this hotel, go to www.mrandmrssmith.com. Register your Smith membership card (see pages 4–5) to enjoy exclusive offers and privileges.

 SMITH MEMBER OFFER A bottle of the Norman apple liqueur known as pommeau.

Château de Saint Paterne 4 rue de la Gaieté, 72610 Saint-Paterne (+33 (0)2 33 27 54 71; www.chateau-saintpaterne.com)

HOW TO... LOOK PARISIAN

Forget the long legs and the blonde hair, and even the grandmother with an attic full of Hermès handbags. All of these are advantages to the fashionably inclined, of course, but the ultimate style gift is to be born Parisian. To be Parisian is to be sexy without trying, cool without caring, which is ultimately what the entire multizillion-dollar fashion and beauty industry is based on reproducing, for those of us not lucky enough to have been born within the *périphérique*.

Can you fake it? Some say not. I say it's worth a go. Here's how:

• Start with the hair. The Parisian hairdo is one that looks as though you've had a fabulous blow-dry, then spent an hour in bed with someone very exciting. If that's hard to arrange, get the most expensive highlights you can afford and learn to backcomb.

• Next, work on your facial expressions. You need to master looking bored, but in an intriguing Left Bank way, rather than in the English way, which gives the impression you're mulling over what to have for tea. Get your eyebrows threaded or waxed for this purpose – all the better to arch them. Once upon a time, smoking cigarettes was an essential element of Parisian life, but this is becoming as retro as a Doisneau kiss.

• Getting dressed. Never, ever copy a whole catwalk look or (shudder) adopt a head-to-toe trend once it has been taken up by the high street. Instead, take a piece of classic French style – a striped Breton top, a fabulous pair of Isabel Marant trousers, a great Vanessa Bruno sweater dress, or a Chanel 2.55 handbag – and build your look around it.

• When in doubt, ask yourself: what would Carine Roitfeld wear? The French *Vogue* editrix has Parisian chic nailed like no one else. Pencil skirts with killer sandals, fabulous tailoring, slender brown limbs, and the confidence to wear exactly what looks good on her. This is where French and American women diverge in their style: the American ideal of beauty exists in the relentless pursuit of a spick-and-span ideal, whereas French chic is all about feeling *bien dans sa peau*.

• Remember that, to a Parisian woman, 'dressed down' means skinny jeans, a cute pair of Repetto ballet pumps, good-quality cashmere and light make-up. The only exception to this is for those who have Birkin/Gainsbourg genes and look incredible in cut-off jeans and last night's eye make-up. As an international rule of thumb, if you are so traffic-stoppingly sexy that men regularly propose marriage when you pop out for a pint of milk, you can be laid-back about your clothes; if not, you can't.

• Look good in a pair of skinny jeans and cute ballet pumps. Remember, Parisian women never, *ever* have more than one teeny corner of someone else's croissant, and even that no more than once a year.

• Wear fabulous lingerie. Putting your cleavage on display is not Parisian at all, but a cream silk blouse unbuttoned so as to display the merest hint of some lacy, *café crème*-toned deliciousness beneath is perfect.

• Wear plenty of black. Especially if you find the croissant rule hard to stick to, since dark colours are always more forgiving.

• Learn to accept compliments (and there will be many, if you have been paying attention) with breezy elegance. When a tribute is paid to your dress, simply smile and say thank you. Refrain from excitedly sharing the information that you picked it up on a sale rail in Zara for a song – such tidbits can shatter that faux-Parisian mystique in an instant.

By Jess Cartner-Morley

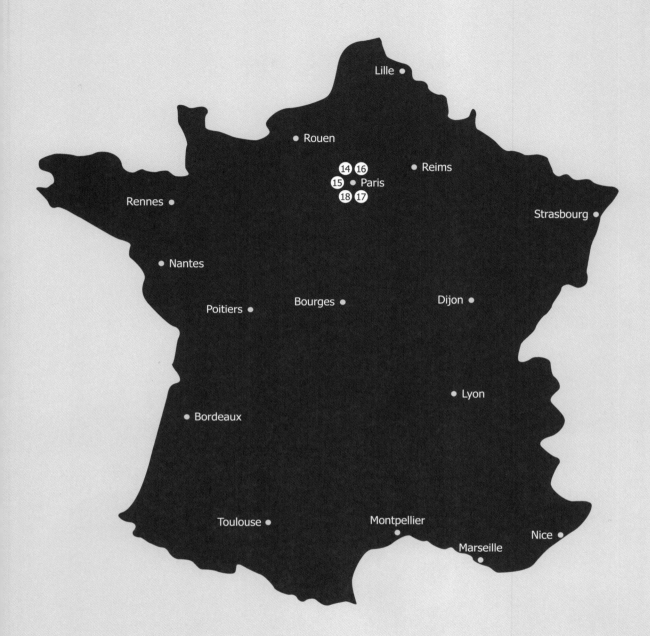

PARIS

14 Hôtel Daniel

15 Hotel Keppler

16 Hôtel Particulier Montmartre

17 Hôtel Récamier

18 La Réserve Paris

PARIS

CITYSCAPE Boulevards, boutiques, brasseries
CITY LIFE Vie bohème

From the top of Montmartre to the tip of the Eiffel Tower, in the Louvre or on the Left Bank, Paris is stylish to its bones: not merely cool and chic, but seriously creative. Between its Gothic cathedrals and grand avenues are flashes of futuristic bravura: the Pompidou Centre and L'Institut du Monde Arabe, proving the revolutionary spirit is alive and relevant. It's the layers of old and new, privilege and punk, that give Paris its ageless verve – the 8ème and 16ème arrondissements are tops for couture-clad swanking; diehard romantics will always have Montmartre (trendier than ever, these days); and Montorgueil is the up-and-coming area to watch.

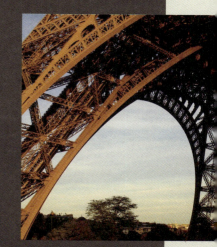

GETTING THERE

Planes BMI Baby (www.bmibaby.com), British Airways (www.ba.com), Air France (www.airfrance.com) and EasyJet (www.easyjet.com) fly to Paris Charles de Gaulle airport from the UK. Most major French regionals have flights into Paris Orly (www.airfrance.com).
Trains From London St Pancras, via Ebbsfleet, Eurostar services reach the city's Gare du Nord in 2hrs 15mins (www.eurostar.com). From the Mediterranean coast, TGV services connect via Marseille or Perpignan and, in the west, Biarritz and Bordeaux (www.tgv.com).
Boats Dover to Calais (www.poferries.com; www.seafrance.com), or Portsmouth to Le Havre (www.ldlines.co.uk) are the most convenient ferry routes.
Automobiles You're better off without one. Many hotels charge for parking, and why risk the passion-killing traffic? Determined drivers need to steel themselves for the infamous périphérique ring road.

LOCAL KNOWLEDGE

Taxis Can be hailed in the street if you're more than 100 metres from a rank (these are all over Paris and have phones if no cab is waiting).
Siesta and fiesta Parisians hit the cafés around 7am for breakfast; shops usually open 10am–7pm. Restaurants get busy around 9pm, and clubs can stay open until dawn.

Do go/don't go Paris shuts down (and relaxes) in August, a national holiday. Go in spring, when the blossom's out, or autumn, not least for Nuit Blanche, an all-night culturefest.
Packing tips Sunglasses, silk scarf, cigarette holder. An arrondissement city map (taxi drivers can be uncertain).
Children La Charlotte de l'Isle is a magical tearoom on Ile Saint-Louis, with witches on the ceiling and incredible chocolate creations in the window (+33 (0)1 43 54 25 83).
Recommended reads Le Spleen de Paris by Charles Baudelaire; A Tale of Two Cities by Charles Dickens; Paris and Elsewhere by Richard Cobb.
Local specialities Paris is all about haute pâtisserie: we love the praline-packed 2,000 Feuilles at Pierre Hermé on Rue Bonaparte in Saint-Germain (+33 (0)1 43 54 47 77; www.pierreherme.com). Buy macaroons, worshipped as the holy grail of sweeties, from the famed Ladurée (also a tearoom) at 75 avenue des Champs-Elysées, 8ème (+33 (0)1 40 75 08 75; www.laduree.fr). Get everything else at glamorous grocer La Grande Epicerie in Le Bon Marché department store, Rue de Sèvres, 7ème.
And… In summer, Paris Plages materialise: three city beaches, two riverside and one canalside. The original runs between the Louvre and Pont de Sully; the others are at Port de la Gare in the 13ème and, in the 19ème, Bassin de la Villette (www.paris.fr).

WORTH GETTING OUT OF BED FOR

Viewpoint Crowded but irresistible, the Eiffel Tower is open 9.30am–11pm (midnight in high season). If all that steel doesn't take your fancy, visit L'Institut du Monde Arabe on Rue des Fossés Saint-Bernard in the 5ème (www.imarabe.org). As well as the amazing Jean Nouvel façade and Islamic art exhibitions, it has a top-floor terrace with great views across the Seine to Notre Dame and Ile de la Cité.

Art and culture There aren't pages enough to list half the capital's cultural and ecclesiastical sights, so here's the speed tour. Catch Mona Lisa's smile and the Venus de Milo's graceful marble drapes at the Louvre (www. louvre.fr; open late Wednesdays and Fridays; closed Tuesdays). The Musée National d'Art Moderne is on level four of the Pompidou Centre (www.centrepompidou.fr; closed Tuesdays); Richard Rogers' radical architecture is another draw. At the Musée National Picasso Paris (www.musee-picasso.fr) in the Marais, the venue is as alluring as Pablo's art – also the case for Musée d'Orsay, a converted train station packed with painterly treats (www.musee-orsay.fr). The white-onion domes of the Sacré-Coeur basilica in the 18ème crown Montmartre hill (www.sacre-coeur-montmartre.com). At grandly Gothic Notre Dame Cathedral, on the Ile de la Cité, make a beeline for the mesmerising South Rose Window (www.notredamedeparis.fr).

Activities The open-top Bateaux-Mouches riverboats are a popular way to see the sights. Most depart from Pont de l'Alma. Ramp things up a notch with dinner for two on a sleek Yachts de Paris launch (www.yachtsdeparis.fr). US-run Fat Tire Bike Tours will show you around on Schwinn bikes, Segways or your own two feet – the night-time tours are fun (www.fattirebiketoursparis.com). For short trips, use a Vélib, one of the city's big, grey communal bicycles. The scheme has evolved quite an etiquette; ask a local about how to put down a deposit, etc.

Perfect picnic Grab a bottle of bubbly from the minibar, and some pastries, smoked-salmon baguettes or tarts from Gérard Mulot at 76 rue de Seine, 6ème (+33 (0)1 43 26 85 77), and enjoy them in the Jardins de Luxembourg on the Left Bank.

Daytripper Live out your Louis XV/Madame de Pompadour/Marie-Antoinette/Sun King fantasies at the incomparable Château de Versailles, just outside Paris (www.chateauversailles.fr).

Shopping For a serious fashion spree, the thoroughfares to scour in the 8ème are Avenue Montaigne and Rue du Faubourg Saint-Honoré. In the 1er, head to the Jardins du Palais-Royal for Marc, Stella, Acne and hip boutique Kitsuné. In the Haut-Marais, an amazing constellation of independent boutiques, explore Rue de Charlot, Rue du Poitou and Rue de Saintonge. Go to Porte de Clignancourt to browse the famous fleamarket for clothes and antiques, open Saturday to Monday until 6pm. Or have a selection of Parisian retro pieces brought to you by Ooh La La! Vintage (ring +33 (0)6 84 76 58 65 to arrange in advance of your trip). If you're a sucker for department stores, head to Le Bon Marché on Rue de Sèvres. Splurge with a healthy conscience at Merci (+33 (0)1 42 77 00 33) on Boulevard Beaumarchais; this hip luxury emporium donates profits from its Annick Goutal scents, Baccarat crystal vases, Stella McCartney and Yves Saint Laurent clothing and hip homewares to a children's charity in Madagascar.

Something for nothing Follow in the footsteps of Degas, Toulouse-Lautrec and Amélie Poulain, wandering through Montmartre and up to the Sacré-Coeur for classic Parisian panoramas. Or visit Oscar Wilde and Marcel Proust at one of the city's smartest addresses, the Cimitière du Père-Lachaise in the 20ème (www.pere-lachaise.com)

Don't go home without… stopping at a boulevard bistro to sip a café crème or a pastis. Whatever your wont (still-walking steak, croque monsieur, rillettes, warm chèvre salad or tarte tatin), it will taste immeasurably better eaten at a cane chair and round table, alfresco.

PERFECTLY PARIS

Play 'Through the Keyhole' with this select handful of establishments and you could only be in Paris. Visit Musée Carnavalet on Rue de Sévigné, 3ème, for an engaging history of the 1789 revolution (www.carnavalet.paris.fr). Turn teatime into an elegant ritual at Mariage Frères, 13 rue des Grands Augustins, 6ème (+33 (0)1 40 51 82 50; www.mariagefreres.com). To enjoy the naff-but-fun, safely air-brushed end of Parisian sleaze, try Le Crazy Horse on Avenue George V, 8ème (www.lecrazyhorseparis.com). It's a cabaret performance in a small theatre where drinks are brought to your seat, meaning you never have to tear your gaze from the semi-naked burlesque dancing girls.

DIARY

May Saint-Germain Jazz Festival gets the Rive Gauche swinging and tapping its toes (www.festivaljazzsaintgermain paris.com). May–June The French Open tennis championship brings grand-slam excitement to the City of Lights (www.fft.fr/rolandgarros). June La Fête de la Musique celebrates the start of summer and sees the streets lined with stages for live bands (www.fetedelamusique.culture.fr). June–July Paris Jazz Festival means free weekend concerts in Parc Floral (www.parcfloraldeparis.com). July Bastille Day, a public holiday with a huge parade down the Champs-Elysées on the 14th, is followed a week later by the opening of Paris Plages, the city's temporary urban beaches. August–September There's an open-air Classical Music Festival in Parc Floral (www.parcfloraldeparis.com). October The city stays up all night for the nocturnal arts party known as Nuit Blanche.

Paris

Hôtel Daniel

STYLE Orientalist opulence
SETTING Elegant huitième

'The Daniel's interiors are a sumptuous
blaze of fanciful fabrics, oriental carpets and
luxurious furnishings – a mood of tasteful
exuberance that proves instantly uplifting'

It must be a sign of the times that the first squeal of delight the Hôtel Daniel inspires in Mrs Smith is uttered when she hears the news that it offers complimentary WiFi. Being a Eurostar regular with a vintage couture business straddling London and Paris, madame is always looking for romantic little hotels where she can happily mix work with pleasure (otherwise known as Mr Smith).

In this respect, the Daniel is a classic example of that hotel discovery you really don't want to tell anyone about. (Well, there are only 26 rooms, including the seven suites, and it would be very tiresome if friends of friends snapped them all up.) On a calm and well-heeled street of the 8ème arrondissement, the hotel occupies six floors, two of which offer rooms with balconies. The Lebanese proprietors, who also own the elegant Hotel Albergo in Beirut, have designed it with great panache to target a refined clientele; we are charmed by the intelligent service, as well as by the luxurious attention to decorative detail.

The Daniel's interiors were created by London-based designer Tarfa Salam, and offer a sumptuous blaze of fanciful fabrics, oriental carpets and luxurious furnishings – a mood of tasteful exuberance that proves instantly uplifting. Talking of which, the lift that takes us to our fifth-floor Paris Suite, lined with colourful hand-painted wallpaper by de Gournay, has to be one of the most inviting in Europe.

Our room is as charming as the inside of a sewing box, with billowing curtains in old gold and jade-green wallpaper painted with blossoms. This is an exception, though, as the Daniel's rooms are generally decked out with 18th-century-style toile de Jouy, which might feature Chinese kite-fliers, swirling ferns, exotic tropical trees or picturesque expeditions by elephant. (If you fancy a snug green boudoir, or rich red walls decorated with whimsical images suggesting dalliance, it's worth mentioning your preferences on booking, since every room is very different.) The Eastern theme continues with bamboo-framed desks, inlaid tables, intriguing curios and butterfly-covered lamps. The bed sheets feel as smooth as cream, and other fine touches in our suite include decent-sized dressing gowns, air-conditioning you can understand, and an iPod.

Within minutes, a welcome pot of green tea arrives, along with willow-pattern cups and a plateful of colourful macaroons from Ladurée. Mrs Smith purrs with approval. Here, at last, is a hotel both classy and feminine, but which also appeals to Mr Smith's decadent side. (And his finickety side: the bathroom comes with a big jar of Dead Sea bath salts and a full-length mirror, and the wardrobe shelves come lined with broderie-anglaise runners.)

Now that we're *bien installé*, it's time to enjoy the City of Light. Stepping out, we find the Daniel surrounded by inviting restaurants that range from simple bistros to the super-smart and stately Apicius, just across the street. Walk south and you hit the grand and congested runway of the Champs-Elysées. Head northwards and there's the oh-so-Paris Parc Monceau, its benches filled with

fine-grained mothers, nannies and *enfants*. Our preference, though, is to stroll east along Rue du Faubourg Saint-Honoré, which gradually builds to a frenzy of window-shopping delights. First up is gourmet food emporium Dalloyau; then comes the newly expanded Hôtel Le Bristol; followed by a parade of famous fashion houses.

As it's a Wednesday, we take advantage of the late-night opening of the Louvre, heading straight for the sculptures in the little-visited galleries devoted to the arts of Africa, Asia, Oceania and the Americas. Mrs Smith pre-booked dinner at nearby Le Fumoir, an untouristy restaurant with colonial trappings and a cosy library at the back. Afterwards, French taxis being the most useless in the world, we whizz back by Métro.

Breakfast the next morning is delivered to our room on a white-linened trolley, a harmonious still life of coffee, newspaper and delicious, what-the-hell pastries. Mrs Smith has work to do that day, and when her Parisian

business partner walks into the Daniel's lounge, which brims with plush cushions, chinoiserie trimmings and gorgeous orchids, she can't help but cry 'Ooh là là!' It's the ideal setting to discuss their new website over an open Mac and a glass of chilled champagne, while Mr Smith gets a few of his own work-related errands in the bag before lunch.

The restaurant at the Daniel is small and intimate, with silky banquettes and wall cabinets filled with dainty coloured glasses. It works equally well whether you're there for a high-powered business meeting or a sexy assignation. We're visiting in high summer, but agree that the Daniel beckons as an appealing wintry love-nest and earmark it for a return trip. The next day, our request for a late check-out is instantly granted, and when our breakfast order is delayed owing to an oversight, relevant charges are immediately waived. This is a hotel that genuinely cares about the time you spend within its exotically decorated walls – whether you're checking in with a laptop, a lover, or maybe both.

Reviewed by Nigel Tisdall

NEED TO KNOW

Rooms 26, including seven suites.

Rates €350–€740, not including breakfast, from €24.

Check-out 11am. Stretched to 6pm at a half-day rate, subject to availability. Earliest check-in, 2pm.

Facilities Free WiFi, PCs and mobile phones to borrow. In rooms: LCD TV, CD, minibar.

Children This hotel is better suited to couples. Check the children in with *grandmère*.

Also Book an in-room beauty or spa treatment. Nicotine fiends can opt for a smoking room.

IN THE KNOW

Our favourite rooms All the Deluxe rooms are on the sixth floor. Room 603 has a big bathroom with a spectacular view of the Parisian rooftops. Standard rooms 102, 202, 302 and 402 are smaller, but equally delightful and quiet. You can enjoy breakfast on your balcony in some of the suites, and watch the sun set over the tip of the Eiffel Tower from the Daniel Suite.

Hotel bar Sip a Kir Royale among sumptuous satin cushions, fresh orchids, shelves of jewel-coloured glasses and de Gournay wallpaper in the hotel's signature sea green.

Hotel restaurant The bar and the lounge do small plates and snacks, including breakfast all day, and steak tartare with chips. Gourmet Restaurant Daniel offers a refined French/Med menu, Monday to Friday; lighter food is served at weekends.

Top table For an intimate dinner for two, cosy up at one of the elegant recessed tables.

Room service It's a 24-hour operation: hot food until the restaurant kitchen closes, then a limited menu until breakfast.

Dress code Sleek silks, nifty tailoring.

Local knowledge Hôtel Daniel guests get discounted use of the pool, spa and gym at L'Espace Payot, five minutes away. Rue de Ponthieu, a few minutes' walk, is studded with nightclubs, such as now-trendy Chez Régine at number 49, and swanky Mathis at number 3.

LOCAL EATING AND DRINKING

You'll need a reservation for super-chef's flagship Pierre Gagnaire on Rue Balzac, which offers boundary-pushing *mer* and *terre* creations (+33 (0)1 58 36 12 50). La Cantine du Faubourg at 105 rue du Faubourg Saint-Honoré (+33 (0)1 42 56 22 22) has a nightlife atmosphere, serving Asian/French fusion in a stylish lounge; it's ideal for a pre-prandial drink. Off the Champs-Elysées on Rue d'Artois, Apicius is a patrician set of white-naped rooms where the top brass eat exquisitely (+33 (0)1 43 80 19 66). The delectable duck tagine is a highlight of the authentic Moroccan menu at 404 on Rue des Gravilliers (+33 (0)1 42 74 57 81). Behind 404 is new and *hyperfun* Derrière (geddit?), also owned by Mourad Mazouz, which is creative and quite, quite cuckoo, serving homely French cooking in a 'sitting room', 'bedroom', 'kitchen', etc. The third hotspot sharing the courtyard is Andy Wahloo, Mazouz's kitschy-cool bar. Simple but spruce, and ultra-useful for lunch, Lô Sushi, 8 rue de Berri (+33 (0)1 45 62 01 00) is one of those instant-gratification conveyor-belt sushi places, just off the Champs-Elysées and minutes from the hotel.

GET A ROOM!

For more information, or to book this hotel, go to www.mrandmrssmith.com. Register your Smith membership card (see pages 4–5) to enjoy exclusive offers and privileges.

 SMITH MEMBER OFFER Mariage Frères tea, served with Ladurée macaroons or other sweet treats.

Hôtel Daniel 8 rue Frédéric Bastiat, 75008 Paris (+33 (0)1 42 56 17 00; www.hoteldanielparis.com)

Paris

Hotel Keppler

STYLE Private Haussmann
SETTING A sashay from the Champs-Elysées

'The rooms feel stylish and serene, with sparing use of Keppler's signature bold prints and colours, and just a smattering of artworks'

To me, an Australian chef and food writer, Paris is not simply the epitome of style, sophistication and romance. It's a place of pilgrimage, a rite of passage, the olde-world yin to Sydney's bright, sunny yang. The French capital is such a finely structured city – with its centuries-spanning architecture and meticulous urban planning, and all those beautifully kept gardens and iconic monuments – that, naturally, we're hoping for a hotel to match. And absolutely, from first impression to last, Hotel Keppler matches our high expectations.

It is located on narrow Rue Kepler (sic), just off Avenue Marceau, in the chic 16th arrondissement, an ideal address for a boutique bolthole, within trotting distance of the Arc de Triomphe and the Champs-Elysées. Perhaps surprisingly, given its proximity to such high-powered shopping, dining and wining, our hotel is not only fittingly fashionable, but also luxuriously tranquil.

Outside, Keppler is all imposing Haussmannian townhouse; inside, designer Pierre-Yves Rochon has signed off a sophisticated meeting of high-society modern style with camped-up classicism. Riddled with alcoves, plastered with frescoes and dotted with intriguing artefacts (note the man-size china vases flanking the door to the winter garden), the hotel has an air of opulence that's nicely tempered by the unstuffy air of its incredibly helpful staff. The concierge and reception staff are friendly and generous with local knowledge, offering advice and tips and chasing up our 'urgent' requests with speedy efficiency.

After checking in, can you blame us for choosing to stay put for our first afternoon? We feel it's our duty, as reviewers, to luxuriate in our style-drenched boudoir and order in champagne. We fling open two sets of doors onto an internal courtyard and let the afternoon light stream in. Our executive room, in case you're wondering, is a decent size without being notably spacious – after all, this is Paris. Rather than the exoticism of the ground-floor communal areas, all objets and orchids, the rooms are designed to feel stylish yet serene, with sparing use of

Keppler's signature bold prints and colours, and just a smattering of artworks. We can't believe the calm and quiet; we plug in our laptops (a necessary evil – at least we're tapping away together) and use the WiFi for an hour before eyeing up a much more fun in-room option: the big bath in the black and white tiled bathroom.

Floating in a sea of fragrant bubbles is the perfect way to ponder where to eat. So many places, so little time... Aux Lyonnais, Ze Kitchen Galerie and L'Atelier de Joël Robuchon are at the top of a very long list, which meanders off into the realms of stratospherically expensive fantasy when it gets to Alain Ducasse au Plaza Athénée and L'Astrance, both within easy walking distance of the Keppler. There are so many phenomenal restaurants in Paris, it really is worth planning ahead and splashing out at least once while you're here. Actually, at least three times, if you're here for a long weekend.

Lazy breakfasts are the perfect kick-off to our Parisian days – particularly when taken in the bright and inviting lower-level winter garden room. Here, pastries and breads are too good to refuse, ripe red strawberries are delicious unadorned, juice is just-squeezed, and espresso is best taken black (a cunning way to sidestep the UHT milk). The luxury service doesn't end there. This is a land where laundry is returned the same day, each article of clothing wrapped in tissue paper and artfully laid in a chic white box complete with ribbon. Yes, it costs a bomb. But that just gives me a feeble excuse to shop for something new; after all, we are in the vicinity of some of the best shopping in Paris, and it's a bit selfish not to contribute to the local economy when you're on holiday – that's what we tell ourselves when we realise we're ordering lobster. Again.

Walking these streets at twilight sums up all that is perfect about Paris; the deep-blue sky with just a sliver of new moon makes a magical backdrop as we promenade with well-heeled locals. Another temptation on our doorstep here is Hédiard. This branch of the ultimate purveyor of to-die-for delicacies is so close by,

it's dangerous, at least it is for someone as food-focused as I am. We can't resist squirrelling a few treasures back to our room for late-night snacking — a perfectly ripe cheese, buttery biscuits, chocolates and fruit jellies — all wrapped in the store's signature red and black packaging. Little wonder we're in heaven for much of our stay.

We do emerge from our boudoir to enjoy the guests-only bar from time to time. The decor is all high-camp sophistication, awash with stripes, animal print and big puffy cushions for fabulous folk to perch on and look the part. My only criticism is that the cocktail list could be shorter and sweeter — we thought the bartender got a bit stuck, thanks to too much choice. The arty/fashiony books in the ground-floor salon make it another lovely spot to ensconce yourselves for tea or a cocktail. There's no restaurant but, as you can probably tell, we're ecstatic heading out to dine spectacularly elsewhere, or calling down to take advantage of a charming in-room delivery of cakes from the famous Angelina tearoom and patisserie on Rue de Rivoli. The most wonderful aspect of our stay at Keppler has been having so many decadent indulgences within our grasp. Our one regret? Not having booked the big top-floor suite with its own private rooftop terrace. Now that sounds like my idea of quintessential Paris.

Reviewed by Christine Manfield

NEED TO KNOW

Rooms 39, including five suites.

Rates €220–€1,000. Breakfast is €22.

Check-out 12 noon, but later is sometimes possible. Earliest check-in, 2pm.

Facilities Sauna, steam room, gym, library, CD selection, WiFi (€17 a day). In rooms: LCD TV, DVD player, iPod dock, minibar. Suites have Hermès products.

Children *Les enfants* stay free, accommodated in cots or extra beds. You can book a local nanny, but there are no other specifically child-oriented facilities.

Also Small pets are welcome for €30 a day. Smoking rooms on request.

IN THE KNOW

Our favourite rooms Designer Pierre-Yves Rochon blends classic with contemporary, putting toiles, checks and animal print against strong colour and dark wooden flooring. We like the black, white and yellow Executive Rooms, with TVs in the bathrooms. The four Superior Suites come with balconies and Eiffel Tower views; the Classic Rooms, though attractive, are somewhat small, if not unusually so for Paris.

Hotel bar Keppler's light-filled lounge has shelves of intriguing antiques and art books to peruse, and a dozen smart sofas and armchairs; it's more of an elegant salon than a bar, for guests only.

Hotel restaurant There's no restaurant, but all the smart bistros of the 8ème are within swift reach. Breakfast is an American-style buffet, served in the chic cream-coloured breakfast room.

Top table Take your café crème and croissants around one of the graceful communal tables.

Room service There's no serious kitchen at Keppler, but you can order from the room-service menu of nearby Hôtel François, 24 hours a day.

Dress code LBD and Holly Golightly sunglasses for Mrs Smith; new-school Barbour and a pastel sweater for Mr.

Local knowledge Arm yourself with a bottle of champagne, stock up on gourmet snacks at Fauchon or Hédiard on Place de la Madeleine and enjoy a Parisian picnic near the Louvre in the Jardin des Tuileries.

LOCAL EATING AND DRINKING

Worshipped for its melt-in-the-mouth macaroons in pistachio, salted-caramel and seasonal new flavours, world-famous confectioner Ladurée has an outpost near the hotel at 75 Champs-Elysées (+33 (0)1 40 75 08 75). Maison de la Truffe is a small deli/café on Place de la Madeleine, majoring in truffle-inspired dishes – a lunchtime must for lovers of the premium fungi (+33 (0)1 42 65 53 22). A few moments from the Champs-Elysées, on Rue Lord Byron, Les Enfants Terribles is toney and theatrical-looking and offers a Modern European menu, including risotto with ceps, fillet of beef Johnny Hallyday, and 'gros baba au rhum'. Seasonal French fare, extravagant decor and Philippe Starck design make for a memorable soirée at La Cristal Room in the Baccarat HQ on Place des États-Unis (+33 (0)1 40 22 11 10). VIP Room on Rue de Rivoli is a swish, futuristic cocktail bar with a glossy clientele to match (+33 (0)1 58 36 46 00).

GET A ROOM!

For more information, or to book this hotel, go to www.mrandmrssmith.com. Register your Smith membership card (see pages 4–5) to enjoy exclusive offers and privileges.

 SMITH MEMBER OFFER Drinks on arrival, and river-cruise tickets.

Hotel Keppler 10 rue Kepler, 75116 Paris (+33 (0)1 47 20 65 05; www.keppler.fr)

Hôtel Particulier Montmartre

STYLE Arthouse original
SETTING Secret garden, Sacré-Coeur

'We find ourselves in a surprising, visually arresting space in which pop-art lips and antiques cohabit with life-size statues of angels, Arne Jacobsen chairs and cowhide rugs'

Mr Smith, good humour dissolving in the fading daylight, has begun to fret. The address we've noted down seems correct, the road is lined with the elegant townhouses we're expecting as neighbours, but there's no sign of the Hôtel Particulier Montmartre. The glass door with the number we've got reveals nothing except yellowed junk mail and a spider family gathering.

I leave Mr Smith fighting to prevent our wheelie suitcases from rolling off down steep Avenue Junot, and follow a dog-walking local to duck down a cobbled alleyway that I suspect may provide some clue as to where we are. Well, we're definitely in Paris: the view that opens out a few feet ahead has all the subtlety of those landscape paintings they flog on the banks of the Seine, with the Eiffel Tower dead centre.

I am still marvelling at this most tourist-thrilling of vistas when a woman, wearing an Agatha Christie-era chambermaid's outfit, appears from behind a tall, black iron gate. She looks at me, I look at her; then she points to a tiny, barely visible brass plaque inscribed with what can only be the hotel's name. Minutes later, trailed by a red-faced Mr Smith, manfully dragging both cases across the cobblestones, I am in the lush gardens of the hotel. It's so peaceful it feels as though someone's thrown a thick blanket over the hilltop of Montmartre. You would never know we are just a five-minute walk from Sacré-Coeur's camera-clicking coach hordes and pavement pierrots.

Stepping through the front door of the hotel, we find ourselves in a surprising, visually arresting space in which pop-art giant lips and aristocratic antiques cohabit with kitsch life-size statues of angels, Arne Jacobsen chairs and cowhide rugs. Though there's a mid-century-modern slant to the furnishings, the overall effect is less dry than that suggests. We contemplate a quick drink at the honesty bar but, liking the aesthetic extravagance of the lobby, we're keen to get upstairs and see our room. We're in the marvellously titled Trees With Ears suite and, on first glance, it's pretty amazing. The walls are covered in fabulous, hand-printed, Japanese-style wallpaper. A bed big enough for an entire family sits next to a huge roll-top bath (happily, there is an all-important separate loo), and this segues into an elegant living area, complete with sofa and chaise longue.

On one wall, facing the window with a view of the drinks terrace and its fairy lights, I discover a rubber earpiece and brass button, next to a little placard reading 'press to hear a secret'. Exploring further, I come across the other end of this tannoy, hidden away behind the sofa. It's a sexy way to relay messages to your lover at the other end of the suite. I wouldn't dream of telling you what Mr Smith whispered through it, but it wasn't 'Fancy a game of Travel Connect 4?'

The hotel does not have a restaurant of its own – it's far too dreamlike to accommodate the sardonic bustle of a hot, clattery kitchen and drums of catering ingredients. Instead, you can order up a seriously good chef to prepare a private dinner for you, to be served in the

garden (amazing for a summer birthday) or around its huge indoor dining table. Our plan, after a long period of luxuriating in the bath, is to head out and find our supper in Montmartre. As one of the touristiest destinations on earth, the neighbourhood is liberally peppered with the kind of restaurants that locals don't even bother deriding, so we're crossing our fingers we'll land luckily.

We end up in a tiny, candlelit bistro, Virage Lepic, as it seems to be full of in-the-know locals. Tablecloths are checked in red and white, and every inch of wall space is covered with posters, film stills and mementos of Doris Day, Judy Garland and Carmen Miranda. It's gloriously gay, in both senses of the word, and we have a fantastic evening drinking champagne and sharing melt-in-the-mouth bone marrow and duck cassoulet. The climb back up to the hotel isn't easy, but at least it's easy to aim for a bed the size of a principality.

Despite Mr Smith's vow that he'll never eat again, he devours plenty of the croissants, freshly baked bread,

marmalade, fruit salad and fresh coffee that's wheeled into our suite. With a little help from me, of course. After breakfast, we head downstairs – past the series of self-portraits by a young Japanese artist who's currently exhibiting in the hotel – and ask for more coffee, so that Mr Smith's got something to accompany his Gitane out on the terrace.

We spend the rest of that day looking for lampshades at Porte de Clignancourt's fleamarket, then mooching around the boutiques of the Marais, but it's not really that important. What is crucial is that we have the Hôtel Particulier Montmartre to come back to. Homely enough to put us completely at our ease, yet filled with the sort of stylish and beautiful touches that makes us feel honoured to be there, it is the perfect Parisian combination. Thank goodness not that many people know about it. If only they'd make a bit more effort to hide the entrance.

Reviewed by Sarah Maber

NEED TO KNOW

Rooms Five suites.

Rates Low season, €290–€490; high season, €390–€590. Breakfast, €20.

Check-out 12 noon, but flexible, depending on the next guests. Earliest check-in, 3pm.

Facilities Garden, library with dozens of contemporary art and design books, CDs and DVDs, free WiFi throughout. In rooms: flatscreen TV, DVD/CD, minibar, Annick Goutal products.

Children Baby cots and extra beds are provided free.

Also The hotel can arrange in-room massages and hairdressing. With shady nooks and a tinkling fountain, the garden is as much a work of art as the hotel interior, thanks to landscaper Louis Bénech, who also redesigned the Jardin des Tuileries.

IN THE KNOW

Our favourite rooms Hôtel Particulier's handful of suites were all designed by Morgane Rousseau, with featured works by different artists, and each is packed with personality. We'd stay in Trees with Ears for the name alone, but it's also invitingly spacious, draped in tactile velvet and full of antiques. Vitrine, created by sculptor Philippe Mayaux, is a saucier stay altogether, with its cabinet of highly suggestive blown-glass objects and a big steam room. The arboreal wallpaper in Jacuzzi-equipped Vegetal makes you feel as though you're sleeping in a light-dappled forest glade.

Hotel bar Le Très Particulier is open Wednesday to Saturday, from 5pm until midnight. It is located in the very cool main salon, where an array of iconic furniture includes an original Arne Jacobsen Egg chair.

Hotel restaurant Hôtel Particulier doesn't have a restaurant, but there is a private dining room, and a chef can be booked. Breakfast consists of fresh fruit, tasty pastries and fabulous coffee.

Top table Take summer breakfast or tea alfresco, at one of the little wrought-iron tables among the flowers.

Room service Soup, ham, cheese and wine are on offer until midnight.

Dress code Glam and quirky: think Weimar or Vivienne Westwood.

Local knowledge Montmartre is awash with art, much of it indifferent. Keep your distance from the Place du Tertre caricaturists and head instead to a gallery such as Espace Dalí at 11 rue Poulbot (+33 (0)1 42 64 40 10).

LOCAL EATING AND DRINKING

Rustic dishes such as duck cassoulet match the country decor in the cosy dining room of Virage Lepic at 61 Rue Lepic (+33 (0)1 42 52 46 79). Light years away, Guilo Guilo at 8 rue Garreau serves up Japanese gastro thrills to the cognoscenti; book way ahead (+33 (0)1 43 54 23 92). Beloved of locals, art deco bistro La Mascotte (+33 (0)1 46 06 28 15) on Rue des Abbesses is famed for its lobster. A relaxed modern bistro at the top of Rue des Martyrs, with a new-classics menu chalked up daily, Le Miroir was launched in 2008 by a distinguished young team who excel at home-made touches (+33 (0)1 46 06 50 73). A boho, shambolically welcoming bar just minutes from the tourist trail atop Montmartre, Rendezvous des Amis, 23 rue Gabrielle, is plastered with photographs of the management's social circle (+33 (0)1 46 06 01 60).

GET A ROOM!

For more information, or to book this hotel, go to www.mrandmrssmith.com. Register your Smith membership card (see pages 4–5) to enjoy exclusive offers and privileges.

 SMITH MEMBER OFFER A bottle of fine wine.

Hôtel Particulier Montmartre 23 avenue Junot, 75018 Paris (+33 (0)1 53 41 81 40; www.hotel-particulier-montmartre.com)

Hôtel Récamier

STYLE Globetrotting glamour
SETTING Sophisticated Saint-Germain

'While the city goes about its business below, our garret hideaway is untroubled by so much as a dove cooing'

Paris! City of Light, city of lovers, city of... remarkably well-behaved prepubescent skateboarders? Admittedly, there's less of a ring to it but, as Mrs Smith and I learn, the best way to locate the slim façade of the Hôtel Récamier, in the southwest corner of tranquil Place Saint-Sulpice, is to look out for the group of skate kids (more Ralph Lauren than Stüssy) politely pulling ollies and kickflips across the road from its front door. In a sense, these gently wheeling garçons summed up the bobo (or, to the Anglophone, bourgeois bohemian) spirit of the 6ème arrondissement. Once the playground of 20th-century philosophical and artistic rebels, from the Existentialists and the Surrealists to the 'Lost Generation' of Hemingway and Fitzgerald, Saint-Germain-des-Prés is now firmly established as the home of grown-up Parisian style, while retaining just enough of its former edge to keep things interesting.

Passing through the doors of the 24-room Récamier, designed by French interiors notable Jean-Louis Deniot, we feel less like we're entering a hotel than the private apartment of a wealthy archaeologist with a taste for the earthier, more textural end of modernist design. In the lobby, black and white chequered marble is offset with warm-toned wooden furniture and fabrics that span the colour spectrum from espresso to macchiato. On a side table, a cast of a bronze West African Ife portrait bust stands, its gaze directing us to the tiny check-in desk across the hall.

With decorous efficiency we're escorted past a twisting staircase to the lift, which we take straight to the top of the supermodel-slender building. Six storeys up and we find ourselves in a perfect lovers' haven. While the city goes about its business below, our garret hideaway is untroubled by so much as a dove cooing. Room 64 is peaceful, full of bright springtime sunlight, snug and well equipped for a city retreat. There's a private terrace from which to look out over the crooked Parisian rooftops, and a fridge full of eminently gluggable wine to celebrate our arrival. The decor continues the safari-meets-1950s-ethnography-museum vibe, with hessian-effect wallpaper and a tent-like canvas canopy sheltering the bed. Relaxing on its great drift of plump cushions and pillows a little later on, we really do feel like the rest of civilisation is far, far away.

Having negotiated the numerous taps that control the twin showerheads, Mrs Smith emerges from the bathroom – which, in contrast to our boudoir, turns out to be all black slate and polished white simplicity – to pass judgement on the range of toiletries. 'Fragonard – herby, fresh, mmm. Very nice. Do we have to go out?' I'm experimenting with the entertainment centre (flatscreen TV, iPod dock) and stumble on a Gallic radio station that seems to play nothing but Bryan Adams and Sting. Even the French, it seems, have their style lapses every now and then. Time to hit the streets.

One of the great advantages of Hôtel Récamier is that we find we don't have to wander very far from its doors to experience the mixture of history and contemporary refinement that make Paris unique.

Dominating the square outside the front door is the Eglise Saint-Sulpice. Dating back to the 13th century, this atmospheric church features in *The Da Vinci Code* – but we don't let that put us off. Much more significantly, it's home to some seriously sensuous murals by the Romantic painter Delacroix, and was the place where the Marquis de Sade was baptised, not that it exactly set history's most celebrated libertine on the straight-and-narrow path. Mrs Smith and I leave the church with far-from-heavenly things on our minds.

As I'm to learn on the short shopping spree upon which Mrs Smith embarks nimbly the following day, flanking the square and the surrounding streets are some of the fashion capital's most chic shops, including a clutch of sophisticated younger French labels such as APC, Vanessa Bruno, Sonia Rykiel and Paul & Joe. For now though we wander through the streets to the local organic café/deli, Bread & Roses, where we eagerly scoff millefeuille knocked back with café crème. A stroll through the Jardin du Luxembourg and back to the hotel brings us to

nightfall, dinner at nearby bistro La Ferrandaise (inventive takes on provincial French classics and delicious Côtes du Rhônes), then drinks in a hip dive bar favoured by art-student locals. Mrs Smith's theory that its jukebox contains '(Everything I Do) I Do it For You' remains, however, sadly unconfirmed.

The following morning we wake to breakfast in bed. The previous night we'd eagerly ticked boxes on the promising menu and are now confronted with a feast of fresh fruit, poached eggs, croissants, bread, yoghurt, freshly squeezed juice, coffee and an impressive cheeseboard. For those who like more company there is a breakfast room and courtyard downstairs. Here, the rustic feel is contrasted by quirky, glittering details: a driftwood sculpture sits on a golden tabletop, and lamps are supported by gilded birds' legs. There's a bookcase full of tomes on contemporary photography, a clutch of board games and a small array of art photos on the walls. But it's not for us – not yet. This is Paris. City of Light. City of lovers. City of lounging in bed long after the rest of the world has greeted the morning sun.

Reviewed by Tom Morton

NEED TO KNOW

Rooms 24.

Rates €250–€420, including tax. Breakfast, from €10.

Check-out 12pm. Earliest check-in, 2pm (earlier if the room's ready).

Facilities Terrace, gym, free WiFi throughout. In rooms: flatscreen TV, iPod dock, bottled water, Fragonard bath products.

Children Cots for babies are free; extra beds cost €30 a night. A local nanny can take over for €18 an hour, given half a day's notice.

Also In-room beauty treatments and massages can be arranged.

IN THE KNOW

Our favourite rooms Each of the rooms has been decadently dressed with exotic furniture and textured trimmings; all have canopied beds. Room 42 triumphs in size and has a chocolate, cream and beige palette, with a striped canopy over the bed, an ornate gold mirror and tactile wallpaper. We also like Room 64 on the sixth floor, which is smaller, but has a balcony overlooking Place Saint-Sulpice. For family stays, each floor has a pair of rooms that can be connected to form a suite. If you prefer a bath tub to a walk-in shower, book a Classic or Club room.

Hotel bar Guests can kick back at a little bar in the breakfast lounge, where a waiter serves drinks in the evenings.

Hotel restaurant There's no restaurant, but a Continental breakfast is put on in the homely lounge every morning — guests help themselves from the old-fashioned dresser. Between 4pm and 6pm, free soft drinks and snacks are served.

Top table Squeeze into the cosy den off the main lounge, and bag one of the brown-velvet sofas or gold-leather armchairs arranged around the fireplace. In summer, step out with your drinks amid the bamboo on the terrace.

Room service A menu of omelettes, cheese platters, risotto and pasta is available until 11pm.

Dress code Nothing leopard-print. You might clash with the carpet.

Local knowledge Succumb to your sweet tooth at artisan chocolatier Pierre Marcolini on Rue de Seine (+33 (0)1 44 07 39 07; www.marcolini.com) — don't miss chocolates delicately flavoured with Earl Grey tea, caramelised cream of pistachio or Madagascar vanilla.

LOCAL EATING AND DRINKING

For inimitable Italian ice-cream, visit Grom on Rue de Seine (+33 (0)1 40 46 92 60). Call in at La Société, a glamorous yet relaxed brasserie on Place Saint-Germain, to admire Peter Lindbergh photographs, sculptures and a marble bar. There's even jazz for your ears (+33 (0)1 53 63 60 60). Good-value bistro La Ferrandaise is known for its well-sourced meats, including the eponymous beef, 8 rue de Vaugirard (+33 (0)1 43 26 36 36). For inventive and inspired South East Asian flavours, try Ze Kitchen Galerie on Rue des Grands Augustins (+33 (0)1 44 32 00 32). La Méditerranée, overlooking the theatre on Place de l'Odéon, serves lipsmacking seafood, including bouillabaisse and monkfish stew (+33 (0)1 43 26 02 30). Bread & Roses, 7 rue Fleurus (+33 (0)1 42 22 06 06), is a rightly famed organic café and purveyor of fine breads, pastries and tarts.

GET A ROOM!

For more information, or to book this hotel, go to www.mrandmrssmith.com. Register your Smith membership card (see pages 4–5) to enjoy exclusive offers and privileges.

 SMITH MEMBER OFFER Two tickets to the Louvre or Musée d'Orsay.

Hôtel Récamier 3 bis, Place Saint-Sulpice, 75006 Paris (+33 (0)1 43 26 04 89; www.hotelrecamier.com)

La Réserve Paris

STYLE Millionaire pied-à-terre
SETTING Eiffel-view Right Bank

'Anonymous from the outside, this chic stay is surely anyone's fantasy Parisian home. Our suite has a view that doesn't merely include the Eiffel Tower – it *is* the Eiffel Tower'

'Is this really a hotel?' Mrs Smith asks, as we approach the discreet entrance to La Réserve Paris, just off the Place du Trocadéro. High-status location notwithstanding (the Eiffel Tower looks near enough to touch from here), we could be walking up to any old door of any old bourgeois 16th-arrondissement mansion block. Nothing indicates that we're about to embark on one of the most amazing hotel experiences a Mr and Mrs Smith could ever know. An inconspicuous bell and an even less shouty sign bring us, clueless lambs that we are, to a place of understated elegance where world travellers – CEOs, rock stars, crown princes – who are used to the best and need a place to call their own will feel more than at home in Paris.

Greeting us impeccably, with genuine smiles, staff convey to us that we are not only expected but seriously welcome, treating us a) as though we are returning from faraway lands and b) as though we own the place. There aren't many establishments that have the capacity to make you feel so relaxed and so important at the same

time. The lobby is tiny – La Réserve Paris has only 10 suites/apartments – and serves purely as a landing pad where staff can greet you and find out what you need from them that day. The premises are full during our visit but we never hear a whimper, and barely cross paths with a fellow guest, though we do end up on nodding terms with someone's avuncular-looking bodyguard. We're thinking hip-hop platinum-seller plus entourage.

No time is wasted at check-in. We are whisked to our quarters by staff who disappear discreetly once they've imparted knowledge. We're agog. La Réserve may be anonymous from the outside but, inside, this chic stay is surely anyone's fantasy Parisian home. Our two-bedroom suite has a view that doesn't merely include the Eiffel Tower – it *is* the Eiffel Tower. Balconies that give you an authentic encounter with the Iron Lady are as rare in Paris as big, ugly dogs.

The bathrooms have Jacuzzi tubs spacious enough for two, as well as robes befitting Henry VIII, and the kind of slippers that Serge Gainsbourg might have padded around in. The living room is fitted with the most enormous flatscreen TV and, of course, there are Bose speakers all around. An Eileen Gray book is nonchalantly exposed on a low coffee table, suggesting one of the designer's sources of inspiration, perhaps. The decor can best be described as simply luxurious: a blank canvas, with the bare minimum of colourful detail. What this means is that, if you were to take an apartment for a few months, you wouldn't be living with someone else's taste; it's more like a very swanky furnished rental, and not remotely like being in someone else's house. It's like being in your own house. If you're in the habit of keeping a residence here, there and everywhere.

Neutral is nice for us northern Europeans, so it's especially easy for us to feel at ease here. Even better, the kitchen is equipped with every possible accoutrement for the home chef. How many hotel

rooms come armed with five different kitchen knives or a fantastic Nespresso machine, may I ask? More than a mere suite, this is a super-serviced five-star apartment. La Réserve proclaims it has 'all the advantages of a palace, without the inconveniences' and it's hard to express it better. Every room has a full-time *gouvernante* on call (by the way, that's French for housekeeper — not a strict governess, whatever you might hope), catering to your every need. From unpacking your luggage to repacking it, to helping you organise private events, this is true 'your wish is our command' stuff.

Keen to share our delight in our plush pied-à-terre, we decide to throw a Saturday brunch for our Paris friends. As we spend Friday night in the nearby Blitz Bar, partying until the wee hours, we wake up late — extravagantly so. I don't know if there are sensors in the room, but it seems our resident angel detects life between bedroom and shower, and starts

preparing breakfast. We don't even have to formulate hungry thoughts: the minute we emerge into the living area in our bathrobes, fresh coffee and orange juice, little pastries and delectable jams – the works – is waiting.

Our friends are due to arrive within an hour and we haven't been to the shops to get the wherewithal for brunch, let alone done any chopping, whisking or devilling up. No problem at all, thanks to Anna, our lovely *gouvernante*. She sits down with us to makes a list of what we want to serve and, 45 minutes later, our requirements are all in the kitchen. This isn't just supermarket fare, either. Every item has been sourced from the best neighbourhood épiceries. Amazing. Anna then melts away, leaving us to get on with the preparation. Four hours later, when the last of our guests has left this magnificent Parisian apartment of ours, she reappears, as if by magic, and offers to clean up. Discretion is not only the watchword of the hotel, but it also applies to the La Réserve way of making things happen.

We've never felt so at home in Paris. We've found a place to stay where we, the guests, are what ultimately matter. At La Réserve Paris, everything is perfect, as it should be, but never overwhelming. *Comme il faut*, you might say. The proportions are just right, from the space and light of the rooms to the excellent service, even the very good but relatively simple breakfast. The thing is, you know that if you desire something a bit (or a lot) more ostentatious than croissants, the staff can probably get you a baby grand piano or a Warhol by teatime.

Reviewed by Rasmus Michau

NEED TO KNOW

Rooms 10 apartments, with one to four bedrooms in each.

Rates €1,850 to €4,330, including tax and Continental or à la carte breakfast, served in the apartment by your maid.

Check-out 12 noon. Earliest check-in, 3pm. Both are flexible, by arrangement.

Facilities In-room beauty treatments, valet parking, on-call chef, trainer, tutor, butler, hairdresser and so on, free WiFi throughout, gardens. In rooms: fully equipped kitchens, multimedia centre with printer/scanner, flatscreen TV, CD/DVD, iPod dock, minibar, bottled water.

Children Cots, extra beds, high chairs and baby monitors are provided, and babysitting can be arranged with a few hours' notice.

Also Clean, quiet pets allowed. Smoking is fine on the terrace or in the garden. No wheelchair access.

IN THE KNOW

Our favourite rooms Best for family trips, Apartment 1 has plenty of space spread over three levels, with its own private entrance, a garden, a huge master suite with walk-in dressing room, and a view of the Eiffel Tower from the dining area. Apartment 2 is also vast, with a big garden and a fabulous view. Apartment 4 has just one double room, but it's still good and big with a living room and dining room for up to eight. Apartment 7 has three doubles, a twin and a dining room in the building's rotunda — ideal for groups of friends. Apartment 10 has an open kitchen and a wonderful terrace where you feel as though you virtually own the Eiffel Tower.

Hotel bar No bar, but you can pre-order the drinks cabinet of your dreams.

Hotel restaurant There's no restaurant, but all the apartments have superbly equipped kitchens, and dining tables seating eight to 10, so you can either shop for groceries, spending a squillionth of the cost of a gourmet restaurant meal (try Bon Marché's La Grande Epicerie) and cook your own dinner, or have a chef called in.

Top table The apartment is your oyster. In summer, the terrace of Apartment 10 is super for aperitifs.

Room service The concierge can arrange delivery, during restaurant opening hours, according to your gastronomic desires.

Dress code Silk Yves Saint Laurent pyjamas.

Local knowledge The Guimet Museum in Place d'Iéna (www.guimet.fr) houses one of Europe's biggest collections of Asian works, including a whole wing of Buddhist, Hindu and Shinto treasures. Palais de Tokyo on Avenue du Président Wilson (www.palaisdetokyo.com) puts on eye-opening contemporary-art shows.

LOCAL EATING AND DRINKING

Two minutes' walk away, fashionable, crystal-strung Café de l'Homme in the Musée de l'Homme on Place du Trocadéro (+33 (0)1 44 05 30 15) has a fabulous terrace offering an incomparable eyeful of Eiffel. Halfway up the Iron Lady, Le Jules Verne (+33 (0)1 45 55 61 44) is a super-exclusive Alain Ducasse restaurant, where alpha Parisians dine on foie gras, turbot and soufflé. Chez l'Ami Jean at 27 rue Malar (+33 (0)1 47 05 86 89) is the oldest Basque restaurant in Paris, now run by star chef Stéphane Jego. Pershing Hall's Lounge Bar (+33 (0)1 58 36 58 00) is a dead cert for glamour, with its contemporary rococo decor, DJs and a stylish crowd. A classical/futurist place to pose with a cocktail, Le Bar at Hôtel Plaza Athénée (+33 (0)1 53 67 66 00) combines a long, blue-lit glass bar and high stools with leather armchairs.

GET A ROOM!

For more information, or to book this hotel, go to www.mrandmrssmith.com. Register your Smith membership card (see pages 4–5) to enjoy exclusive offers and privileges.

 SMITH MEMBER OFFER Two half-day passes for a nearby spa, usually €100 each; members staying three nights or more also get a free treatment each.

La Réserve Paris 10 place de la Trocadéro/3 avenue d'Eylau, 75116 Paris (+33 (0)1 53 70 53 70; www.lareserve.ch)

déjeuner

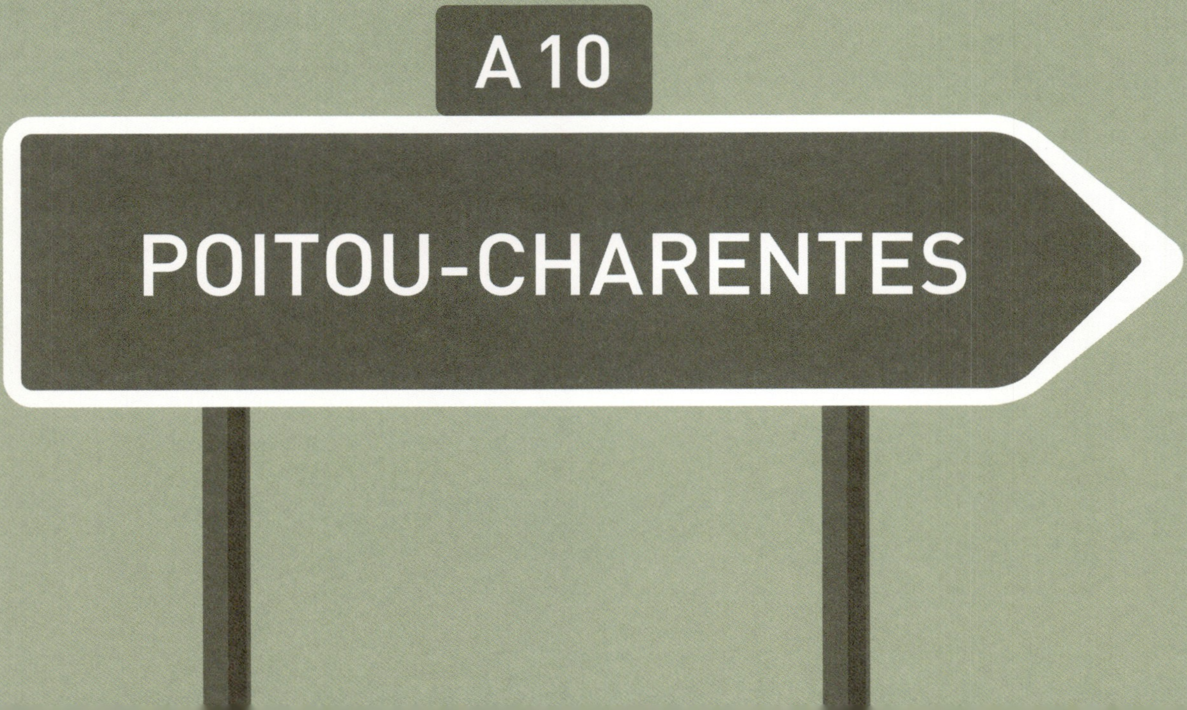
A 10
POITOU-CHARENTES

Lille

Rouen

Reims

Paris

Rennes

Strasbourg

Nantes

Poitiers

Bourges

Dijon

La Rochelle

20

Angoulême

19

Bordeaux

Lyon

Toulouse

Montpellier

Nice

Marseille

POITOU-CHARENTES

19 Château de la Couronne

20 Le Logis de Puygâty

POITOU-CHARENTES

COUNTRYSIDE Grand castles, sandcastles
COUNTRY LIFE Brandy-soaked suppers

Topped by the Loire valley, tailed by Bordeaux, cooled by Atlantic breezes, Poitou-Charentes is the home of cognac, and a coast-to-country destination *par excellence*. Beautiful beaches are the main draw, with bucket-and-spade Royan and yachtie La Rochelle the star-billed sands, and Ile d'Oléron and Ile de Ré the offshore jewels. Meandering from north and east, a network of rivers once vital for paper mills and vineyards is now populated by kingfishers and canoeists. Gourmets will easily fall for this green and fertile land, where oysters and sirloin of beef are equally prized, and eaux de vie flow sociably. Whether you take your apéritif countryside or seaside, it's the region's easygoing calm you'll raise a glass to.

GETTING THERE

Planes The region's airports include Angoulême, Poitiers, Limoges and La Rochelle. For internal flights, try Airlinair (www.airlinair.com) and Brit Air (www.britair.com). For direct flights from the UK, Bordeaux is 90 minutes from Angoulême, and British Airways and EasyJet can convey you from London. Ryanair flies from Stansted to La Rochelle, Limoges and Poitiers, and to Angoulême between Easter and October (www.ba.com; www.easyjet.com; www.ryanair.com).

Trains Poitiers and Angoulême are on the Paris–Bordeaux TGV route (www.tgv.com). UK travellers can take the Eurostar and connect at Lille (www.eurostar.com).

Automobiles Angoulême is four and a half hours by road from Paris, seven hours from Calais. You can rent a car at the airport at Bordeaux, Angoulême, Limoges and Poitiers, where Hertz and Europcar both have desks. Book car-hire pick-up at Poitiers rail station with Europcar (www.europcar.com).

LOCAL KNOWLEDGE

Taxis It should be easy to hunt down a cab in bigger towns such as La Rochelle, Rochefort and Angoulême. In villages, *c'est pas évident*, so ask your hotel to organise one for you.

Siesta and fiesta Shops and banks shut between 12pm and 2pm. Outside high-season months (June to August), many shops and restaurants take a two-day weekend on Sundays and Mondays. Dining is always a serious business, so whatever time you want to head out to a restaurant, it's best to book.

Do go/don't go When schools break up for summer, the region's beaches fill with families; only go in July and August if you don't mind sharing with them. Autumn is a great time to visit: the Atlantic is as warmed by the summer sun as it will ever be, and the grape harvest (September to October) brings festivals.

Packing tips Riding boots – the region has many horse trails. A hip flask for your cognac. Deck shoes and a Breton top for mingling on the marina at La Rochelle.

Children Adrenaline-junkie kids (and dads) will love Aventure Parc in Massignac, open April–October, for rope swings and bungee jumps (www.aventure-parc.fr).

Recommended reads Maigret comes to La Rochelle in Georges Simenon's *Le Voyageur de la Toussaint*. Or pack mid-20th-century novels *Claire* or *Les Destinées Sentimentales* by local writer Jacques Chardonne, for light social commentary against a Charentais backdrop.

Local specialities Tourteau fromagé is a sponge cake made with goat's cheese, identifiable by its raisin-dark crust. The handmade butter from the dairy at Echiré is acclaimed worldwide as a connoisseur's choice. Head to the coast for sumptuous seafood: langoustines, oysters, crabs, mussels... Livestock farming takes place throughout the region, too, so your beef, mutton or pork shouldn't have travelled far. The area was prized for its truffles in the 19th century, though all that remains now are the truffle cheeses, such as Jonchée and Chabichou, sold in local markets.

And... Ile d'Oléron is France's second-largest island after Corsica, and is home to some of the nation's most revered oyster farms, some specialising in the much-prized Marennes-Oléron variety.

WORTH GETTING OUT OF BED FOR

Viewpoint Patrol the mediaeval ramparts in Angoulême, where 2km of ancient wall remain intact. Only a gilded frame could better the city views along the stretch between Rempart du Midi and Place Beaulieu.

Arts and culture At the comic-strip museum in Angoulême at 121 rue de Bordeaux (+33 (0)5 45 38 65 65), the graphic genre is illuminated via drawings, magazines and murals. In Cognac, Camus is one of the last family-run cognac houses, and offers half-day 'blend your own' brandy masterclasses, as well as tours and tastings (+33 (0)5 45 32 72 96; www.camus.fr). King of the region's castles is Le Château de la Rochefoucauld (+33 (0)5 45 62 07 42; www.chateau-la-rochefoucauld. com; open daily, April to December). Take the guided tour for access to vast libraries (18,000 volumes from the 18th and 19th centuries) and the archives of historic documents and parchment letters.

Activities Enjoy a canter in the countryside – you'll find dozens of stables open to the public across Poitou-Charentes (www.cheval-poitoucharentes.com). Take to the region's rivers: try kayaking at Aubeterre-sur-Dronne (www.aubeterresurdronne.com), or at Montbron on the Tardoire. Or take a trip on a *gabarre* – a flat-bottomed barge made for ferrying premium booze down to the coast – from the pretty village of Saint-Simon, west of Angoulême (www.village-gabarrier.com).

Best beach La Grande Conche at Royan is a 2km arc of tan-gold sand, sweeping south from Royan to Saint-Georges de Didonne. On Ile d'Oléron, the sheltered beaches around Saint-Trojan-les-Bains, including gorgeous Gatseau, are family-friendly and edged with pines.

Daytripper Ile de Ré is worthy of a day's exploration. Either take the toll bridge from La Rochelle if you're driving, or cross by boat from its old harbour to Saint-Martin-de-Ré (+33 (0)5 46 34 25 67; www. inter-iles.com). The marina there is the place to yacht-spot, enjoy an ice-cream, and browse galleries and boutiques. Have lunch at Les Embruns at 6 rue Chay Morin (+33 (0)5 46 09 63 23), before heading out to La Flotte, Ars-en-Ré or viewpoint Saint-Clément-des-Baleines. If you're staying on Ile de Ré, a trip to Angoulême, with its atmospheric old town, ramparts and engaging museums, is worth the mileage.

Shopping There are night markets in summer in Saint-Martin-de-Ré, selling the usual arts/crafts/jewellery. In La Rochelle, follow your nose to Rue Marché to admire the fantastical, fragrant fruits of the sea. Nip into Chocolaterie Duceau at 18 place de l'Hôtel-de-Ville in Angoulême (+33 (0)5 45 95 06 42). Its artisans have been creating chocolates by hand since 1876, and their Marguerite sweets, made of dark chocolate with orange peel, have stood the test of time.

Something for nothing The first two hours are free when you hire a yellow bicycle in La Rochelle, which, in 1997, became the first city in France to instigate car-free days. Secure yours at Autoplus on Place de Verdun and Quai Valin (+33 (0)5 46 34 02 22).

Don't go home without... taking a sunset stroll around the fortified marina at La Rochelle, accompanied by the 'ting ting' of yacht stays on masts. Yachts rub bows with gin-palace cruisers and the sun bathes the cream-stoned harbour walls in rosy light.

POTENTLY POITOU-CHARENTES

The Atlantic waters help create the eaux de vie that Cognac is famous for. White wine is double distilled, and aged in barrels until fierily strong and caramel smooth. Visit the cognac houses (in Cognac, of all the places) and go home with your own labelled bottle. Camus, at 29 rue Marguerite de Navarre (+33 (0)5 45 32 28 28), is a fifth-generation family firm; Rémy Martin, at 20 rue de la Société Vinicole (+33 (0)5 45 35 76 66) is famous for champagne cognac; Hennessy, on Quai Richard Hennessy (+33 (0)5 45 35 72 68) is good for a quick tour and a general overview.

DIARY

January Angoulême hosts a festival of comic strips, with exhibitions, author Q&As and prize-giving (www.bdangouleme. com). July Les Franco Folies is La Rochelle's festival of French music, usually held mid-month and involving full-scale gigs, as well as acoustic performances (www.francofolies.fr). August–September The Grand Pavois, held at Port des Minimes at La Rochelle, is a boat show, first and foremost, with events around the exhibition including a 'night sail', a kind of *son et lumière*-meets-yachting spectacular (www.grand-pavois.com). September Bugattis, Jaguars, Bentleys, among assorted vintage and classic cars, vroom to the starting line for the spectacular Circuit Des Remparts in Angoulême. Expect car shows on the Saturday, and the race itself on the Sunday (www.circuit-des-remparts.com). October In the north of the region, Pamproux hosts the annual Festival des Vendanges. Locals celebrate the grape harvest with exhibitions, plays, concerts, comedy, dance and, of course, a glass or two. November Tastings and cookery classes draw the crowds to Angoulême's food festival, Gastronomades. Over three days, you'll get to sample regional produce and see Charentais chefs showcasing local fare (www.gastronomades.fr).

Marthon

Château de la Couronne

STYLE Modern-day fairy tale
SETTING Pretty Charente parkland

'Boudoir-bound, we climb the spiral wooden staircase and walk down corridors lit with pools of green light, hung with dappled black and silver canvases and salvaged wooden doors'

It's 3am and I'm playing billiards with Mr Smith. I say playing but I mean beating, despite – or perhaps because of – the merlot we demolished over dinner. With balls still to kill, Mr Smith is getting desperate. He resorts to accusations of cheating, and bad gags about ball-play. I keep my cool, balance buttocks on the baize for a tricky backwards shot, and expertly pot the black. 'Never mind, darling. Fancy a film?'

It may sound like Mr Smith and I are out on the town but, in fact, we're in a 16th-century château in the sleepy village of Marthon in south-western France. Outside, in the inky darkness, apple-green fields surround ivory-stone streets and terracotta-roofed buildings. The craggy-faced elders we admired in the village earlier are snoring now, and contented dogs are dozing off their baguette and bavette scraps, whimpering fitfully as they picture fat rabbits.

But here in Château de la Couronne, the night is young. We lounge on the cream leather sofa in the cinema room, and watch Bond blow things up, play with some gadgets and perform his vanishing-knickers trick on the ladies. It looks quite tiring; we think 007 would be better off here, where it's warm, snug and free of explosives. He could play seducer by strumming on one of the electric guitars hanging on the wall, or croon on the microphone and caress the keyboard. He could shake his martini at the Stone Salon's wood and glass honesty bar, crunch on pistachios, relax fireside on the battered Chesterfield, and rest his dragon flamethrower on the table fashioned from tree roots.

He'd love our suite: a white expanse set in a turret, with bold red and black splodgy paintings on one wall, two silver Chesterfields, a palatial bathroom with two tubs, and a beautiful bed framed with wood and ochre fabric, piled high with marshmallow-like duvet and pillows. As the film continues, our thoughts turn to the bed with increasing frequency. Soon we're boudoir-bound – climbing the spiral wooden staircase, walking down corridors lit with pools of green light, hung with dappled black and silver canvases and salvaged wooden doors. Back in our suite, blankety bliss envelops us.

The next morning, we wake early, having left the shutters open so that our Vitamin D-deprived Blighty complexions will absorb optimum sunshine. Beyond our balcony, the grounds are looking good: an emerald park, with rows of perfectly pruned hedges, white tables with parasols and spidery black chairs. The warm spring air exerts a pull on us, and we ask owners Mark and Nicky (fellow Brits) for breakfast alfresco. Nicky lays a spread of feather-light pastries, creamy cheeses, sweet jams and zingy orange juice. In the past, I've classed fruit salad in the 'safe but boring' category, along with soup – but the specimen Nicky serves up is divine: slices of sunshine-yellow pineapple and mango, scattered with plump blueberries, raspberries and ruby-red pomegranate seeds, served up in sundae glasses. Breakfasting outside is marvellous – as well as eyeing up each other, we admire the glimmering pool and lush grounds, and plan a ramble in the gardens later on.

After breakfast, we view the château in its sunlit glory. Rooms are sprinkled with a buccaneer's bounty. I like the glittering art deco lipstick case and vanity mirror, and the piano is a handsome beast. Mr Smith is keen on the battered top hat adorning a radiator, and the lobby's acid-green and white armchair. We could praise the château all day, but there's exploring to be done, so we clamber into our hire car.

Our Peugeot 1007 has doors that newfangledly slide back to open. The button to release these is identical to the button that works the windows. Except that this button is positioned far from the windows, whereas the ones to operate the doors is within easy reach. Several near-death experiences later, we arrive in Brantôme, a historic town that Nicky has recommended.

Walking around, we check out Dordogne hotels with jade-green shutters and antiquated black lettering, the Benedictine abbey flanked by wooded slopes, the stone bridge and, above all, the Dronne river, flowing through

the town. A short stroll leads us to irresistible delis where we stock up on rich tasty cassoulet and pretty candy. Next stop is at a seemingly unremarkable café where steak, topped with fragrant chopped onion, accompanied by slender, salty frites are far superior to what you'd find in an equivalent establishment back home. We've crossed bridges, we've eyeballed the abbey, we've shopped, but now we're pining – our château awaits. Resistance is futile, so we hop into our chariot.

Back at boutique basecamp, we run baths. Regally occupying individual tubs, we sip champagne plucked from the bathroom's minibar. The artfully tarnished mirrors steam up, herby bubble bath scents the air, and it's all deliciously intoxicating. A dinner reservation at an Angoulême restaurant stirs us from our perfumed paradise. Several plates of foie gras, salmon parmentier and an extremely phallic lamb shank later, and we're back. It's as though we never left. In the Stone Salon, by the flickering fire, Mr Smith pours me a drink and, with a challenge in his eyes, necks a handful of peanuts.

'Billiards, my sweet?' As if he needs to ask.

Reviewed by Mr & Mrs Smith

NEED TO KNOW

Rooms Five suites (nine if you take the entire château).

Rates €145–€315, not including breakfast, €15. Rent the whole château, which sleeps up to 26, for €2,000 a night or €12,000 a week.

Check-out 11am. Later, subject to availability. Earliest check-in, 4pm.

Facilities Heated outdoor pool, cinema/billiards room with guitars, keyboards and amps for guests' use, games room with table tennis, DVD and CD library, free WiFi in the Piano Salon. In rooms: flatscreen TV, DVD/CD, fully stocked fridge.

Children There are plenty of activities, indoor and outdoor, for the bairns, including pool and tennis. Cots are available free; extra beds are €40 a night.

Also Massages, manicures and pedicures by arrangement.

IN THE KNOW

Our favourite rooms We were seduced by Suite 4, which has a vast double-tubbed bathroom and natural-stone walls snaked with exposed copper piping. It's one of the château's biggest suites, with modern iron and glass furniture, lime-green cushions, and a toe-enveloping fluffy black carpet. Suites 1, 2 and 5 have turrets; the latter also has twin corner baths with a coloured-glass mosaic between them.

Hotel bar There's an extremely well-stocked honesty bar in the Stone Salon. You can also kick back with a glass of local wine in front of the original open fireplace in the Seventies-feel White Salon or in the Piano Salon, by the bay window overlooking the gardens.

Hotel restaurant There's no restaurant, but Château de la Couronne can prepare a dinner for 10 or more, if requested in advance. A fine buffet breakfast is served in the high-ceilinged *réfectoire*.

Top table Nurse a cognac on the green leather chesterfield in the lovely Stone Salon.

Room service Nope, but you can help yourself to a glass of Bordeaux from the honesty bar.

Dress code Casual cashmere.

Local knowledge Château guests are free to use Marthon's village tennis club facilities (rackets available to borrow).

LOCAL EATING AND DRINKING

Of the handful of places to eat near the château, the pick of the pile is nearby Les Glycines (+33 (0)5 45 70 23 90), a salt-of-the-earth eatery serving simple, satisfying traditional fare. It's open for lunch and dinner; book for the evenings. Chez Steph is a busy brasserie, a 10-minute drive from the château, on Rue Halles in La Rochefoucauld (+33 (0)5 45 62 09 11), where you can eat excellent pizza, pleasing meat dishes and home-made puddings. In the cobbled hilltop town of Angoulême, 25km away, Jardin de Kashmir, on Rue Raymond Audour in the old quarter, is an excellent Indian (+33 (0)5 45 95 03 03), and Le Terminus on Place de la Gare (+33 (0)5 45 95 27 13) is a great spot to stop – no pun intended – for seafood.

GET A ROOM!

For more information, or to book this hotel, go to www.mrandmrssmith.com. Register your Smith membership card (see pages 4–5) to enjoy exclusive offers and privileges.

 SMITH MEMBER OFFER A bottle of champagne.

Château de la Couronne 16380 Marthon (+33 (0)5 45 62 29 96; www.chateaudelacouronne.com)

Le Logis de Puygâty

STYLE Refined Renaissance retreat
SETTING Cognac country

'Everything we see and touch has elegance and originality, from the china and silverware we use at breakfast to the reclaimed trough redeployed as a washbasin'

Emerging through the massive arched entrance into Le Logis de Puygâty's great expanse of walled courtyard, we're met by complete silence. For a moment, all we can hear is our own footsteps. But we're not alone – Max, who owns Puygâty along with his partner, Pierre, is standing by with one of their dogs to greet us. An American/Belgian pair with a passion for furniture collecting and interior design, they restored the property to be their own holiday home – and then, I suppose, the guest list just got out of control. We're here to relax and reflect, just me and Mrs Smith, and to enjoy some precious time alone together; we've left our four children in the care of their grandparents and we've got two days of rural peace and quiet ahead of us.

If the exterior of this 15th-century fortified manor looks authentically austere – strong stone walls, beautiful proportions, a fine-looking turret – the interior design is pretty modern in style. Max and Pierre have used simple, rough-hewn materials and lots of wood, steel and animal skins, to keep an artisanal feel. The biggest, most attractive fireplace in the house (and there are quite a few) is in the living room. Adorned with a sort of chainmail curtain, it's what you're drawn to first, even when it's hot outside. Next to it is a pair of big armchairs and a low table with fresh flowers, candles and design books. Though much of the furniture has a 20th-century look, the colours used feel warm and antique, and the monumental beams and stone give the place a unique solidity.

I was born and bred in the southwest of France; my home town of Dax – also the first side I played rugby for, for eight years, before I moved on to Perpignan – is some 250km to the south of here. So the terrain around Le Logis de Puygâty feels familiar enough to represent a kind of homecoming, especially since I now live in the UK. All I can say is that I've finally found the most peaceful place in the south-west of France. It's funny, though: when we go into town, people start to recognise me – perhaps it would have been better to lie low at Le Logis. Max has recommended a good spot for dinner in Angoulême. Usually, the kind of places you find by the train station are, ahem, not that great, but Le Terminus is terrific, with very good fish – unexpected here in landlocked Charente. Afterwards, we continue our date at the cinema, where

we watch *Avatar*, supposedly as a test to see if it's suitable for the kids, but we love it.

When we want a drink back at Le Logis, there's an honesty bar: a few bottles of wine and brandy by the television. The house cocktail, made with cognac and lemon, will be whisked up in front of you if your hosts are around, and very good it is, too. Everything we see and touch has elegance and originality, from the china and silverware we use at breakfast (brought to us in our room) to the reclaimed trough redeployed as a washbasin. Our bathroom is very simple, absolutely nothing like the standard hotel facility; the massive shower, with natural stone walls like a cave, honours the countryside context perfectly.

On Sunday we spend the whole afternoon hanging out in our room, which is ideally kitted out for 'staying in', with a fireplace, sofa and soft armchairs. The white-clad bed is up on a mezzanine, decorated with more natural wood, stone walls, hessian and animal-skin rugs, which are an acquired taste, but definitely add to the warm atmosphere. Our windows are deep-set and small, which means it's blissfully shady and cool when the summer heat gets heavy, even if you can't fling them open to admire the view. Because

I work for the BBC and French TV as a rugby pundit, I'm used to my phone going off 10 times an hour. But here, inside these 500-year-old walls, the pinging is definitely less relentless, although that might just be my network, since Max and Pierre have made sure their ancient home is well and truly wired up for modern telecommunications.

There are animals living here, too: Max and Pierre's dogs, Nelson the black cat, the sheep, ducks, geese and a couple of donkeys who kindly provide our alarm call. It's OK, though – it's late morning by the time they rouse us. Actually, if you want to sleep soundly, definitely come and stay at Le Logis de Puygâty. The only traffic noise around here is made by the sheep, who we notice having their breakfast at the same time as us, three or four metres away. And the custom-made cotton sheets are so comfortable we ask Pierre to order us a set.

On our second and last night, we take a nice fireside table for Pierre's table d'hôte – refined country cooking that's nothing less than awesome, especially the magret de canard, which, we understand, has achieved a measure of fame in *Côté Ouest* magazine (a sort of regional *World of Interiors*). Nelson is at our side throughout, which technically could mean we didn't get to spend as much time alone together as we'd planned. Feline gooseberry aside, we have luxuriated in 48 hours of the sleepiest, least hectic, most calming time possible. Le Logis has given me a lot of inspiration, space to reflect on my goals, and consider the potential of the next few months. It's amazing what elegant interior design, historic architecture, great cooking, a beautiful location, friendly hosts and a bunch of cute farm animals can do...

Reviewed by Raphael Ibanez

NEED TO KNOW

Rooms Four rooms, including a suite and a one-bedroom cottage.

Rates €120–€250, including tax but not Continental breakfast, €12.50.

Check-out 11am, but flexible subject to availability. Late check-out is free for Mr & Mrs Smith guests. Earliest check-in, 3pm.

Facilities Gardens, outdoor pool, library, including DVDs and CDs. Daimler limo taxi service for guests (transfers and short journeys only). In rooms: free WiFi, flatscreen TV, CD/DVD, kettle, fridge and minibar.

Children The pool is unsupervised, and some of the farm tools scattered around the property are not child-friendly, but youngsters aged 12 and up are welcome.

Also Owners Pierre and Max have three dogs among their menagerie. They therefore prefer guests canine-free, but occasionally make exceptions, charging a dog fee of €15 a day. No smoking inside – ashtrays are left on the terraces.

IN THE KNOW

Our favourite rooms Pierre d'Arceluz has a lofty ceiling, wooden beams, an exposed stone wall and a swathe of white fabric above the bed, suspended from hooks. For extra seclusion, book Maison d'Amis, a one-bedroom cottage with space to add extra beds for children. François de Lâge, named after the Logis' first owner, is an uncluttered space decorated in neutral shades, with local-limestone flooring and sturdy oak beams. The Marie de la Laurencie suite has an impressive rusty fireplace, in contrast to the pretty, muted decor; floating iron stairs lead to the mezzanine bedroom, and the bathroom is hidden under the staircase.

Hotel bar Drink like a thirsty farmer, with an ice-cold beer in the barn/bar/boutique, Sorti de Grange. There's also a cocktail menu to explore: the Cocktail Puygâty is a blend of cognac, sirop and freshly squeezed lime juice.

Hotel restaurant The Logis offers a versatile table d'hôte, owner Pierre rustling up French and international dishes. Give 24 hours' notice and you can have a three- or four-course feast.

Top table For privacy, take a table in the bar. If you feel sociable (and provided you're staying more than one night), you might dine with your hosts, around their whitewashed wooden table overlooked by dramatic paintings.

Room service None.

Dress code After all Pierre's efforts, it'd be churlish not to scrub up. Match the hotel's design quirks with a smart shirt or a tea dress.

Local knowledge Action Smiths are well catered for at Le Logis. Ask the owners about hiking/walking routes from the property; they'll also lend out mountain bikes, and can arrange horse riding for experienced equestrians.

LOCAL EATING AND DRINKING

Succulent seafood is the speciality of Le Terminus at 3 place de la Gare in Angoulême (+33 (0)5 45 95 27 13). Don't be put off by the frill-free exterior and opposite-the-station locale: food and service are fantastic. For modern French cuisine cooked to gourmet standards, dine at Restaurant du Château at 15 place du Château in Jarnac (+33 (0)5 45 81 07 17). Charismatic chef Thierry Verat owns gastronomic La Ribaudière in Bourg-Charente (+33 (0)5 45 81 30 54), known as one of the region's best restaurants, and serving superb food at reasonable prices.

GET A ROOM!

For more information, or to book this hotel, go to www.mrandmrssmith.com. Register your Smith membership card (see pages 4–5) to enjoy exclusive offers and privileges.

 SMITH MEMBER OFFER A bottle of sparkling Charlemagne wine.

Le Logis de Puygâty 16250 Chadurie, Charente (+33 (0)5 45 21 75 11; www.logisdepuygaty.com)

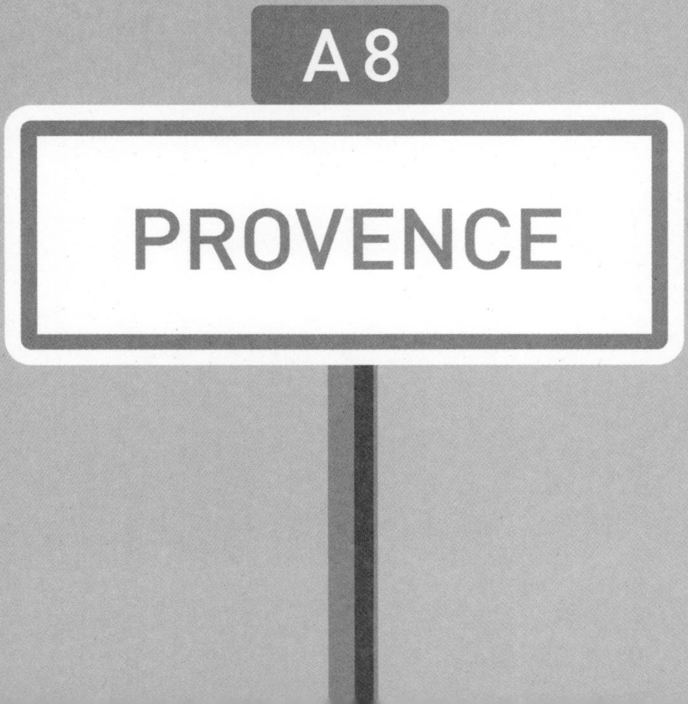
A8
PROVENCE

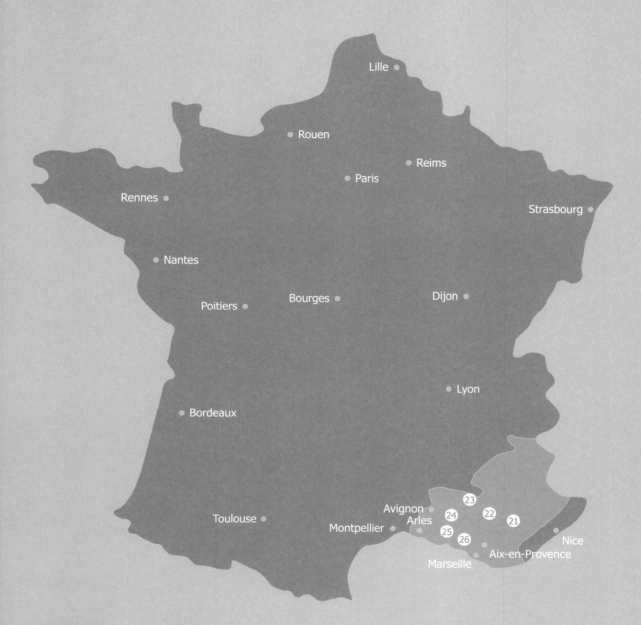

Lille

Rouen

Reims

Paris

Rennes

Strasbourg

Nantes

Bourges

Dijon

Poitiers

Lyon

Bordeaux

Toulouse

Avignon

23

Arles

24

22

21

Montpellier

25

26

Nice

Marseille

Aix-en-Provence

PROVENCE

21 La Bastide de Moustiers
22 Le Couvent des Minimes Hôtel & Spa
23 Hôtel Crillon le Brave
24 La Maison sur la Sorgue
25 Le Mas de la Rose
26 La Villa Gallici

PROVENCE

COUNTRYSIDE Scenes from Cézanne
COUNTRY LIFE Pétanque and pastis

A land of light and colour, cultural but earthy, where the artist and the wine-maker are king, Provence is a true beakerful of the warm south. To the west is the great river Rhône, flowing south to the Camargue and the Med. Inland, the Vaucluse is fruitful with vineyards, olive groves and lavender fields; to the east rise the highlands of alpine Provence. Proud cities, from mediaeval Avignon to elegant 18th-century Aix, offer charming squares, sun-dappled boulevards, galleries and café culture. You could make elaborate plans to explore the Roman ruins, contemporary Marseille, the summer music festivals, truffle markets, wine tastings – or you could simply tug down the brim of your straw hat and lie back until it's time for sunset pastis.

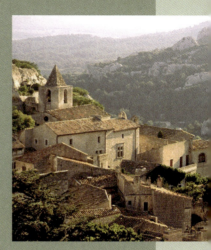

GETTING THERE

Planes Access the region from Nîmes, to the west in neighbouring Languedoc-Roussillon, or Marseille. From the UK, Ryanair flies to Nîmes from Liverpool and Luton (www.ryanair.com); or travel to Marseille from Gatwick with EasyJet (www.easyjet.com) or British Airways (www.ba.com).

Trains From the UK, put your car on the Autotrain at Paris, catch a separate train and be reunited in Avignon (0844 848 4050). Or take the Eurostar – probably the most civilised option – and change at Paris for Avignon or Aix (www.eurostar.com). Trains from Paris Gare de Lyon to Avignon take around three hours (www.tgv.com).

Automobiles Avis, Hertz and Europcar do car hire from Avignon TGV station, as well as Nîmes and Grenoble airports (www.avis.com; www.hertz.com; www.europcar.com). The A7 is the main artery from the north.

LOCAL KNOWLEDGE

Taxis There are taxi ranks in the main towns, railway stations and airports. Prices are cheaper than on the Côte d'Azur, but there may be a charge for luggage. Your hotel should be able to arrange transfers by cab.

Siesta and fiesta Businesses are normally open 9am–12pm, and 2pm–6pm. Banks shut at 4.30pm. Lunch is observed strictly between 12pm and 2pm; restaurant kitchens serve dinner between 7pm and 9.30pm. Outside high season, restaurants often close on Mondays and Tuesdays.

Do go/don't go Spring and autumn are perfect, with warm weather and sparser crowds. May sees flowers abloom and warm sunshine, and September brings the grape harvest. Winter's often bleak, and the chilly Mistral wind can be relentless, whatever the season.

Packing tips Take cobble-friendly sandals, rather than stilettos, and his 'n' hers straw hats. Pack binoculars for bird-spotting in the Camargue.

Children Let your brood clamber over the Roman ruins in Arles. The great amphitheatre, builit around 80AD, has a watchtower still intact (+33 (0)8 91 70 03 70).

Recommended reads The Yellow House: Van Gogh, Gauguin, and Nine Turbulent Weeks in Arles by Martin Gayford. Caesar's Vast Ghost: Aspects of Provence by Lawrence Durrell. The Man Who Planted Trees by Jean Giono. Market Day in Provence by Michèle de La Pradelle.

Local specialities Provence's cuisine is bursting with sun-ripened olives, garlic, melon, peach, tomatoes… Order bouillabaisse in Marseille, game in the hills, spelt risotto in the Vaucluse, and terrific lamb dishes and sheep's milk cheese everywhere. Expect lashings of olive oil, aromatic herb flavours and, of course, regional wines.

Côtes de Provence rosés are dry and refreshing; world-class reds are made in Rhône valley villages such as Gigondas and Vacqueyras. Make like a pétanque-playing village elder and order a Ricard (a famed brand of pastis), starting with one part pastis to three parts water. And... The Camargue is almost as famous for its mosquitoes as for its horses. If you're venturing to its boggy expanses, go armed with box-fresh repellent.

WORTH GETTING OUT OF BED FOR

Viewpoint There's a wonderful view towards the Camargue from the battlements of the fortress in Les Baux-de-Provence. In summer, go early in the morning to avoid crowds. High above the village of Beaumes de Venise (ask a local for directions), Domaine de Durban offers not only a superb vista but also some of the finest pudding wines in the world (+33 (0)4 90 62 94 26; www.domainedurban.com). Or you can take the twisty route up Mont Ventoux.

Arts and culture Arles and Orange each has an impressive amphitheatre, used for cultural events, such as open-air opera. Just outside Les Baux, you can wander among vast art images projected onto the walls of a huge quarry cave, the Cathédrale d'Images (www.cathedrale-images.com). The Granet Museum in Aix-en-Provence has a special room dedicated to Paul Cézanne, born in Aix in 1839. Avignon's Unesco-protected architectural finery includes the famous *pont* from the song (aka Saint-Bénezet bridge), and the Popes' Palace, a powerhouse in the Gothic style, left beautifully bare within (+33 (0)4 90 27 50 00; www.palais-des-papes.com).

Activities The best way to see the Camargue is on horseback (+33 (0)4 90 97 91 38). Kayak down the Gardon river to the towering Roman aqueduct of Le Pont du Gard, with Kayak Vert in Collias (+33 (0)4 66 22 80 76; www.canoe-france.com/gardon; March to October). Provence Vélos (+33 (0)4 90 60 28 07; www.guideweb.com/provence-velos) will deliver bikes and tandems from their base in Carpentras, for half or full days of back-road cycling. There's quad biking on the slopes of Mont Ventoux; contact Ventoux Quad in Crillon-le-Brave (+33 (0)6 19 06 05 92). Station du Mont Serein has skiing in the winter and go-karting in the summer (+33 (0)4 90 63 42 02; www.stationdumont serein.com). Wine-tasting routes criss-cross the region; see www.rhone-wines.com for details. Oenologist Julien Poujol arranges walking tours of Gigondas' vineyards to give visitors an understanding of *terroir* and *cave* culture (+33 (0)6 78 70 55 93; www.viti-oenotourisme.com).

Perfect picnic Head to the market (Carpentras on Friday is one of the biggest and best) and fill your bicycle panniers with bread, goat's cheese, onion tart, figs and rosé. Then find a shady spot off-road to enjoy your feast.

Daytripper Between Aix-en-Provence and Avignon, the perched villages of the Luberon cling to craggy ridges, among cedar glades. Gordes, Ménerbes, Roussillon and Bonnieux are a treat to admire from afar; pack a picnic and gaze up from the walking trails of the Luberon Regional Park (www.parcduluberon.fr).

Shopping Apart from giant blocks of *savon de Marseille*, the best buys are olive-wood kitchenwares and lavender products (we like the Popée family's tiny shop on the road from Sault up to the Ventoux). In Sault, nougaterie André Boyer (+33 (0)4 90 64 00 23; www.nougat-boyer.fr) sells sweet treats amid historic decor. Isle-sur-la-Sorgue hosts a famed antiques market every Sunday morning. Aix-en-Provence has enticing design boutiques on Rue Fabrot, and a food market every day on Place Richelme.

Something for nothing Vincent Van Gogh painted almost 200 canvases during the year or so he spent in Arles. Many of the places he worked are marked by a series of panels dotted around the city.

Don't go home without... a few bottles of well-chosen wine. A good tasting *cave* in Gigondas is family-run Domaine Saint-François-Xavier (+33 (0)6 20 52 64 54; www.gigondas-vin.fr).

PLEASINGLY PROVENCE

The Camargue is a coastal wilderness of marshes, dunes and flamingo-specked salt flats, where *gardians* (cowboys) watch over the famous herds of black bulls and white horses. Explore the area by 4x4, boat or on horseback (Arles' tourism website, www.tourisme.ville-arles.fr, has a list of operators). To spot feathered residents, head to the Ornithology Park (www.parcornithologique.com).

DIARY

April The Feria de Pâques takes place in Arles, opening the bullfighting season in France. Some half a million revellers turn up to watch the spectacle in the Roman amphitheatre. **May** Gypsies from all over Europe gather in Saintes-Maries-de-la-Mer to pay their respects to St Sarah, the Black Madonna. Les Baux holds its annual Fête des Vignerons, when you can join villagers in tasting local vintages (www.lesbauxdeprovence.com). **July** The Festival d'Aix-en-Provence attracts world-class opera singers (www.festival-aix.com). The Festival d'Avignon (www.festival-avignon.com) sees all manner of street art around the city, as well as formal concerts, and a fringe festival (www.avignonleoff.org). Mid-month, Carpentras stages Les Estivales de Carpentras, a two-week celebration of music, theatre and dance (www.estivales-de-carpentras.com). Opera and classical music fill the magnificent amphitheatre in Orange for France's oldest festival, the Chorégies d'Orange (www.choregies.com). **Mid-August** Sault, the heart of the region's lavender industry, hosts the fragrant Fête de la Lavande. **September** With paella, sangria and bull-running, the Rice Festival in Arles feels decidedly Spanish.

La Bastide de Moustiers

STYLE Alain's inn
SETTING Lavender, herbs and olive trees

'Most of the produce is plucked from the sprawling gardens, planted with 30 varieties of tomatoes, along with peppers, courgettes, verveine, mint, lavender, beans and carrots'

Early December isn't everyone's choice for a French sojourn, but we find it perfect. We arrive to crisp, cold days and clear skies. Dramatic snowy peaks are the delightfully clichéd backdrop as we head towards La Bastide de Moustiers, along what has to be the most enjoyable stretch of road I've encountered in a long time. It's lavender central, with row upon row of bushes patiently waiting for the spring sunshine – we can only imagine the aroma when they flower.

Still owned by legendary chef Alain Ducasse, La Bastide de Moustiers is his former home, located in the foothills of the Alps, near the Gorges du Verdon and the Luberon. During a spell on the Riviera, Ducasse set off on his motorbike to explore, and happened upon a grand stone building, the former home of a master potter. Moustiers' green, gold and blue beauty cast a spell on him, and he decided to buy it and turn it into a luxurious inn.

As we climb out of the car, we're greeted warmly by Jeremy, the assistant GM and, during our stay, very much the man who makes things happen. Although Ducasse doesn't preside over Moustiers himself, the hotel and restaurant are imbued with his spirit and passion. We immediately get that lovely 'staying at a friend's home' feeling. There's no concierge nor formally clad staff; the clobber of choice here is smart-casual, and they pull it off fantastically. A charming welcome, by people who really make you feel like a long-lost pal, is hard to top.

Coffee cravings calling, we make for the view-rich back terrace. It is hard to imagine we left a rain-drenched London just hours ago. Then, easy though it would be to sit for hours in the cool winter sun, we drag ourselves from our wicker chairs to explore the magnificent grounds, finding tunnelled pergolas, meandering paths and a swimming pool. There's no danger of time inside playing second fiddle, though. We've been given the Olive Suite, surrounded by mistletoe and arbutus trees in fruit. The rooms have discreet mod cons (including a handy iPod dock, and air-con for summer) yet they are, in essence, light-filled, airy and elegant.

Local artisans restored La Bastide and supplied furnishings for its interiors, resulting in a property that has a distinctly Provençal flavour, with hand-embroidered linens, painted ceramic sinks, handmade crockery

(Moustiers is an historic centre for earthenware faïence) and gleaming copper pots hanging in neat rows in the tiny original kitchen. Heavy wooden antique furniture and a wall of framed botanical prints by the main staircase add gravitas, and vases of freshly cut flowers inject the rooms with colour and scent.

By 7pm, activity in the salon beckons us to enjoy an aperitif and have a sneaky peek at the other guests – mainly overnighters from further afield in France, rather than locals from nearby. On our way to join them, we steal a gander at the small but lavishly stocked wine cellar, with wines from Bordeaux and Burgundy, as well as some star bottles of Côtes du Rhône.

As one would expect in a dining room belonging to the holder of the most Michelin stars in the world, eating at the Bastide is a highlight. It won Ducasse one of his stars, but don't expect a barrage of unnecessary extras. It's all simple, intelligent and seasonal. Even the crudités are mini flavour-bombs: zingy radishes, cool, crisp cucumbers, delicately steamed carrots and plump peas. Most of the produce is plucked from the sprawling gardens – planted with 30 varieties of tomatoes, along with peppers, courgettes, verveine, mint, lavender, beans and carrots – or the olive grove or herb gardens.

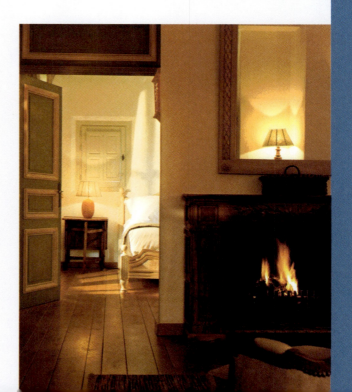

Like the hotel, the restaurant is a love poem to the surrounding area, with seats on the terrace so you can admire the Provençal hills as you eat, drink and make merry. The interior is divided into four separate rooms, each with its own allure. Le Salon des Amoureux is the choice for Mr & Mrs Smiths: a single private table – very romantic. Another has a splendid log-burning fire. We eat *en famille* in the library room, surrounded by Ducasse's personal collection of cookery books. Out comes fantastic wild boar and silken potato gnocchi, accompanied by superb wine; the list is admirable, as you'd expect, but we stick with local, small, artisanal producers.

It's hard to get out and about when you're made to feel so at home at La Bastide, but the local attractions are not to be scoffed at: the Gorges du Verdon are a must for sheer rugged scenery. We also find a wonderful food market in Riez, where just-in clementines are a real treat. Years ago I made a pilgrimage to the *marché aux puces* at Puimoisson, hoping to bring home beautiful antiques sold at knockdown prices by poor farmers clearing out the attic. The offerings couldn't have been more flea-ridden but, determined to return with something, I bought an old child's chair I thought the kids would love. I fought with the attendants to get it on the plane, and it now sits at home in *our* attic. Still, we return to peruse the 60 stalls of bric-à-brac, and we're rewarded with some fantastic old tin toys.

We're happy to have a memento of our trip. La Bastide de Moustiers has much to offer families and food-lovers, romantics, weekend recluses and countryphiles. Yet what touches us most about our time here is the staff. We're always made to feel comfortable and relaxed – nothing is ever too much trouble. They even make time to indulge me my shocking conversational French. That personal touch and natural hospitality will stay in our minds for a long time.

Reviewed by Anthony Demetre

NEED TO KNOW

Rooms 12, including one suite.

Rates €190–€400, not including tax or breakfast, €20.

Check-out 12 noon. Earliest check-in, 4pm. Both are flexible, depending on availability.

Facilities Private park, outdoor pool, gardens, book and DVD library, free WiFi. In rooms: flatscreen TV, DVD/CD, iPod dock, minibar, Bains Plus cotton nightshirts.

Children Children are very welcome. Cots cost €25; extra beds, €45. Babysitting with a local nanny can be arranged.

Also Banish any residual pre-holiday tension with a massage by the pool. Should you like to make a dramatic entrance, the hotel has a helipad.

IN THE KNOW

Our favourite rooms Antique birdcages hang from the ceiling of La Volière, which translates as 'the aviary'. This room has burnt-orange walls, a four-poster dressed with a lemon-yellow quilt, and French doors leading to a patio. La Chambre Pigeonnier is named for its location in the old pigeon house. It has a downstairs sitting area, a mezzanine bed with a hand-carved frame, and a bathroom with chequerboard tiles.

Hotel bar There is a small, well-stocked bar area, in a cosy room next to reception. Silver ice buckets stand on a bar made of antique carved wood; green glass lamps hang from above, and an open fire blazes in winter.

Hotel restaurant Alain Ducasse's gastronomic restaurant, headed by one of his protégés, Wilfred Hocquet, is a foodie's fantasy. Vegetables, herbs and edible flowers are plucked from the gardens to ornament delectable dishes such as roasted young pigeon with polenta, beetroot and turnip.

Top table Take a terrace table for views as beautiful as Hocquet's creations. For a really romantic dinner, book the intimate Salon des Amoureux (lovers' salon), which has just one table.

Room service None, but with such a serious restaurant a mere stroll from your boudoir, you won't want to graze.

Dress code Relaxed and comfortable but with an eye on glamour.

Local knowledge Explore the Gorges du Verdon canyons with a guided climb or hike, and go windsurfing or canoeing on the turquoise waters of Lake Sainte Croix (www.moustiers.fr). Wander among the lavender fields in the Verdon National Park (ask the hotel to pack you a picnic before you set off). La Bastide de Moustiers can arrange a hot-air-balloon ride with a professional pilot, who can also instruct you in paragliding and hang-gliding.

LOCAL EATING AND DRINKING

Unless you're staying for a while you won't want to eat anywhere else. However, if the day's adventures should lure you away, we recommend La Treille Muscate on Moustiers-Sainte-Marie's Place de l'Eglise (+33 (0)4 92 74 64 31), where the emphasis is on fresh, seasonal ingredients and regional cuisine: beef with artichokes, turnips, chorizo and red wine sauce is a hearty example. There's also Ducasse's second country inn, Hostellerie de l'Abbaye de la Celle, an hour and 15 minutes' drive from the hotel, at 10 place du Général de Gaulle in La Celle (+33 (0)4 98 05 14 14). The restaurant showcases Provençal produce in dishes such as courgette flower with crispy bacon, and fruity puds with local cherries.

GET A ROOM!

For more information, or to book this hotel, go to www.mrandmrssmith.com. Register your Smith membership card (see pages 4–5) to enjoy exclusive offers and privileges..

 SMITH MEMBER OFFER A basket of seasonal fruits and flowers in your room, and a complimentary after-dinner drink of Génépi, an Alpine liqueur.

La Bastide de Moustiers Chemin de Quinson, 04360 Moustiers-Sainte-Marie
(+33 (0)4 92 70 47 47; www.bastide-moustiers.com)

Mane-en-Provence

Le Couvent des Minimes Hôtel & Spa

STYLE L'Occitane-enhanced convent
SETTING Aromatic Luberon gardens

'Taupe linens, limed-oak flooring and framed pressed lavender in our spacious suite nudge us further into relaxation mode'

Centuries-old cream stonework, terracotta roof tiles – little about Couvent des Minimes' exterior betrays that this former home to the Order of the Minimes has been reincarnated as an elegant hotel. Barely past the pastel-painted cafés and houses in the village of Mane-en-Provence, a driveway brings our car up past the hotel, beyond rows of olive trees. We amble towards the bell-towered main house, past the striking moat-like pond. Mr Smith looks at me with befuddlement. 'How can such a charming old house contain two pools, a spa, a bistro and a fine-dining restaurant? Are you *sure* we're at the right place?'

'Bonjour,' smiles a friendly receptionist as we pass through the discreet front entrance. Polished stone floors and vaulted ceiling are the only echoes of this building's past: in its sleek entrance hall, a glass cabinet of L'Occitane products and chill-out tunes welcome us to a modern-day sanctuary. Signing-in formalities complete, the friendly front-of-house offers us a fresh raisin juice each. Mr Smith looks bewildered again.

I picture his brain cogs at work, conjuring a tiny juicing contraption with someone struggling to individually press halved raisins. Once we've swilled the sweet grapey nectar, it's time for a freshen-up in our room before supper. We shun the stairs – our next pick-me-up is a lift so brightly lit we need sunglasses. A timely reminder that our tired complexions are ripe for a L'Occitane facial, perhaps? (The sweet-smelling Provençal cosmetics brand is in cahoots with Le Couvent.)

Taupe linens, limed-oak flooring and framed pressed lavender sprigs in our spacious suite nudge us further into relaxation mode. Morsels of chocolate cake wink from beneath a small glass cloche. Perched on the end of the bed, we greedily demolish our unexpected treats. How different this is to my last brush with a nunnery: I can still see Sister Kevin (no, really) waving that big, well-thumbed book at me, aged 12. No, it wasn't the all-time bestseller you'd usually associate with a nun, but a tome by the rather less saintly Jeffrey Archer. I'd been caught reading *Kane and Abel* in an RE lesson, which didn't go down so well. To my habit-wearing teachers, it signalled that my time in their establishment had run its course. But hey, being expelled from a convent school is up there with swimming with dolphins, doing a marathon and visiting Provence, don't you think? It has to be done at least once in your life. Although please don't ask me to do a marathon.

Toying with the notion of making a quick a tea in our room, Mr Smith decides an aperitif in the bar would be more like it. On a balmier evening, we'd hit one of the foliage-fringed terraces or the lavender-sown inner courtyard. Tonight, a G&T by the fireplace in the library is our cosy rendezvous. Olives, roasted almonds and blue corn chips take the edge off an appetite built up during the hour's drive from Marseille airport.

People-watching in upmarket French hotel restaurants is first-class grist to overactive-imagination mills. Le Cloître doesn't disappoint, providing a cast of couples of all ages. A chap accompanied by a decades-younger blonde, joined after a while by another woman? It's a perfectly respectable family celebration, no doubt. My imaginings are probably the repercussions of that spell at a Catholic girls' school. If only my convent had served bistro-style red mullet and king prawns, like they do here. And tasty Côtes du Ventoux by the glass. I don't think it's even legal in France to serve custard as lumpy as they used to in Buckinghamshire.

The following day has been set aside for steaming, swimming and mostly staying supine; just the thought of such an Elysian afternoon elicits a heavenly night's slumber. I'm pretty sure that Sunday mornings don't get easier than choosing between a banquet of a breakfast or a splash in one of two pools. Croissants, cold cuts, muesli, yoghurt and eggs win over a mooted visit to the hotel's gym. After eating more food groups in one sitting than I'd usually have over a week, we're fuelled for a quick explore. Ideal for this lazy pair, Forcalquier is on our lap, a 10-minute drive away. The hilltop Haute-Provence town provides us with a 12th-century

cathedral, stylish *brocante*-filled shops, a bustling market and many cafés and bistros. Nice. Now our postcards can legitimately say we did more than lie around like beached whales in white towelling for most of our trip.

Mmm, laconium and caldarium. No, not prescription drugs, nor fungal infections but, rather, the bathhouse delights awaiting us back at Le Couvent des Minimes. Robed and slippered, we drift down to the pool and collapse on a double lounger. (If we made furniture at Mr & Mrs Smith, this would be one of our signature pieces.) Squeezing into our respective saunas, our next challenge is some competitive sweating. I emerge the victor, surviving 20 minutes in the 85º heat. My beet-red colour has my Scandinavian-heritage Mr Smith smiling as he luxuriates in the cool pool. Chuckle he may, but a quick pummelling on the thighs from the jets in the indoor pool, and my circulation is boosted to turbo.

More steaming and water-dipping is punctuated by top-ups of verbena tea. The relaxation room doubles as a *tisanerie*, blessed with the same soothing view of the gentle Luberon hills flanking the outdoor pool. After floating into a candlelit therapy room for a facial, I surrender, finally, to a succession of smearings of local-herb-infused creams. It's so relaxing I nod off, waking up with a loud toad-like snort – an embarrassing interruption to the new-agey swimming-with-dolphins soundtrack. What a contrast to our usual hedonistic boutique boltholing: this salubrious escape has been uplifting to mind, soul and body. *Merci bien*, Couvent des Minimes. Careful though – one more day in your clutches and I'll even be considering that marathon.

Reviewed by Mr & Mrs Smith

NEED TO KNOW

Rooms 46, including six suites.

Rates €170–€850, including tax but not breakfast, €29.

Check-out 12pm but flexible, subject to availability and half a day's room charge, until 6pm. Earliest check-in, 3pm.

Facilities Outdoor and indoor pools, spa with sauna and hammam, gym, aromatic gardens, wine cellar, pétanque pitch, tennis court, former church used for art exhibitions and social functions, pool table, DVD and CD library, free WiFi throughout. In rooms: flatscreen TV, DVD/hi-fi, minibar and L'Occitane toiletries, created exclusively for the hotel.

Children *Les petits* are welcome, with cots and extra beds provided free for under-12s. The restaurant does a special menu, and staff can provide babysitting for €15 an hour, booked in advance. Guests must be at least 16 to use the spa.

Also Dogs weighing 5kg or under are welcome. Smokers can light up on the outside terraces.

IN THE KNOW

Our favourite rooms If you like the sound of space, white walls and calming pastels, book one of the mid-range Restanques rooms. If you have friends or family in tow, opt for the hotel's biggest suite, La Maison de Mane, which can be arranged as a two-bedroom apartment. Newlyweds may want to follow the oak steps that spiral up to the honeymoon suite, La Cassine, tucked away behind a small wooden door in the oldest part of the building. Walls are whitewashed, with regal purple furnishings adding pools of colour; the bedroom has a vaulted ceiling and overlooks the gardens.

Hotel bar Le Pesquier lounge bar is decorated in shades of ocean grey, caramel and cream, with plump sofas and armchairs, and sleek bar stools. Open during high season, Le Caveau des Minimes is a bar and terrace overlooking the pool. The wine cellar, La Cornue, can be reserved in the evenings for special tastings, for four or more people.

Hotel restaurant Le Cloître is one of the area's most renowned restaurants, serving simple but refined dishes, such as sea-bass with crystallised lemon and dried fruit and nuts. The menu often features vegetables and herbs plundered from the hotel's gardens. In balmy weather, buffet lunch is served at Bancaou, the restaurant next to the swimming pool.

Top table In summer, the restaurant moves out into the courtyard. Sit indoors by the open fire in winter.

Room service A selection of salads, sandwiches, starters, mains and puddings is available 7am–11pm.

Dress code Floral prints, understated colours.

Local knowledge Take a wander round the hotel's 15-acre scented gardens, and have a treatment in the L'Occitane spa, open 10am–8pm (be sure to book). There's a market in Mane on Sundays – buy goat's cheese, lavender and honey, then relax on a café terrace with a hot chocolate. Visit the Château de Sauvan (+33 (0)4 92 75 05 64), an 18th-century manor nicknamed Le Petit Trianon Provençal, owing to its resemblance to Marie-Antoinette's home at Versailles.

LOCAL EATING AND DRINKING

The crispy pizzas come stacked with fresh ingredients at La Manne Céleste on Le Grand Chemin (+33 0(4) 92 75 05 70). Dine on the terrace at La Bastide de Moustiers, the award-winning Alain Ducasse-owned country-house hotel located at Chemin de Quinson in Moustiers-Sainte-Marie (+33 (0)4 92 70 47 47). La Bonne Etape at Chemin du Lac, Château-Arnoux-Saint-Auban, is another pretty Provençal hotel with a gastronomic restaurant and a second, equally appetising eatery. If you like what's on your plate, you can request a cookery class at the hotel (+33 (0)4 92 64 00 09).

GET A ROOM!

For more information, or to book this hotel, go to www.mrandmrssmith.com. Register your Smith membership card (see pages 4–5) to enjoy exclusive offers and privileges.

 SMITH MEMBER OFFER Free use of the L'Occitane spa throughout your stay (usually €25 a day each), plus home-made macaroons or other treats in your room on arrival.

Le Couvent des Minimes Hôtel & Spa Chemin des Jeux de Maï, 04300 Mane-en-Provence
(+33 (0)4 92 74 77 77; www.couventdesminimes-hotelspa.com)

Crillon le Brave

Hôtel Crillon le Brave

STYLE Trad turreted eyrie
SETTING Seven-house hamlet

'The gentle, traditional furnishings
perfectly suit a suite that essentially
acts as one giant window seat'

Usually, our problem on holiday is finding the hotel in the village. This time, it's different: Crillon le Brave *is* the village.

Salt flats, rivers and ravines traversed, we've at last reached our intended peachy-hued Provençal hilltop. But a bistro with postcard stands outside seems the only show of hospitality. We pull into the carpark by the *mairie* and admire the town hall's pristine white woodwork and a proud red, white and blue flag. It's perfection. 'He looks like he wouldn't tolerate anything less,' says Mr Smith, gesturing towards the mustachioed statue of Crillon the Brave himself. After a gulp of the countryside view rolling out from the hillside, we seek out the luxurious hideaway that bears his name.

Seven houses clustered around the 16th-century church make up this hip *hostellerie* – there are just a handful of private homes in the village. Neon arrows are conspicuously absent. All we get to nudge us discreetly towards reception are subtle grey signs on the pale stacked-stone exteriors. Pretty chalky-blue shutters flung open to the panorama indicate which boudoirs are among the hotel's 32 bedrooms. There's one thing baffling Mr Smith, as we enter the hotel. 'Why the abundance of fluoro Lycra?' he asks, tilting his head towards some folk clad in eye-wateringly tight get-up. 'Unusual sartorial choice for a boutique hotel,' he says, clearly feeling like a bit of a cliché in his beige linen. Then we spot our fellow guests' wheels. 'Now *that's* what we should do tomorrow!' he declares, puncturing my hopes of fitting in a Cowshed spa treatment with talk of gears, gradients and pedal power.

We're not staying in the main house but in a separate enclave – it's worth splashing out on a suite here. With keys in hand (and facial covertly booked), we are chaperoned by a kindly attendant through a maze of footpaths, which make hand-holding navigation necessary. (Not literally: it may be romantic here, but the staff don't go that far.) A skip down some stone steps, over a cobbled terrace, and we're at our suite. Unlocking a little iron gate at the end of an alleyway, it's like having our own pied-à-terre in this charming hamlet.

Without a shred of nostalgia for metropolitan style, we admire the gentle, traditional furnishings. They perfectly suit a room that essentially acts as one giant window seat. 'Just try and take your eyes off that view,' says Mr Smith, as I gaze out over the pale terracotta roof tiles and rocky ramparts. Fluffy oak and cherry trees, neatly coiffed vineyards and bedheady fields give way to gently sloping limestone-topped hills. What is especially beguiling about the Vaucluse is how untouched it feels. On this balmy late-summer afternoon, we're as far from the rat race as weekend-awayers can be. It's impossible not to daydream about living here.

Taking our fantasies to the main terrace, we're soon picking at pre-dinner olives and almonds, glugging crisp local rosé. The peaceful patio is set to become a glass-walled all-day bar in the near future, giving this stylish retreat a new hub where guests can breakfast or cocktail. Lights a-twinkle below, we ponder Crillon le Brave's year-round allure; as we admire the farmland in the distance, our charming waiter tells us of cherries, strawberries, apricots, peaches, nectarines, blackberries, grapes dominating the restaurant menu in summer. We're just in time for fresh figs, but we'd love to come back for truffle season in November and March.

Salmon tartare and a steak cooked perfectly *à point* are superb compensation for trufflelessness. Then,

suddenly, in the candlelit restaurant that we thought was packed with couples and groups of cyclists, we realise we're all alone. As the purr of voices drifts from one of the sitting rooms above, we resist the temptation to gatecrash a game of poker, and sneak back to our suite. Seven church bells gently prod me from my slumber, eight hours later, but a peek outside says the rest of the world has yet to start the day. I collapse back in bed to ponder a day of swimming, cycling and spa treatments. Following a lion's helping of croissants, naturally.

The headline act of my lazy morning is that herbal treatment, care of the Babington House-inspired Cowshed mini-spa. An expert therapist gently talks me through sweet-smelling unguents that rival the local lavender. An hour later, I muster just enough energy to roll from my towel-enveloped cocoon, down the few steps to the view-drenched pool. I listen to the sound of trickling water, and wonder what Mr Smith is up to. Rather than picture him whizzing through the hills on a bike, I suspect he's logged onto the WiFi in our room, downloading music. He told me he wanted to create the perfect Gallic soundtrack for our cycle ride; hopefully by now he's noticed the CD already provided in the room. Crillon has most things covered, leaving guests to do very, very little if they choose.

Bicycles aren't my usual request from the concierge, but eventually I get my derrière into gear for that promised excursion. (We skip the skin-tight shiny threads. I don't care how de rigueur Lycra is here – no one needs to see Mr Smith's details.) A wobble or two later and we're cruising... for all of half an hour. If only we could get our act together and seek out the antiques markets or gorges we've heard all about. But a glass of red on Crillon's terrace beckons. What better endorsement of a hotel than having its guests race back there – to do absolutely nothing?

Reviewed by Juliet Kinsman

NEED TO KNOW

Rooms 32, including seven suites.
Rates Rooms, €240–€270; suites, €590–€740. This includes tax, but not breakfast, €19.
Check-out 12 noon. Earliest check-in, 3pm.
Facilities Heated outdoor pool, gardens, mini Cowshed spa, book, CD and DVD libraries, free WiFi throughout.
In rooms: TV, DVD, Bose Wave with iPod connection, minibar.
Children Young Smiths are welcome. Cots are provided free; beds for older children cost €40 a night. Babysitting with a local nanny starts at €15 an hour. It's appreciated if you give plenty of notice.
Also You can borrow bikes, book a cheese-tasting session and arrange beauty treatments.

IN THE KNOW

Our favourite rooms Room 33 is a vast suite on two levels, containing a pair of roll-top baths, separated by a 'champagne table', so you can sip as you soak. Room 32 has an open-plan living area, bedroom and bathroom, and a huge shower room built into the wall of the old citadel.
Hotel bar Take aperitifs in the brand-new glass-fronted bar, and sip cool kirs accompanied by serene, green views over the acres of vineyard below.
Hotel restaurant Slow-roasted leg of lamb, roasted sea-bass, and tomato and goat's cheese tart are typical of the refined but not precious Provençal dishes served in the cellar dining room.
Top table At the front of the terrace in summer; by the fire in winter.
Room service Order anything off the restaurant menu until 9.30pm.
Dress code Linen, sun hat, nothing too outré.
Local knowledge Ask the sommelier to organise a wine-tasting tour to suit your palate: elegant (at a Châteauneuf-du-Pape winery, perhaps) or earthy (with a local *garagiste*). In October, you can attend a mini *vendange* at Château Pesquié in Mormoiron (www.chateauuupesquie.com), hosted by Frédéric Chaudière, who will show you (hands-on) what grapes to harvest and when, and explain the fermentation and blending process, with an all-important tasting analysis.

LOCAL EATING AND DRINKING

Le Vieux Four on Bas de Crillon is the village's other option for dinner, and a fine, informal one it is, too, with a terrace (+33 (0)4 90 12 81 39). Chalet Reynard, near the summit of the Mont Ventoux, is an Alpine-style pitstop, popular with view-seekers and Lycra-clad cyclopaths (+33 (0)4 90 61 84 55). Loved by locals, with welcoming service, Le Clos du Pâtre in Caromb specialises in robust rustic fare, featuring lots of goat's cheese, olives and herbs (+33 (0)4 90 62 38 49; www.leclosdupatre.com). On market day in Carpentras, the best staging posts are Le Rich on Place 25 Août (+33 (0)4 90 63 11 61), and the bars on Place Charles de Gaulle, near the cathedral. Bistrot de l'Industrie on Quai de la Charité in L'Isle-sur-la-Sorgue (+33 (0)4 90 38 00 40) is recommended on the riverside for a cold beer and a pizza on market day. Or, for a special occasion, book a table in the garden of Le Jardin du Quai on Avenue Julien Guigue (+33 (0)4 90 20 14 98).

GET A ROOM!

For more information, or to book this hotel, go to www.mrandmrssmith.com. Register your Smith membership card (see pages 4–5) to enjoy exclusive offers and privileges.

 SMITH MEMBER OFFER One champagne breakfast for two.

Hôtel Crillon le Brave Place de l'Eglise, 84410 Crillon le Brave (+33 (0)4 90 65 61 61; www.crillonlebrave.com)

L'Isle-sur-la-Sorgue

La Maison sur la Sorgue

STYLE Well-travelled townhouse
SETTING Waterside brocante market

'The white stone walls act like gallery space for a collection of finds from all over Asia – dark-wood furniture, decorative chests, Buddhas – all beautifully and unpretentiously put together'

My husband is a strong contender for 'Most Stereotypical Parisian of the Year'. He can't stand the countryside, he detests the South of France, and he'd rather spend a week trapped in a lift than amble around the villages of Provence. There's no tribal-regional-football reason behind this; he doesn't even like soccer. No, he just claims that, the minute you leave the capital, the heat is oppressive, the local markets are absurd, and the houses look rather on the old side. He's a bit of a one, my husband. So it is with a certain sadistic joy that I ask him to accompany me to La Maison sur la Sorgue, a ravishing *hôtel particulier* located in one of the most attractive market towns in the South of France, L'Isle-sur-la-Sorgue.

We're in the heart of things, which isn't at all a bad place to seek relaxation and romance. The town square and its baroque church are virtually on our doorstep so, when the mood takes us, we can nip out to sit on a sunny café terrace with a coffee and *Le Monde*. And, let's face it: for out-and-out urbanites, it's vital to be *somewhere;* in France, the middle of nowhere means just that.

We're no more than a 25-minute drive from Avignon TGV station, itself two and a half hours from Paris, but we're deep in prime husband-riling holiday territory, a part of France where grapes, olives and lavender are cash crops, and second-homers are a fact of life for locals. And here's this pretty little island, where the pace is slow and the air is warm, with plane trees doing an admirable job of providing shade when the heat gets a bit much.

This charismatic region, to the east of the river Rhône and the papal city of Avignon, is still sometimes known by its historic name of Comtat Venaissin, and L'Isle-sur-la-Sorgue has been called its Venice. The town was built on piles driven into marshland during the 12th century, and it is criss-crossed by canals. Venice it ain't, before your expectations mushroom, but it is lovely, its streets charmingly skew-whiff and its stone-built houses solid and attractive. The River Sorgue meanders lazily here and there, going underground and re-emerging, and turning massive, mossy waterwheels as it flows.

It's not easy pulling off a truly excellent maison d'hôte – guests should feel perfectly at home, but it must offer a degree of elegance that puts their own abode just slightly in the shade. The achievement of La Maison sur la Sorgue's proprietors, Frédéric and Marie-Claude, is remarkable. They took on the property in 2002 and opened house in 2006, after extensive works. There are just four suites, each vast and subtle in style. I'm not keen on over-complicated, artificial deco or low-lit loungey retro, so I'm in the right hotel. In terms of interiors, fashion, design, I crave simplicity, originality, integrity and craftsmanship – the values Frédéric and Marie-Claude seem to have written into their design credo.

Via the magnificent, heavy wooden door, you enter a splendid residence, whose white stone walls act like gallery space for a collection of finds from all over Asia: dark-wood furniture, decorative chests, Buddhas. It's beautifully and unpretentiously put together. Through the picture windows, we make out the courtyard, shaded by a great plane tree, with laurels, pots of aromatic herbs, a teak swimming pool and an artful smattering of wrought-iron garden furniture. Back in the luminous kitchen/dining room, on a big tiled worktop near the enviable black Lacanche stove, stands an immense platter of hazelnuts and walnuts and – twinkling at us by way of greeting – two glasses of Côtes du Rhône. My husband abandons his wariness of the warm south and lets the hospitable welcome melt away his Parisian tension.

Our room, Chambre à la Loggia, has theatrical red walls, sisal-type flooring, a superbly big bed and, instead of a TV, shelves of Murakami novels; we also find a music system in a little carved-wood wardrobe, not to mention CDs by Pink Floyd and their psychedelic ilk (did I mention that my husband is a card-carrying old hippie?). The suite opens onto a terrace decked out with sofas and an inviting day-bed; we're delighted by so many opportunities to take things lying down. In the morning, it's Frédéric who mans the stove, serving us a fine breakfast – fresh melon and strawberries, scrambled eggs, home-made pannacotta – on refined white porcelain. He was a Parisian in a former life, until he joined his wife, a Vaucluse native, to breathe contemporary chic into Isle's accommodation offering. They've even rethought the old épicerie that belongs to La Maison sur la Sorgue, piling it with an ever-changing stock of statues from Thailand, hand-blown glass lamps and other objets trouvés and trinkets. Retour de Voyage is not your usual hotel boutique.

As far as the rest of the local shops go, L'Isle just happens to be the third most important world hub for vintage furniture and brocante finds, with treasures from every era, including the old-hippie years of the Sixties and Seventies. There are 12 permanent markets and 40 boutiques, and up to 300 dealers crowding in at weekends. We aren't in materialistic mood, so we take a drive out to Velleron, a village known for its farmer's markets; and further on to Gordes, a perched settlement with protected status. To avoid the tapenade shops and save our ankles from mediaeval cobbles, we repair immediately to a locals' café with three outdoor tables. Here, we look up at the sky and down at the Luberon valley, and surrender to wine, foie gras and the inimitable pleasures of French country living. Back at La Maison sur la Sorgue, we sprawl on our terrace, warmed by the sun, the wine, the freedom. And – can it really be? – my husband's eyes seem a little mournful as he checks the Avignon–Paris return tickets are in order for the morning.

Reviewed by Valérie Abecassis

NEED TO KNOW

Rooms Four, including two suites.

Rates €190–€310, including breakfast and tax.

Check-out 12 noon. Earliest check-in, 3.30pm.

Facilities Boutique, outdoor pool, CD, DVD and book libraries, WiFi downstairs and in the garden (€12 for your whole stay). In rooms: flatscreen TV, CD, Compagnie de Provence toiletries.

Also In-room beauty treatments can be arranged. Smoking is allowed in some outdoor areas, including the terraces of the two suites.

IN THE KNOW

Our favourite rooms Room on a Loggia is spacious and loft-like, with deep-crimson walls and a huge private terrace overlooking the gardens and market square. Just down the steps, book the Suite of Shadows for spectacular light effects involving the shutters at sunset. And for the best bathroom, pick Room with a View; it has an antique roll-top bath, wood panelling and a pretty vista of an 18th-century chapel.

Hotel bar Drinks are served downstairs on request, where a carefully curated soundtrack flits from classical and jazz to George Michael (in a good way).

Hotel restaurant There's no restaurant, but the hotel can arrange for a local chef to prepare dinner for small groups. Breakfast is served in the ground-floor dining room or in the garden, between 8.30am and 10.30am.

Top table Poolside, beneath the sycamore tree in the garden.

Dress code Well-travelled, informal chic.

Local knowledge Isle, as locals abbreviate it, is a major antiques centre, famed for its top-drawer (and pricey) *brocante*; dealers flock to the market on Sundays, and shops are open round the week. Shipping can be arranged. The hotel can arrange classic-car tours around the area, taking in the lavender fields and nougat factory in Sault, and a stop to taste goat's cheese in Banon. There's a terrific market in Carpentras on Fridays – go early, do the rounds, then stop for a treat at Jouvaud pâtisserie, 40 rue l'Eveché, which is so amazing it has a branch in Tokyo. Due north are celebrated wine villages such as Vacqueyras, Gigondas and Beaumes de Venise.

LOCAL EATING AND DRINKING

Minutes from the hotel, Café Fleurs (+33 (0)4 90 20 66 94) on Rue Théodore Aubanel is a pretty, elegant lunch spot with plenty of shady outdoor seating. Café de France (+33 (0)4 90 38 01 45) on Place de la Liberté is our tip for evening drinks and watching the town go by. For marvellous menus set by Daniel Hébet, head to Le Jardin du Quai on Avenue Julien Guigue (+33 (0)4 90 20 14 98). It's charming inside but, in the summer months, try to book a table in the flower-filled garden. Finally, find holiday treatsville at Gelateria Isabella (+33 (0)4 90 20 85 42) on Esplanade Robert Vasse, which makes all comers happy with enormous portions of home-made ice-cream and sorbet.

GET A ROOM!

For more information, or to book this hotel, go to www.mrandmrssmith.com. Register your Smith membership card (see pages 4–5) to enjoy exclusive offers and privileges.

SMITH MEMBER OFFER Drinks every night of your stay, and 10 per cent off in the hotel boutique.

La Maison sur la Sorgue 6 rue Rose Goudard, 84800 L'Isle sur la Sorgue
(+33 (0)6 87 32 58 68; www.lamaisonsurlasorgue.com)

Le Mas de la Rose

STYLE Genteel farmhouse
SETTING Van Gogh view

'Waking up is a delight. A sweet morning light washes over the room's natural tones, and sunshine tells us it is breakfast time'

Orgon

In a parallel universe, my grandmother is French, and she has a house just like Le Mas de la Rose, in the countryside near Saint-Rémy-de-Provence. There's always a bed made up for me, a pot of herbal tea is ever-brewing and lunch is laid out at half past 12, in the garden, beneath the shade of a huge mulberry tree.

In the real world, the owner of Le Mas de la Rose is not my *grandmère* but Mme Luron-Huppert, who arrived from the north-east in 2004 to turn this traditional 17th-century smallholding into a luxury maison d'hôte. Driving from Avignon in our little rented car, after an hour or so, we find the right tiny woodland road and reach a charming gate that opens automatically. We are already being looked after.

The house looks very old and very solid, with its vast square stone walls and tiled roofs. The lit-up windows blaze welcomingly in the dark, and the night-sky stars seem magically bright to these fugitives from the big city. Paris is instantly forgotten when we see the shapes of

cypresses in the garden, vines on the terrace, and the glowing blue swimming pool.

Our quarters occupy the same building as Mme Luron-Huppert's kitchen and dining room, but with their own entrance. As it is late, I suggest to Mr Smith that we skip the full exploration until morning, and we head straight to the bedroom. We are led first into our own salon with a little open kitchen for tea-making, noting the antiques, woven-coir flooring and profound quiet. The bedroom walls are limewashed, the colours soft and neutral. It's Provençal for sure, but minus any rustic patterns or too-cheerful hues. The cushion-covered, linen-clad bed looks especially enticing. We press pause on reviewing until daybreak.

Waking up is a delight. A sweet morning light washes over the room's natural tones, and sunshine tells me it is breakfast time. Mr Smith, however, is impervious to nature's alarm call, wantonly asleep under the white sheets and duvet. I exchange bedded bliss for hot-bath heaven, exploiting the ensuite's huge-windowed view of countryside and woodland. I don't recall savouring such quiet. Finally Monsieur opens his eyes and declares he's famished. Outside, all is fresh; the Mistral that welcomed us yesterday is still blowing, erasing any wisps of cloud in the sky. I'm glad of the shawl that travelled with me from Paris: even in summer, that wind can be bracing.

Astonishing: the only word to describe this estate. Bordered by rocky hills, grounds bursting with fragrant lavender, pine and cypress trees, this is unmistakeably Mediterranean terrain. We dip our toes into the swimming pool, which has a sandy-looking edge. Wow, we have our own beach – well, beachette – right here in the garden. And there's a Jacuzzi set into one of its curves. Two cats come twining along a wall and chaperone us into the house. We find Mme Luron-Huppert in her kitchen. 'Vous avez bien dormi?' she asks. *Mais, bien sûr.*

Tables set for two, a big couch, lots of books and a wide fireplace greet us in the dining room. Breakfast is on the terrace, ample and fragrant: great coffee, croissants, baguette, fromage frais, fruits... There's even jam from the Moulin du Calanquet – strawberry with black olives, how Provençal is that? Armed with advice from our hostess about local beauty spots and activities, we decide on a morning outing, with plans to flop by the pool when it hots up. Although we have a car and Saint-Rémy-de-Provence is not so far away, we decide to walk. One thing, Madame warns: wild boar wander hereabouts. We're unsure about whether to feel worried, or hopeful that we see one.

We step bravely (OK, gingerly) over the electrified barriers, Mr Smith propelling me with a gentlemanly hand. A scrubby path takes us swiftly among the vineyards and olive trees of Domaine de Valdition, a well-known Alpilles wine producer. The land was given by François I to his daughter as a wedding gift in the 1500s, its stony clay soil cultivated for wine and olive oil since Roman times. We consider calling ahead to make an appointment for a wine tasting, but sense

Le Mas de la Rose pulling us back to its terrace for a lunch of tomato salad, fresh bread, onion tart, ham and cheese. Reading in the shade and basking in the sun, our afternoon tails off into balmy evening. The air is sweet, time is slow, and there's nothing to worry about. We pull ourselves together sufficiently to consider a visit to St-Rémy in the morning, but that's it for organising.

If lunch is homely, dinner is a more refined affair of Provençal cuisine: we are served iced gazpacho, and a 'duo' of local lamb with vegetable tian and olive-oil mash. For our second night, a table has been booked at Sous Les Micocouliers. Three miles away in the village of Eygalières, the restaurant's name translates, long-windedly, as 'Beneath The Mediterranean Hackberry Trees'. The food is refined and contemporary, but the chef is clearly proud of local tradition, since our risotto is made with spelt, and the roast pork sourced from Mont Ventoux slopes. Our bottle of red wine, Vallon des Anges, is from the Domaine de Valdition, our rambling rendezvous yesterday. I look at Mr Smith. His face looks different. It has more colour, and there's something about his jaw... Ah, it's a huge smile. A bit like mine. They go nicely with our tans and our flapping white linen shirts.

After two days at Le Mas de la Rose, I no longer even dream of having a Provençal grandmother. So long as Mme Luron-Huppert is in charge, brewing herbal teas, ensuring the chic furnishings are just-so, and providing a kind and discreet welcome, I know there's a patch of the South of France we can call our own.

Reviewed by Ligia Dias

NEED TO KNOW

Rooms Eight, including three suites.
Rates €180–€350, including tax but not breakfast, €22.
Check-out 12 noon, but flexible, subject to availability. Earliest check-in, 3.30pm.
Facilities Heated pool, gardens, tennis court, golf range, library with DVDs, free WiFi in certain spots. In rooms: flatscreen TV, bottled water, Côté Bastide products.
Children Little Smiths are welcome, with cots provided free, and extra beds at €30–€40 a night. The hotel can arrange babysitting with a local nanny at €10 an hour.
Also Smokers, it will come as little surprise that you are expected to wait till you're outside to light up.

IN THE KNOW

Our favourite rooms Room 6 is light and spacious, overlooking the front garden. Room 9 has a private patio, with a little bistro table positioned by a jasmine hedge. Families or pairs of couples should book the apartment, which is separate from the main building and has two bedrooms decorated in milk-white and dove-grey hues. Lovebirds may lust after Room 14, the honeymoon suite, which has an ornately carved headboard in the boudoir and a vintage roll-top tub in the bathroom.
Hotel bar There's no bar in this family-farmhouse hotel, but if you ask nicely you'll get whatever you're thirsting for.
Hotel restaurant Dinner is a traditional affair, with Provençal meals prepared on request. Expect regional, seasonal specialities, such as roasted lamb with tapenade and tagliatelle of local vegetables.
Top table Sit at a wrought-iron table in the courtyard, enjoying candlelight by night and countryside views by day.
Room service None as such, but you can request to have breakfast or lunch in your room.
Dress code Cool and casual: a linen shirt or dress teamed with tousled hair and a dash of citrussy scent.
Local knowledge Sharpen your gustatory skills with a wine and olive oil tasting at the beautiful Valdition estate, next door to the hotel (+33 (0)4 90 73 08 12; www.valdition.com).

LOCAL EATING AND DRINKING

Chez Bru, aka Le Bistrot d'Eygalières, is a place of pilgrimage for gourmets. The salt-marsh lamb is perfection, and the cheese course almost a meal in itself. Head to Route de Jean Moulin (+33 0(4) 90 90 60 34) and see for yourself.
Sous Les Micocouliers, at the end of Traverse Montfort (+33 (0)4 90 95 94 53; closed December–January), is owned and run by a smart young chef, whose innovative seasonal cuisine is served beneath the eponymous elms. Enjoy moreish Mediterranean fare at **Bistro L'Aubergine**, 18 avenue Jean Jaurès (+33 (0)4 90 95 98 89). Dine at another Provençal hotel, L'Oustau de Baumanière, in **Les Baux-de-Provence** (+33 (0)4 90 54 33 07), where delicacies include caviar, foie gras and a dazzling cellar of Premiers Grands Crus.

GET A ROOM!

For more information, or to book this hotel, go to www.mrandmrssmith.com. Register your Smith membership card (see pages 4–5) to enjoy exclusive offers and privileges.

 SMITH MEMBER OFFER Wine tasting at a neighbouring vineyard.

Le Mas de la Rose **Route d'Eygalières, 13660 Orgon (+33 (0)4 90 73 08 91; www.mas-rose.com)**

Aix-en-Provence

La Villa Gallici

STYLE Chintz with chutzpah
SETTING Cultured vieille ville

'Our bedroom, with its creamy Louis XV
furniture, sky-painted ceiling and rich
fabrics is definitely liaison-worthy'

Beeswax, honey and lavender scent the air, and a haughty, dark-haired beauty watches as we take in our surroundings. It's one of several portraits we spy of an aristocratic lady who must be Madame Gallici, the wife of Villa Gallici's original owner. Little is known about the wealthy bourgeois couple who built this fine-looking house in the hills above Aix-en-Provence, but they'd surely have approved of the classical opulence that greets their 21st-century guests. As a stylish bourgeois type myself, though my west London estate is a little more modest (and I haven't yet been captured in oils), I'm qualified, hopefully, to check this place out.

We enter by way of an alleyway attended by Italianate statues and dripping with roses, glimpsing Florentine gardens and detecting the melodious sound of a fountain. It's dark, but far from gloomy – rather, the 18th-century mansion is enveloped in velvety Mediterranean night.

The detailed elegance of Villa Gallici's decor, combined with its mini-grand scale, make it intimate and welcoming; the hotel 'reception' looks nothing like one, and the restaurant is more reminiscent of an elegant period sitting room, with fireplaces, upholstered armchairs and little sofas in alcoves. We find antique furniture and perfectly polished, centuries-old wooden floors, set off by scenic toile de Jouy wallpaper in sunny yellow and pink. The salon area opens onto a terrace adorned with classical statues of goddesses, who seem to look kindly upon the villa's guests; below, a swimming pool is surrounded by blooming pink bay trees in terracotta pots.

Details that make us smile include big jars of home-made calissons, the local sweetmeats made with almonds and fruit paste, and armfuls of roses decorating almost every surface. Only the kind and discreet staff, smartly uniformed, remind us we aren't, in fact, in a luxurious family home, but guests at a superb small hotel.

Before we enter the bedroom, ascending an airy staircase illuminated with tea lights, Mr Smith notices that the wall above the door is painted with a rural scene, all saucy shepherdesses frolicking in haystacks. And, indeed, the villa was originally built during the century that saw the French flowering of libertine love, when spirited conversation was offered as essential foreplay to more earthy pastimes. The bedroom itself, with its creamy Louis XV furniture, sky-painted ceiling and rich fabrics, is definitely liaison-worthy, with ample charms for entertaining jaded aesthetes.

We're enfolded in boudoir-appropriate toile de Jouy, with libidinous cherubs decorating the canopy bed, the sofa and the heavy drapes that separate the bedroom proper from the little sitting room. From here, great big windows and French doors open onto our private balcony. As I run a bath in the marble bathroom, I can easily imagine dropping my white-lace bodice on the floor, before I step into the bathtub filled with asses' milk – a beauty ritual popular historically popular among Provençal belles (they copied it off the Romans), who swore by it to soften their skin. Today, you can substitute savon de Marseilles, the traditional local soap made of olive oil, almond oil and lavender essence.

After a lazy night and an ample breakfast in bed, Mr Smith and I extract ourselves from Villa Gallici in order to explore charming, prosperous Aix, cultural capital of Provence. The post-impressionist Cézanne and prolific 20th-century composer Milhaud were both born here, and the opera festival is up there with Glyndebourne and Bayreuth. This is also a city of churches: mediaeval, Renaissance, big ones, small ones. Food comes a close second to culture, as demonstrated on Thursdays, when the market is held on Place de Verdun. Wonderful local products include tapenade (the savoury paste made with olives), anchoïade (ditto, made with anchovies), speciality vinegars, flavour-packed tomatoes and super-sized ceps.

Appetites duly whetted, when evening comes we're treated to refined Provençal dining in the restaurant, back at Villa Gallici, where the white linen tablecloths are decked with fresh flowers and gleaming wineglasses,

topped up by the charming waiters with rosé, then red and, finally, Beaumes de Venise dessert wine. We start with pumpkin velouté with morels and quail's egg, then I opt for magret of duck cooked in white truffle honey, while Mr Smith goes for John Dory with ricotta ravioli. It isn't too indulgent, provided you keep off the bread, and share one thyme crème brûlée between you. On our second night, we dine in Aix at Mitch, a stylish and extremely good restaurant off Cour Mirabeau, the city's main drag. Even though they're already fully booked when we ring, Mitch himself arranges us a table in the mediaeval cellar, cheered by candlelight and the piano where he sometimes plays for guests at the end of the evening.

We're not inclined to linger long away from Madame Gallici and the shepherdesses. Aix is attractive but we'd rather make the most of our private, comfortable hotel. It's near enough to the centre to let you walk down in 10 minutes, but its seclusion from the busy streets sustains a gentle, rustic atmosphere behind the heavy iron gates. The languid, timelessly romantic feel of the place both slows our thoughts and makes our hearts beat a little faster; the sense of privacy is incredibly restful, so whatever we do and see when we leave the hotel, we know we can relax completely when we return. We're none the wiser about Monsieur and Madame Gallici by the time we check out, but we do believe they were a pair of generous souls, for building their sensual, classical villa and sharing it with us present-day libertines.

Reviewed by Frédérique Andreani

NEED TO KNOW

Rooms 22, including five suites.
Rates Low season, €230–€470; high season, €390–€900, not including taxes or breakfast, €28.
Check-out 12 noon, but flexible. Earliest check-in, 3pm.
Facilities Outdoor heated pool, flatscreen TV, valet parking, free WiFi throughout.
Children Cots are provided free; extra beds are €50 each. Babysitting with a local nanny, €10.
Also Pets are welcome for €50 a day.

IN THE KNOW

Our favourite rooms Superior Room 8 has a grand four-poster bed and hand-painted chinoiserie wallpaper in eau-de-nil tones. Suite Room 1 has a terrace overlooking the pool. We love the romantic bathroom with slipper bath and separate shower in Deluxe Room 24. Suite Room 20 is a cream and taupe split-level sanctuary with the bedroom downstairs and a smart black and white bathroom.
Hotel bar The bar is lavish-looking, with trompe l'oeil walls, and florals and stripes on soft furnishings. Any cocktail you want can be magicked up as you unwind to lounge and jazz classics. It's open all day, closing when the restaurant does.
Hotel restaurant It's sumptuous and formal but cosy, with sofas and squashy chairs pulled up to linen-draped tables. The candlelit terrace has a more relaxed summer-dining look. The fine-dining menu features pan-fried foie gras with cherries, roasted John Dory and chicory-anise ice-cream.
Top table Out on the terrace for romantic seclusion.
Room service The simple menu offers cheeseboards, smoked salmon, soup and omelettes, available any time. You can also summon afternoon tea wherever you choose to take it – on the terrace, in your room or in the grounds.
Dress code Don labels, by all means, but opt for understated.
Local knowledge Let the spring waters of Aix-en-Provence soothe ailments and aches, with a hydrotherapy treatment at the Sextius Thermal Baths (www.thermes-sextius.com). The aquatic centre, built on the site of the Roman original, offers hydro-massage baths, jet massage and a range of cures, including thermal-mud treatments.

LOCAL EATING AND DRINKING

To dine among a fashion and film crowd, head to unpretentious **Antoine Côté Cour** at 19 cours Mirabeau (+33 (0)4 42 93 12 51). Try **Le Grillon** at 49 cours Mirabeau for people-watching and afternoon tea (+33 (0)4 42 27 58 81). On the same street, **Brasserie des Deux Garçons** has a listed interior and specialises in seafood (+33 (0)4 42 26 00 51) . Down the road, hit **La Bastide de Cours** (+33 (0)4 42 26 10 06) for a cocktail in one of its cool private rooms. **La Rotonde** on Place Jeanne d'Arc is flamboyantly decorated with chandeliers, velvet-covered chairs and silk lampshades, and stays open from breakfast to digestif (+33 (0)4 42 91 61 70).

GET A ROOM!

For more information, or to book this hotel, go to www.mrandmrssmith.com. Register your Smith membership card (see pages 4–5) to enjoy exclusive offers and privileges.

 SMITH MEMBER OFFER A bottle of Provençal rosé.

La Villa Gallici Avenue de la Violette, 13100 Aix-en-Provence (+33 (0)4 42 23 29 23; www.villagallici.com)

SAY
CHEESE

HOW TO... EAT CHEESE

The French don't just like cheese. They respect it and revere it. They make grand tributes to it, such as 'Dinner without cheese is like a pretty girl with only one eye' (18th-century epicure Brillat-Savarin) or 'How can you govern a country that has 246 varieties of cheese?' (Charles de Gaulle). And they are mighty proud of their regional varieties, from Normandy's rich and buttery Camembert to the spicy goat's cheeses of Provence, and all creamy, crumbly points between.

For the visitor, cheese culture combines gastronomic pleasure with rural tradition and a true sense of *terroir* (that magical word meaning 'of its place'), and it couldn't be more accessible, whether you stop at the *fromagerie*, the market or the farm gate. The French shop for bread first thing in the morning, and again on the way home in the evening, when they tend to add a quick detour for cheese – just enough for that evening's meal – to enjoy with a glass of wine. Buying little and often means there is no waste and no need to store, and you can buy exactly what you have an appetite for that day.

Small independent shops, thriving in every village, town and city, are part of the culture, and who can resist those painstaking displays of produce: those perfect little turrets of goat's cheese, or Gruyère-style wedges like mountain peaks? Don't be afraid of aromas – the French shopper prefers the gamey perfume of a perfectly ripe cheese to the blank sterility of the vacuum pack. Madame will want to ask a question, prod a soft cheese, smell a Camembert to see if it is worth buying. Whether you are a novice or a bit of an expert, you will get good advice from your cheesemonger, who will guide you through seasonal varieties, as well as flagging up unusual or different styles you may not have tried before.

Choosing your selection at dinner is very much part of the pleasure. The French like to eat cheese before pudding, partly because there might be a lovely wine to finish after the main course, but also because a selection of different textures and styles works so much better before you indulge in something sweet. How you put your plate together needs a little thought. The basic rule, as far as I am concerned, is to have a fresh or medium-matured goat's cheese to start – its natural acidity cleanses the palate beautifully, in readiness for the more robust flavours to follow. A white bloomy-rind soft cheese should come next, followed by a harder, crumblier cheese. Then you go onto the more pungent aromas of the washed rinds and firm ewe's milk cheeses, especially those from the Pyrénées, with their lovely earthy, nutty flavours, before ending with a blue cheese.

Simply served with thin slices of walnut bread or sourdough, and a glass of wine – this is how the French enjoy their cheese course. They might add a tart, crisp apple or a delicious Beurre Hardy pear as an accompaniment. Personally, I love raw, unskinned almonds alongside a Beaufort d'Alpage, the wonderful prince of Gruyères from Savoie, and the cheese that started me off on my odyssey...

By Patricia Michelson

A 48

RHONE-ALPES

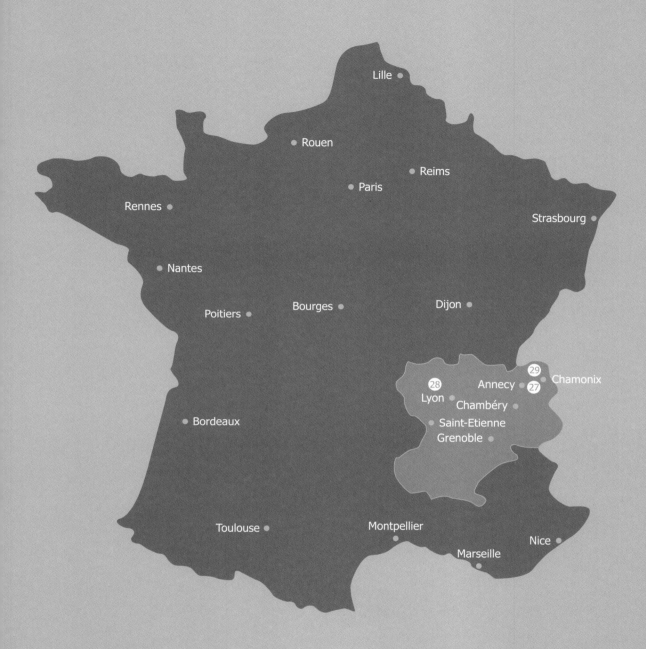

Lille

Rouen

Reims

Paris

Rennes

Strasbourg

Nantes

Bourges

Dijon

Poitiers

28 Lyon Annecy **29** Chamonix **27**

Chambéry

Bordeaux Saint-Etienne

Grenoble

Toulouse Montpellier Nice

Marseille

RHONE-ALPES

RHONE-ALPES

COUNTRYSIDE River deep, mountain high
COUNTRY LIFE Wine, wandering, winter sports

Named for the river running through it and the mountains at its edge, Rhône-Alpes is a region of vinous valleys, mighty peaks, lakeside spa towns and scenic drives – the home of Evian water and hot-air ballooning, distinguished vineyards and world-famous cuisine. Honey-coloured châteaux watch over farmland and forest, and the snow-speckled tips of the Alps line the region's pockets, drawing the flashest skiers to white velvet slopes at Courchevel, Chamonix and Val d'Isère. There's Europe's highest summit, Mont Blanc, and its deepest gorge (in Ardèche). And the culinary traditions of France's second city, Lyon, are among the most revered in the world, Beaujolais and the Côtes du Rhône providing the accompanying nectar.

GETTING THERE

Planes In the east, Geneva airport is the best gateway to the Alps, 80km from Chamonix via the toll motorways. EasyJet, British Airways and BMI Baby all fly from the UK (www.easyjet.com; www.ba.com; www.bmibaby.com). In the west of the region, Lyon-Saint-Exupéry airport receives visits from BA and Air France (www.airfrance.com) from Heathrow, and other carriers from throughout France and Europe.

Trains The TGV speedily links Lyon with the rest of France. London to Lyon takes four to six hours on Eurostar (www.eurostar.com), via Lille or Paris. The Rhône-Alpes region is spiderwebbed with railway lines and bisected by the high-speed LGV Rhône-Alpes, which crosses four *départements*, so getting around by train is easy, mountain climate permitting (www.sncf.com).

Automobiles Pick up a hire car at Geneva or Lyon. Make time to enjoy the winding valley roads, dotted with timber chalets, and vineyard-lined routes overlooked by châteaux and historic towns. Lyon is at the heart of central France's motorway network, linked to Paris by the A6.

LOCAL KNOWLEDGE

Taxis In bigger towns and cities, cabs can be flagged down on the street or picked up at a rank. In remote areas, book in advance, or prepare for a long walk.

Siesta and fiesta Most restaurants observe mid-afternoon downtime between 2pm and 4pm. A lot of small shops, even in city centres, also close for lunch, and most shut on Sundays.

Do go/don't go The ski season lasts from early December to April, and the high-altitude slopes mean you're in for good snow. Hikers and mountain bikers will love meandering over the grassy hills in high summer. Cherry blossom blooms in May, and there's more spectacular colour in autumn, when the leaves are turning. At lower altitudes, winter can be rainy.

Packing tips A Prada ski suit for the slopes; an appetite for rich repasts if you're spending time in Lyon.

Children Get your little Smiths up to speed on the slopes with lessons from the Ecole du Ski in Les Carroz (www.esf-lescarroz.com).

Recommended reads *Frankenstein* by Mary Shelley; *French Women Don't Get Fat* by Mireille Guiliano.

Local specialities Brimming with fine restaurants, Lyon is one of the centres of French gastronomy, and Beaujolais is a Milky Way of Michelin stars. Regional specialities include tender Charolais beef, creamy Saint-Marcellin cheese, and saucisson sec, as well as quenelles (fish or meat dumplings) and boudin noir (black pudding). The countryside is dominated by vineyards, the source of wonderful wines such as Chablis and some Côtes du Rhône appellations. Towards the mountains, Savoyard cuisine offers more than just raclette, tartiflette and fondue; delicious pike, perch and trout swim in Lake Geneva and the surrounding Alpine rivers. There's a noticeable influence from Italy – it is just the other side of Mont Blanc, after all.

And... One of the earliest film recordings ever was made by the Lyon-schooled Lumière brothers in 1895. Auguste and Louis only shot workers leaving a factory, but it earned them a place in cinema history.

WORTH GETTING OUT OF BED FOR

Viewpoint You get classic pastoral panoramas and vineyard vistas all over Beaujolais and the Côtes du Rhone. At the Alpine end of the region, in Haute-Savoie, there are misty mountain eyefuls in every direction. In Lyon, you can sometimes climb the north tower of the Basilica Notre-Dame de Fourvière, which gives you spectacular views over the city; when you can't, the esplanade beside the church is a good second choice. In Chamonix, the slopes offer dazzling views of the mighty Bossons glacier, dusted by year-round snows.

Arts and culture Lyon is famed for fashion, and its silk industry in particular. Visit the Maison des Canuts (www.maisondescanuts.com) to see the looms that powered the 18th-century weaving boom. There is a top-class opera house on Place de la Comédie, with a glass-roofed extension designed by Jean Nouvel that is spectacularly lit at night (+33 (0)4 72 00 45 45). The Musée des Beaux-Arts in Palais Saint-Pierre is one of the finest in France, containing ancient Greek art, as well as works by Monet, Picasso and Gauguin (+33 (0)4 72 10 17 40).

Activities In the west of the region, cycle through peaceful villages between Cluny monastery and Juliénas; it's hilly, but the views are wonderful. In the Alps, brace yourself for sky-soaring activities along the lines of heli-skiing, paragliding and zip wiring. Evolution 2 (www.evolution2.com) can organise these in the Mont Blanc-Chamonix area. Get yourself a guide and hike the biggest glacier in France: the Mer de Glace is 7km long and 200m deep, accessed by cog railway from Chamonix.

Daytripper Visit the waterside town of Annecy, on the northern tip of Lake Annecy. It's home to the Palais de l'Isle – a 12th-century prison on an island in a canal – the Château d'Annecy and the Cathedral of Saint-Pierre. Wander beneath the arches of Rue Sainte-Claire, dating

back to the 17th century, and Rue Royale, with its shops and gardens. On the mountain-flanked lake itself, pedalos, boats and canoes can all be hired, and a cycle path lets you loop the lake on two wheels.

Shopping Chamonix has a Saturday market where you can pick up some of the region's renowned cheeses: Beaufort, Reblochon and Morbier. Villefranche-sur-Saône has a covered market every morning except Tuesday and Thursday. In Lyon, Saint-Marcellin cheese and boudin noir are on sale at stalls on Croix-Rousse hill and Quai Saint-Antoine. Lyon has Paris-rivalling designer boutiques (head to Rue Emile Zola, Rue Président Edouard Herriot and Place Kléber) and is famous for silk scarves.

Perfect picnic Take your hamper up to Evian-les-Bains, on the shores of Lake Geneva, then board the solar boat over to the Pré Curieux water gardens. While you're in the mountain town, make the most of the thermal waters with a trip to the spa at the Royal Resort (www.evianroyalresort.com).

Something for nothing Drive through the Aravis Massif from Annecy through the valley of Thônes and St Jean de Sixt, past La Clusaz, an old village that's been hosting winter sports for over 100 years, and up to Col de la Colombière, an Alpine idyll.

Don't go home without... following the traboules of Vieux Lyon – some 40 ancient, labyrinthine passageways used by the city's silk-makers during the 18th century to carry their delicate fabrics under cover from Silk Hill down to the river barges.

RESOUNDINGLY RHONE-ALPES

After winter, wine is Rhône-Alpes' favourite thing. Follow the wine route through Beaujolais, calling in at the villages of Brouilly, Saint-Amour, Fleurie, Morgon and Moulin-à-Vent. The Rhône valley also produces great Côtes du Rhônes reds. And the Alps don't miss out on the action – Savoie produces its own white, in vineyards clinging to the hillsides.

DIARY

June Spanning 42km and climbing 2,511m, the Mont Blanc Marathon in Chamonix is not for the faint-hearted (www.montblancmarathon.net). June–July The Jazz à Vienne festival brings scat-happy scenesters to the town (www.jazzavienne.com). Lyon's Roman theatres host Les Nuits de Fourvière, a festival dedicated to the performing arts (www.nuitsdefourviere.fr). August The Guides Festival in Chamonix is one of the oldest events in the region, a series of parades, markets and music in honour of the mountain guides (www.fetedesguides.com). September–October Le Festival d'Ambronay, at the abbey of the same name, concentrates on baroque music (www.ambronay.org). October Lyon's film festival, Lumière, sucks in the cineastes (www.onlylyon.org). November The year's Beaujolais Nouveau is unveiled in the town of Beaujeu, at midnight on the third Wednesday of the month. December The Festival of Light is held just before New Year in Lyon, when windows are lit with candles and there's a lantern procession through the city. Concerts and operas are put on, too (www.lyon-france.com).

Alpaga

STYLE Perfectly lodgical
SETTING Alpine playground

'We soak lazily in the warm spa pool, unwind to pruning point in the dark steam room, and float back to our room for a siesta before supper'

The French for horse-drawn carriage is *calèche*. You may think this nugget only marginally relevant to anyone planning a stay in the upscale Alpine resort of Megève, best known for its five-star skiing and glut of gastronomic restaurants. But had my vehicular vocab been better, I might not have accidentally booked one within five minutes of arrival at the resort's Alpaga hotel.

The mistake is mine. Guillaume the concierge is confirming our weekend arrangements in French, when he asks if Mr Smith and I want to 'promener en calèche' into town for dinner the following night. Feeling blasé about my powers of interpretation, I hear 'walk' but not the 'en calèche' bit. It is only when Guillaume picks up a pen to make a note of our plan to stroll into town that I realise we've signed up for something. Cue enquiry, explanation, embarrassment, then polite but firm refusal to take the horse and (tourist) trap.

Offers of twee equine tours aside, Alpaga makes an exciting first impression, its slick, contemporary Alpine style exuding the promise of luxurious touches and attentive service. By the time we've followed the porter through shades of cream and mink in the lobby, glimpsed the crisply linened tables in the restaurant, and ascended to our room, we are giggling with delight.

We find that our room itself – a Deluxe, located above the restaurant, with a balcony and mountain views – calls less for giggling, more for seduction. The decor is sumptuously touchy-feely, with textural detail galore. Faux-fur throw and pillows, a velvet armchair, unvarnished wooden floor and walls, and a slate bathroom all demand to be fondled (as does Mr Smith, judging by his come-hither sprawl on the bed). Even a painting in the bedroom – a modern picture of sheep – is daubed in rough-to-the-touch acrylics.

Bundled up in slippers, robes and swimwear, Mr Smith and I use Alpaga's underground network of tunnels to get from our chalet to the spa, located in the basement of the entrance building, without ever stepping outside.

Mr Smith overrules my pleas for a massage, pointing out that, at these prices, the masseur must be on two euros a minute. I'm not sure whether to sulk or consider a change of career. We soak lazily in the warm spa pool, unwind to pruning point in the dark steam room, and float back to our room for a siesta before supper.

Dinner at Alpaga's restaurant is another fantastic feat of texture. I start with a glorious glass of seafood – layers of shredded crab and pulped avocado, crowned by a moreish cheese crumble – while Mr Smith tucks into duck foie-gras pâté. We continue with perfectly pink filet mignon en croute and cod fillet with olive mash, both delicious, and all the better accompanied by a soundtrack of jazzy reworkings of pop tracks. We're particularly taken with an Austin Powers-style version of 'Rehab' complete with jazz flute.

A cloudless indigo sky greets us the next morning; with fresh powder coating the pistes, the sunny conditions confirm it's going to be a great day to ski. Which is just

as well, given that it's our only day to ski. Luckily, taking Alpaga's *navette* to town, and nipping to Ski Concept to hire our kit right beside the Chamois lift means we're on the mountain in no time, gently shooshing down tree-lined red and blue runs.

At twilight, restored by a steaming bath and a well-earned catnap, Mr Smith and I stroll arm-in-arm into town, delighted with ourselves for having body-swerved the jingle-bell cart ride. It's a 25-minute walk, so perhaps we should have taken a cab, but we know we have *cuisine savoyarde* ahead of us (Guillaume has booked us a table at L'Alpage au Fer à Cheval) and we want to make room for all the cheese. A crackling wood fire and traditional decor greet us. It's the perfect setting for a textbook Savoie feast.

Mr Smith and I are ushered to a cosy, candlelit table, where we tuck into a fondue so fine it makes me want to use words such as 'heavenly' and 'simply tremendous'. We have smiles on our faces and cheese on our chins.

Well-to-do French families soon fill the remaining tables, the waitress disappearing under a pile of patent quilted jackets, aka *doudounes*, and floor-length furs. Mr Smith and I are riveted by Megève's aristo set – fragrant billionaires here, fur-clad bottle blondes there – but if you cut through its flashy reputation (take a left by Hermès and go straight past Tod's), there's still a beautiful and charming resort beneath.

By the time we leave L' Alpage au Fer à Cheval, the first snowflakes are beginning to fall. Undeterred, Mr Smith and I elect to walk home. Several wrong turns and 40 minutes later, we're less than happy with our decision. The snow now falling thick and fast, we look like a couple of yetis – frost-covered, our cheeks red-raw with cold – as we pester the night porter of a (hopefully) neighbouring hotel for directions. 'Are you in a car or on foot?' he asks. 'Er, c'est pas evident?' I can't help but smirk by reply. Thankfully, his instructions are better than his powers of observation, and 10 minutes later we are back at Alpaga.

It's not the perfect ending, even if the frostbite on my nose is only temporary, but it is the perfect stay. We can imagine returning in June or July, say, when this low-altitude resort is covered in grass and wildflowers, its pine forests at their glossy summer best, the Alpine trails beckoning to be walked. Better still, we can really, truly consider returning in June or July: in the shadow of Mont Blanc, only 80 minutes from Geneva, Megève is much nearer the UK than we'd realised. And Alpaga is irresistible and close to town – especially if you take a horse-drawn carriage.

Reviewed by Mr & Mrs Smith

NEED TO KNOW

Rooms 22, as well as six three-storey chalets with space for up to 12 people, and four apartments, sleeping up to four.
Rates €280–€550, including Continental breakfast and taxes. Chalets are €1,400 a night; apartments, €535–€670.
Check-out 10am. Earliest check-in, 4pm. Both are flexible, subject to availability.
Facilities Spa, with pool, steam room and treatment rooms; free WiFi throughout. In rooms: flatscreen TV.
Children Smiths of all ages are welcome. Cots and extra beds are provided free. The restaurant caters to younger palates with a kids' menu.
Also Pets can stay for €25 a night. Minimum two-night stay during high season. Alpaga runs a transfer service to/from town – just ring reception when you're ready.

IN THE KNOW

Our favourite rooms Deluxe rooms strike a happy medium in terms of space and luxury. Ask for one in the restaurant chalet (rooms 10 to 19) for the shortest hop to breakfast or dinner. Families can opt for a spacious Prestige room (which sleep two adults and two children, or three adults), two of which have mezzanines. Or request interconnecting rooms; the hotel has two pairs.
Hotel bar The bar, located by the lobby, is open all day, and serves coffee, cognac and all strengths in between. A small menu of light dishes, sweet and savoury, is also available.
Hotel restaurant Work your way through a delicious Modern European menu, accompanied by a thoughtfully crafted, mainly French wine list. The decor is smart, and the staff are friendly and efficient. Dishes such as brioche filet mignon or roast bream with fennel and lemon compete with the gourmet scene in town.
Top table Near the buffet for breakfast. By night, head for the cosier left-hand side.
Room service A short menu of hot and cold dishes is available 24 hours.
Dress code Mountain casual: nobody bats an eyelid at slippers and jeans.
Local knowledge The hotel spa offers a range of massage and beauty treatments, but you'll need to book. Alpaga's concierge can organise restaurant reservations, carriage rides and taxis, hot-air-balloon trips and ski lessons.

LOCAL EATING AND DRINKING

L'Alpage au Fer à Cheval on Route du Crêt d'Arbois is an upscale hotel restaurant serving superlative Savoyard fare (+33 (0)4 50 21 30 39). On the mountain, L'Alpette has gastro standards as high as its altitude, and does brilliant burgers (+33 (0)4 50 21 03 69). Lunch on melting, flaky tartes salées, followed by handmade meringues and truffles, at patisserie-café Le Comptoir du Père Sotieu on Rue du Général Muffat St Amour (+33 (0)4 50 21 67 51). For a change from Megève's plentiful supply of Savoyard eateries, Le Restaunome at 201 rue de la Poste offers a globetrotting menu in a dark-wood contemporary dining room (+33 (0)4 50 55 86 24). Succulent seafood and grilled meats lead the menu at Les Enfants Terribles (sister restaurant to L'Alpette) on Place de l'Eglise, a spacious, modern restaurant with theatrical flourishes and eye-catching murals (+33 (0)4 50 58 76 69).

GET A ROOM!

For more information, or to book this hotel, go to www.mrandmrssmith.com. Register your Smith membership card (see pages 4–5) to enjoy exclusive offers and privileges.

 SMITH MEMBER OFFER A bottle of champagne.

Alpaga Allée des Marmousets, 74120 Megève (+33 (0)4 50 54 65 36; www.lodgemontagnard.com)

Château de Bagnols

STYLE Five-star aristocrat
SETTING Cultivated Beaujolais

'Next to the bed, the water tumblers are made of silver, giving us a sensory suggestion of what it might have been to be a French aristocrat'

For more than a decade, I had dreamt of the Château de Bagnols. When I was editor of *Elle Decoration*, I saw incredible pictures that lodged in my imagination, images from childhood: 'Beauty and the Beast', 'Bluebeard's Castle', 'The Princess and the Pea'... The extravagant interiors looked about as far from the usual idea of a boutique hotel, and from the modern design that filled the pages of my magazine, as was possible. Intensely beautiful, the pictures that struck me most were of its beds, which simply beggared belief – insane four-posters piled high with mattresses and hung with heavy red-brocade drapes or antique silks. This was the stuff of the films of Peter Greenaway and Luchino Visconti. However, it was a dream, and I never went.

Now, finally, invited to review the hotel with my husband, it is time to visit Bagnols in the heart of Beaujolais. Will I be horribly disappointed? Are those pictures a stylised sham? As we arrive in the village of Bagnols, 17 miles from Lyon, and spy the extraordinary castle walls, the answer is, clearly, no. This is a really staggering

building in a tiny village, its historic might absolutely apparent. Complete with moat, bridge and towers in the honey-coloured stone called *pierre dorée,* the schoolbook stronghold is punctured by neat, cruciform arrow holes. (You might call it a hole-istic experience, perhaps, to be the recipient of an arrow from one of those.)

The interior of the château does not disappoint. It is the brainchild of a truly cultured woman, Lady Helen Hamlyn, who also owns the house by architects Mendelsohn and Chermayeff in Old Church Street, London – one of England's first modernist houses. The rooms in both the original 13th-century castle and the 'new block' (15th-century) are beautiful. Our bed is as sublime as I had hoped, decorated with fragile antique textiles and made up with tactile Irish bedlinen (which you can buy, too). Next to the bed, the water tumblers are made of silver, giving us a sensory suggestion of what it might have been to be a French aristocrat. The bathroom is grand, too, with an antique marble bath and local products, including a really, really strong lavender bath foam – the type that works against typhoid and tigers. We also have a huge sitting room, filled with bleeding-heart-coloured sofas, and another tiny room covered with frescoes. It blows your mind.

The kitchens are central to the building and, thanks to a clever sleight of design, you walk through them on your way to anywhere, past the teeming, steaming theatre of food preparation. The grounds are lovely, with dense borders of lavender and a formal garden where we take drinks before dinner. The swimming pool is round, with grass growing right up to its edge. Alas, all this whimsy and wonder has to fit into a 21st-century reality, and the food and service at Bagnols are of a very French kind, rather than tallying, to my mind, with the beyond-beautiful environment. The human contact is formal and, operationally, the hotel deals in star ratings and status rather than princesses and peas. But the Château de Bagnols is certainly the most

beautiful hotel I have ever stayed in. To have a heavenly time, order room service (after all, how often do you have your own four-poster?). The rooms are so exquisite it is mad not to stay in for the evening and do your own variation on 'You be Louis and I'll be Marie Antoinette.' Just don't lose your head. We also dined in the very grand Salle des Gardes, where we had cherry clafoutis for pudding; as a contrast, we lunched under the trees, on goat's cheese and red wine.

During the day, go out and explore, do your own thing. The château has bicycles you can go off on for picnics and jaunts. We make use of their attractively produced book of trips to enjoy by bike or car, which take us to just the sort of places we love. We spend a morning at an over-the-top food market at Villefranche, where we do the rounds among vast quantities of local produce, buying huge bags and bundles to take home, including an array of fresh goat's cheese and a

sausage called Jésus (the old ladies laugh when I ask them why, leaving me none the wiser), as well as admiring all those great, artistically ordered piles of fruit and vegetables.

Hanging out in yeasty cellars and debating the relative values of 2004 and 2002 is very much our idea of fun, so we also pay a visit to a much-awarded local winemaker, Alain Chatoux, who makes Beaujolais and some very decent white. If you think there is no significant difference between men and women, you might think again after a session of wine tasting. Down in Mr Chatoux's chilly cave, we note that Mr Smith prefers the powerful kick of a 2003 or a 2005 vintage, while Mrs Smith puts her money on the lighter, chillable 2002 or 2004. An interesting experiment, and not one without its non-scientific compensations.

For a change of aesthetic, we drive an hour to see the modernist convent La Tourette by Le Corbusier. One of his last works, it is a building that expresses the interior life of man, and embodies his search for intensity and soul. Built around the progress of the sun, the building allows light to enter the building in many different ways. Slits of illumination accompany you down corridors; you enter a chapel through a transformational wall of light; and altars are dramatically lit with wizard fingers of brightness. It is incredibly moving. We aren't sure how to follow that, except by plunging back into the brocade-draped, fresco-covered, sumptuous worldliness of our quarters at Château de Bagnols — from the sublime to the luxurious, you might say.

Reviewed by Ilse Crawford

NEED TO KNOW

Rooms 21, including eight junior suites, four suites and one apartment.
Rates €480–€990 for the rooms, or €2,435–€2,700 for the Lady Hamlyn apartment, not including tax. Breakfast, from €32.
Check-out 12 noon, but flexible where possible. Earliest check-in, 3pm.
Facilities Heated outdoor pool in summer, library with internet access, WiFi from €15 a day, DVD selections, bicycles to borrow. Horse-drawn carriage rides, picnics, hot-air-balloon flights, wine-tasting by arrangement. Luxury chauffeured cars available for transfers and touring. In rooms: flatscreen TV, DVD, CD on request, bottled water.
Children Welcome. Extra beds (no charge for under-15s) are available in some rooms. Cots, changing mats, nappies, bottle heaters, baby baths and potties can all be provided, and there's a children's menu. English-speaking babysitters charge from €20 an hour, with 24 hours' notice.
Also Book a body treatment in your room; hairdressing can also be organised. Small dogs can be accommodated. Smoking is allowed in some rooms. Helicopters can land in the neighbouring field.

IN THE KNOW

Our favourite rooms We love the arched ceiling, 17th-century frescoes and gilded four-poster in junior suite Gaspard Dugué (Room 8). The room was once part of the chapel where its namesake wed in 1609. Deluxe room Les Seigneurs d'Albon (Room 1) has a circular bathroom in the tower.
Hotel bar There's no official drinking den here, but you can order wine or soft drinks to enjoy on velvet sofas beside the fire in the Grand Salon. In summer, staff will bring you drinks alfresco on the terrace.
Hotel restaurant La Salle des Gardes serves modern French cuisine, as well as traditional dishes and spit-roasted meats and game, in the former guards' room and on the south-facing terrace.
Top table Dine by the fire in winter; in summer, eat in the Salon Ombragé, an outdoor dining space shaded by 100-year-old lime trees.
Room service Available round the clock. Also served in the public lounges when the restaurant is closed.
Dress code No jeans: châtelaine chic for her; jacket for him.
Local knowledge Vines grow all around Bagnols. Ask the concierge to point you towards a friendly *cave* for tastings.

LOCAL EATING AND DRINKING

Le Vieux Moulin on Chemin du Vieux Moulin in Alix (+33 (0)4 78 43 91 66; www.lemoulindalix.com) is a stone-built Rhôneside mill, where you can fill up on mustardy sausages or frogs' legs. Request a table in the conservatory at Les Terrasses de Pommiers at 706 montée de Buisante in Pommiers (+33 (0)4 74 65 05 27; www.terrasses-de-pommiers.com), where beautiful Beaujolais views accompany classic cuisine such as roasted sea bream or fillet of beef. Exposed brickwork and low beamed ceilings create a cottagey feel at La Vieille Auberge, at 201 rue Paul Causeret in Oingt (+33 (0)4 74 71 28 79; www.la-vieille-auberge-restaurant.fr). The food is simple (chicken with cream of mushrooms, andouillette), but superb in flavour. Just north of Lyon, L'Auberge de l'Ile on Place Notre Dame, L'Ile Barbe (+33 (0)4 78 83 99 49; www.aubergedelile.com) is a romantic 17th-century house serving divine dishes such as foie gras ravioli and slow-poached cod in garlic cream. Guy Lassausaie, on Rue de Belle Cise in Chasselay, is another excellent option with a contemporary atmosphere (+33 (0)4 78 47 62 59; www.guy-lassausaie.com).

GET A ROOM!

For more information, or to book this hotel, go to www.mrandmrssmith.com. Register your Smith membership card (see pages 4–5) to enjoy exclusive offers and privileges.

 SMITH MEMBER OFFER Wine tasting at a local vineyard or, when the *vendange* intervenes, two bottles of Beaujolais red or white.

Château de Bagnols Le Bourg, 69620 Bagnols (+33 (0)4 74 71 40 00; www.chateaudebagnols.fr)

Les Carroz
d'Arâches

Les Servages d'Armelle

STYLE Convivial contemporary chalet
SETTING Slopes of Mont Blanc

'I am hit by the smell of pine and the sound of a crackling fire. The dark honey colour of the untreated timber mingles with our hostess Armelle's smile to create instant warmth'

I like driving south to the sea. Mr Smith likes driving north to the mountains. We are driving north. I watch as the signage changes to 'edelweiss this' and 'glacier that'. We pass a big white peak. We take the turning off towards Les Carroz and I realise I am cold, and nervous. Cold because the temperature has dropped, and nervous because Mr Smith, an artist, a gourmet cook and a man of impeccable taste, can be a very difficult man to please.

When we enter Les Servages d'Armelle, I am hit by the smell of pine and the sound of a crackling fire. The dark honey colour of the untreated timber mingles with our hostess Armelle's smile to create instant warmth. And yet all I can think about, as we follow her up the ample staircase, is when Mr Smith is going to launch his redesign. Will he bang on about the golden section? And what particular curse will he cast upon the fittings and fixtures?

Once Armelle has shown us to our suite and the door has closed with a wholesome click, Mr Smith gets to

work. He circumnavigates the enormous timber bed with its clouds of white linen. He listens to the hushed action of the dimmer switches. He contemplates the ceiling-height log fire. He releases water from the chrome showerhead, and runs his finger over the sophisticated knobs that await the bathrobes, still snug in their wrapping. Then he parts the wooden louvred shutters and slides the glass doors open to reveal a panorama of mountain peaks floating in a sea of cloud like *oeufs à la neige*. All of this he does without saying a word. Could this, I wonder, be the day on which Mr Smith is silenced by another's good taste?

Outside the hotel, work is being done on ski slopes and lifts by men in quilted jackets; inside, we are naked and being pummelled to jelly in our private hammam. We collapse in a sweat, first on the granite bench of the steam room, and then on the firm but giving mattress, and finally we stand under a cascade of water illuminated so beautifully that it is like standing under a sunlit Victoria Falls. Now we are playing with our Anglepoise reading lamps. 'We should get some like this,' I say. 'This,' says Mr Smith, finally, as he pours himself a glass of Badoit, 'is perfect'. Yes! I think. 'Yes, we should,' he says. 'But why would anyone need a reading lamp here? I suppose if you were too old for sex or just starting out and needing a manual...' 'Dinner?' I say.

We are seated on leather chairs in a cosy corner of the restaurant and, though it seems we are the only guests, we feel completely at ease. In fact, although we have come face to face with the ultimate irritants to a musician and a painter having supper – a speaker above us piping unwanted music and a blood-red painting glaring down at us (we only ask for one of them to be turned down) – we are laughing. With our view, through the glass, of industrious chef Pascal Flecheau, the logs sizzling in the grate, the sturdy antique furniture and white linen and, of course, the cheerful attention of Armelle, we are as comfortable and content as if the restaurant were buzzing. And it soon is – minutes later, half the village and their children turn up to bask in the glow with us.

From the excellent wine list, Mr Smith chooses a Burgundy that smells properly of camembert. Through the wooden hatch and onto our plates comes freshwater shrimp bisque, stuffed squid, fillet of beef, roasted kumquats and wild mushrooms. A big green salad, though not on the menu, is prepared for us. Everything is *comme il faut*. Our wine glasses are refilled somewhat over-eagerly by the waiter, who reassures us, when we gesture helplessly at the cheese platter (which boasts *tommes de* this and that, a melty Reblochon and a mammoth Beaufort), that the cheese will still be there in the morning. And indeed it is, along with fresh crusty bread, home-made jam, eggs, ham, Savoie yoghurt and an excellent bowl of Illy coffee prepared by Armelle, with a country jug of steamed milk. A perfect pre-ski breakfast.

Behind every great hotel there is a great host: Armelle, dainty and Alpine-pretty, is at reception to welcome you. She is in the restaurant at breakfast, lunch and dinner, happy to answer questions about anything from the local pottery they use to walking itineraries. When I ask for a sandwich before a trek,

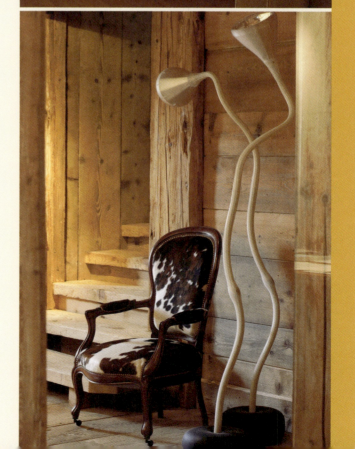

though she is busy serving, she makes it with the same care with which she seems to do everything else, and it is the best sandwich I have ever eaten (admittedly after a two-hour climb, while gazing at Mont Blanc).

It is clearly Armelle's standards that are being met at every turn, and her love of elegant but functional design that prevails. And it is she who finally manages to silence and, indeed, satisfy Mr Smith. Even the gutters are fashioned from logs, for goodness sake, and Mr Smith is very fussy about gutters. I realise, as we drive south after two delectable nights, that I love Armelle, and the mountains, and log cabins, and the north, and above all I love Les Servages, where we have relaxed more than we have in the eight years of marriage we came here to celebrate.

Reviewed by Ruth Phillips

NEED TO KNOW

Rooms 10, including three suites. There's also a self-contained chalet, sleeping up to six.

Rates Low season, €190–€680; high season, €220–€800, not including breakfast, €21. The chalet costs €1,000 a night.

Check-out 10am, but flexible if there's availability. Earliest check-in, 4pm.

Facilities Flatscreen TV, DVD, Annick Goutal products, Balneo bath tubs, in-room spa treatments, free WiFi in the main farmhouse and restaurant. The chalet has a well-equipped kitchen.

Children Under-10s stay free; extra beds for older children are €50 a night. Babysitting can be arranged with a local nanny. The restaurant has a children's menu.

Also Pets can come, too, by arrangement. During the winter, there's a two-night minimum stay.

IN THE KNOW

Our favourite rooms The suites above the restaurant in the farmhouse have their own mini-spa: a hot tub and hammam to soothe away après-ski aches. Their French doors open out onto an Alp-facing terrace, and there's an extra bedroom and bathroom upstairs.

Hotel bar The bar, tucked away in a corner of the restaurant, is decked out with ponyskin stools, big wooden tables and grand mirrors. Iced buckets of champagne line the counter, ready for owner Armelle to pour you a Kir Royale. It's open until 11pm, when an honesty bar takes over.

Hotel restaurant The restaurant is divided between a terrace, a conservatory and an indoor bit. You can watch chef at work in the kitchen, preparing inventive takes on traditional French and Italian dishes: black risotto with langoustines, fantastic steaks and appetite-whetting charcuterie. It's all open and inviting, and buzzing with activity – you'll feel completely at home wandering into the kitchen with a request. It's elegantly rustic, with handmade crockery and a whole table topped with baskets of fresh bread.

Top table If it's warm enough, eat out on the terrace; if not, cosy up by the window of the conservatory.

Room service Breakfast and a selection of cold dishes on request.

Dress code Your usual off-piste attire: snug sweaters will fit in nicely.

Local knowledge Most activities in the Grand Massif are mountain-based, even in the snow-free summer. Slow the pace by swapping downhill speed for horse-drawn sedateness: Cheval et Montagne in Les Carroz (+33 (0)6 10 80 05 99; www.lescarroz.com) will take you skijoring. And there's a golf course at Flaine-Les-Carroz – the highest in Europe, open in summer only (+33 (0)4 50 90 85 44).

LOCAL EATING AND DRINKING

In Chamonix, head to hotel restaurant Albert 1er on Route du Bouchet for creative, much-lauded menus featuring foie gras, caviar and lamb baked in hay and thyme (+33 (0)4 50 53 05 09). Atmosphère on Place Balmat does fine dining by the river, with speciality game dishes on offer in the autumn (+33 (0)4 50 55 97 97). La Cabane des Praz on Route du Golf is an Alpine cabin open for lunch, afternoon tea and dinner. The menu gives a gastronomic flourish to wild boar, Reblochon cheese and other regional flavours (+33 (0)4 50 53 23 27). Flocons de Sel on Route de Leutaz in Megève has a creative dynamo in the kitchen, and a suitably pine-panelled dining room (+33 (0)4 50 21 49 99).

GET A ROOM!

For more information, or to book this hotel, go to www.mrandmrssmith.com. Register your Smith membership card (see pages 4–5) to enjoy exclusive offers and privileges.

 SMITH MEMBER OFFER A bottle of Savoie wine.

Les Servages d'Armelle 841 route des Servages, 74300 Les Carroz d'Arâches (+33 (0)4 50 90 01 62; www.servages.com)

Rive

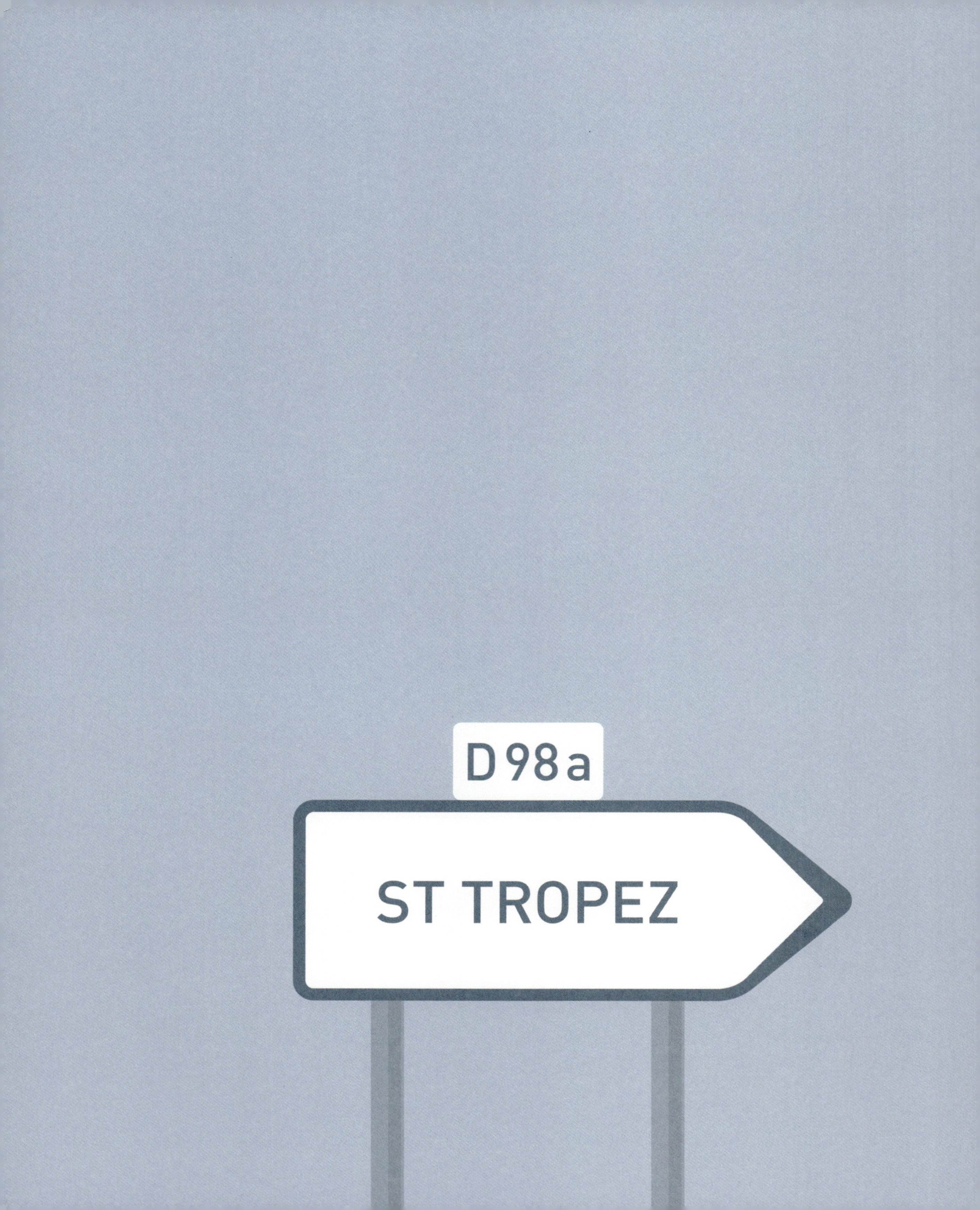
D98a
ST TROPEZ

Lille

Rouen

Reims

Paris

Rennes

Strasbourg

Nantes

Bourges

Dijon

Poitiers

Lyon

Bordeaux

Toulouse

Montpellier

Nice

Marseille

31 30
St Tropez

ST TROPEZ

30 Hotel Pastis

31 La Réserve Ramatuelle

ST TROPEZ

COASTLINE Yacht-sprinkled bay
COAST LIFE Models and millionaires

Rock-star villas, luxury boutiques, Chanel bikinis... For a seaside fishing village, St Tropez has evolved admirably. Under the hot sun, jet-setters pose on the promenade, basking in the enviable gleam of super-yachts and super-tans. Honeymooners, movie stars and millionaires mingle in slinky cocktail lounges, while the party crowd soak each other with champagne at Nikki Beach. But step back a little, away from the port and its A-list shenanigans, and a different Riviera light shines. Welcome to a more insouciant St Tropez, where pétanque balls clack in sandy, tree-lined squares, and senior citizens sup pastis in humble cafés. To be stylishly simple *and* flagrantly status-hungry takes confidence – and this town's got it in spades.

GETTING THERE

Planes From the UK, British Airways, BMI Baby, EasyJet and Flybe fly to Nice, 90 minutes from St Tropez by car (www.ba.com; www.bmibaby.com; www.easyjet.com; www.flybe.com). The nearest airport is Toulon, served from Bristol and London Stansted by Ryanair in summer.
Trains From London, take the train via Lille to Marseille (www.eurostar.com); from Paris, board the TGV (www.tgv.com). From Marseille to St Raphaël (as near as the railway gets to St Trop) the train offers deckchair views.
Automobiles It's a long way from the UK to this easterly port, and only a masochist would take their motor into St Tropez itself. Determined drivers can use the Autotrain from Paris to Avignon or Nice, instead, and clock up the mileage from there (0844 848 4050).

LOCAL KNOWLEDGE

Taxis You risk paying €25 to travel a distance that would take minutes on foot, so stick to walking or hotel shuttles.
Siesta and fiesta It can be 11pm before bars start to buzz. Most shops are open 9am–12pm, then 3pm–7pm. Banks ply their trade Tuesday to Friday, 8am–12pm and 1pm–5pm.
Do go/don't go The season in St Tropez follows the sailing calendar: May to September are the best months to go. Check your dates for diary clashes with regattas, when crowds and congestion may potentially mar your trip.
Packing tips Deck shoes, nautical designerwear, and the glitziest jewellery, accessories and beachwear Mrs Smith can pile on.
Children Bundle your progeny on board a boat across the bay to fellow coastal town Sainte-Maxime. In St Tropez, continue the nautical theme at the Naval Museum in the 16th-century citadel.
Recommended reads *Out to Lunch in Provence* by Mike Aalders; anything by Colette or Anaïs Nin, both cult 20th-century eroticists and St Tropez residents.
Local specialities The delicious and ubiquitous Tarte Tropézienne is a brioche-style cake filled with kirsch-laced cream and sprinkled with pearl sugar. The fresh catch includes sardines, red mullet, lobster and crevettes; fans of the loaded seafood platter are in the right place for a frequent fix.
And... Club 55 is a restaurant, bar and beach club that embodies the spirit of St Tropez. Named for the year of its arrival – 1955, when Brigitte Bardot allegedly mistook a fishing hut for a beachfront café – it's a bamboo-screened, tamarisk-shaded favourite of the A-list. Lunch tables disappear faster than the Dom Pérignon, so you'll need to book (+33 (0)4 94 55 55 55).

WORTH GETTING OUT OF BED FOR

Viewpoint The ramparts of the 17th-century *citadelle*, which houses the naval museum, give the best lookout over the tiled rooftops. In the tiny hill village of Gassin, clamber up through the winding streets for a magnificent view over woodland, wine country and the bay – you should be able to see the three Golden Isles (Porquerolles, Port Cros and Levant).

Arts and culture The Musée de l'Annonciade on the port houses works by Matisse, Bonnard and Seurat (+33 (0)4 94 17 84 10). Galerie Abrial Côté Art on Avenue Paul Roussel (+33 (0)4 94 97 31 08), has some huge pastel pieces to tempt art deco collectors. Movie geeks might wander over to the Gendarmerie Nationale, where comedy flick *Le Gendarme de St Tropez* was shot. On Rue Etienne Berny, the Maison des Papillons, with its 220 species of pin-skewered butterflies, makes for an eccentric afternoon's lepidoptery (+33 (0)4 94 97 63 45). There's plenty in the way of ancient architecture to ogle in the nearby village of Grimaud, including a mediaeval water system.

Activities Pampelonne Beach at St Tropez is the region's water-sports capital. Water-skiing, parascending and cat-sailing are all on offer to restless baskers, who are also at liberty to attach themselves to a boat and go wakeboarding over the waves. For coastal walking with wonderful bay views, head east of the port to the Cap, continuing to Pampelonne beach, where a trail cuts back across the peninsula into town. Between May and September, horse-ride through L'Estérel forest near Saint Raphäel (+33 (0)6 85 42 51 50; www.les3fers.com). Hire bicycles from Location Mas at 3 rue Joseph Quaranta (+33 (0)4 94 97 00 60; www.location-mas.com). You can also bike or hike your way through the mighty Massif des Maures, whose rugged mountain terrain encompasses forests, monasteries and sleepy towns. Explore the Mediterranean gardens of Domaine du Rayol in the village of Le Rayol Canadel (+33 (0)4 98 04 44 00; www.domainedurayol.org), on a glorious headland above the bay of Figuier. For more of an off-the-beaten-track excursion, visit the lighthouse at Cap Camarat: it's the second largest in France and on a clear day you can see Corsica from the top.

Best beach The long golden strip at Gigaro, at La Croix Valmer, tapers to a spit with sea either side. Plage de la Bouillabaisse is a lovely bit of blond shoreline west of the port. For seclusion (and nudity) try Plage de la Moutte or Plage de l'Escalet. Lined with clubs and restaurants, bustling Plage de Pampelonne is St Tropez's largest, and sees more celebrity towel action than a Beverly Hills day spa.

Daytripper Head to the hills and Saint-Paul-de-Vence, a mediaeval village colonised by artists from Picasso to present-day painters. Walk the battlements, stroll down Rue Grande in the castle walls and pick up a sunhat or a Cubist painting; there are dozens of boutiques and galleries. For lunch, head to La Colombe d'Or (decor: Gaudi meets Kandinsky and goes nuts). Make sure you book in advance – it takes weeks to get a table (+33 (0)4 93 32 80 02).

Shopping St Tropez is a potted (or should that be ported) Milan, with designer boutiques such as Dior and Cavalli crammed into the tiny streets around Place de la Garonne and Rue Gambetta. For a more low-key spend, browse and barter in the markets at Place des Lices (Tuesday and Saturday mornings), where you can fill your bags with traditional bedlinen, Provençal cooking ingredients and desirable presents.

Something for nothing For a super-chilled walk to find a secret beach, make your way to L'Escalet nudist beach, south-east of St Tropez, and keep walking until you come across the small, peaceful Cap Taillat strand.

Don't go home without... visiting the yachtie hang-out Café de Paris on Le Port. Wander in for lunchtime noodles, salad and seafood, or book a table to see it liven up at night (+33 (0)4 94 97 00 65).

SUITABLY ST TROPEZ

If the streamlined vessels moored at the marina whet your appetite for the ocean wave, you can charter a yacht for the day and take to the Riviera seas with your own captain, from €500 a day, at L'Echo Nautique (+33 (0)4 94 97 73 66; www.echonautique.com). They can supply anything from a 10-metre yacht up to an Abramovich-proportioned monster with a helipad. For a more pocket-friendly option, hire a smaller-scale motor boat from Suncap (+33 (0)4 94 97 11 23; www.suncap.fr).

DIARY

May Processions of sailor-suited locals mark the three-day Bravade festival, a tribute to local patron saints. June The Giraglia Cup is a 50-year yacht-racing tradition that's one of the port's busiest regattas. July The St Tropez elite turn their attention to the turf as the International Polo Cup comes to town (www.polo-st-tropez.com). August Ramatuelle brings out the brass and blue notes at its annual jazz gathering (www.jazzfestivalramatuelle. com). September–October The international yachting competition Les Voiles de St Tropez sends the port populace sailing-giddy (www.ot-saint-tropez.com).

St Tropez

Hotel Pastis

STYLE Graphic detail
SETTING Sea and be seen

'A Lichtenstein print here, a collection of
pastis jugs there – we could feel St Tropez
chic running through the hotel, with
a distinct underlay of London know-how'

'Quick, take this — and read it later,' urged the gentleman, slipping a note under my croissant. Then, with a wistful look, he picked up his cases, wove through the lobby and was gone for ever. I didn't come to this boutique hotel in St Tropez to have an affair. In fact, I hadn't even noticed my fellow guest, let alone encouraged him to pass me a love letter when Mr Smith wasn't looking. But hey, that's St Tropez for you. Something about the sun-drenched, A-list ambience makes people do crazy things, I guess. Obviously it's tempting to proffer mystery man's hand-written love poem ('If you were a bird, I'd want you in my sky...' and so on) as an analogy for the romantic, poetical virtues of our hotel. But Pastis is way too cool for such a chick-lit cop-out.

Arriving late, drenched from a freak Mediterranean storm, we're ushered into our room in a whirl of umbrellas, howling winds and rain-battered pastel shutters. Pulling billowing curtains — and dressing gowns — tightly together, Mr Smith and I are happy to be tucked in for the night. It's only upon waking to a turquoise-infused St Tropez light that we see this hotel for what it is: total design heaven. Art is everywhere at Pastis. Splashes of colour from framed canvases hit us between the eyes as we spiral our way down the staircase to breakfast. 'That's a Hockney,' nudges Mr Smith, as we take our table in the lobby and breathe in the coffee fumes from the huge silver Gaggia behind the bar. Nibbling on pistachio and hazelnut bruschetta and sitting on basketweave chairs, it's just the two of us, though a murmuring from the terrace tells us fellow guests are nearby — next to the outdoor pool, steaming in the morning air. Yes, the sea view from our table is interrupted by a road (the hotel is on the route into St Tropez), but we spy waves over our mini pain au raisin, so who cares?

Walking through the hotel, a 360-degree melange of dazzling design pieces in a pastel-cool French setting, we look up and clock the owners' rock 'n' roll side, ie: a framed Sex Pistols LP over the bar telling us to Never Mind The Bollocks. Having swapped the London lifestyle for St Tropez, Pauline and John have stamped their personalities all over this place. Ex-graphic designers turned retail designers (they were responsible for rebranding one of the UK's biggest supermarkets a few years back, they inform us), they know what they like, and everything is just so. A Lichtenstein print here, a collection of pastis jugs there — we could feel St Tropez chic running through the hotel, with a distinct underlay of London know-how.

Eyeing the hotel's palm-fringed pool, we decide to head Tropezwards before making the most of promising mercury fluctuations. St Tropez is tiny. Craning, portside, to view the fibreglass monster yachts, to Mr Smith's horror I manage to trip, almost acrobatically, over a huge electricity cable. Stumbling into the path of a man wearing a blindingly white suit being filmed at the waterfront, I'm thankful that no one yells or yanks me away. Dignity dashed (and praying I won't end up the butt

of some comedy out-take), we head past the gleaming mega-vessels and on up to the main square, the Place des Lices. A jumble of dusty boules games and cafés, it's worlds away from the ostentatiously OTT bars and boats below at the port. It's the St Tropez behind St Tropez — metaphorically and literally.

Popping into famed La Tarte Tropézienne, we pick up some pistachio-sprinkled tarte aux pommes for later, resisting the risotto in favour of our so-touristy-but-so-what lunch reservation at Café de Paris. Perched on plushly upholstered chairs beneath lavish chandeliers, we feel distinctly uptown, hanging out at this iconic beast. In the company of a pipe-smoking sailing fraternity and stiffly coiffed dames who've seen too much sun, we dine on succulent sushi, crème caramel and nerve-janginglyly strong coffee. Then, as I promise Mr Smith it's safe to go back to the scene of the love-letter crime, we head back to Pastis.

Distressed Louis XV decor and a chrome ceiling fan with the proportions of a plane propeller welcome us back at the room; then a hammered-silver platter of Côté Bastide products tempts us to soak in bubbles for an hour. Outside, as guests drape themselves on rustic poolside seats next to twinkling twilight candles, and a group of guys start sinking Dom Pérignon at the zinc bar, the sky turns an indigo-blue colour across the bay and out towards the mountains.

Later on, watching a gaggle of WAG types totter out of a black limo and straight onto the black-sand floor of yacht-side bar Le Quai Joseph, we pop into Hotel Sube for our before-bed cocktail. You either have to sharpen your elbows or bribe the barman to nab a table on Sube's balcony (the best viewpoint in St Tropez, we reckon). We did neither but still somehow managed to score a table. In a world where Dior dominates café culture and stilettos strut the beaches, chalky-toned Hotel Pastis is a serene break. It doesn't try too hard, it just is – a pastel-shuttered heaven after the hot Tropezian hustle. And hey, there's even the prospect of being propositioned by fountain pen under your partner's nose at the breakfast table. If you're very lucky.

Reviewed by Charlotte Crisp

NEED TO KNOW

Rooms 10, all with a terrace or balcony, one with wheelchair access.

Rates Low season, €175–€300; mid-season, €275–€425; high season, €450–€650. Rates don't include breakfast, €20.

Check-out 12 noon. Earliest check-in, 4pm. Outside high season, timings are flexible, subject to availability.

Facilities Outdoor heated pool, gardens, DVD library, free WiFi throughout, parking. In rooms: flatscreen TV, CD/DVD, minibar.

Children Extra beds are €50 for under-14s. Cots are free, subject to availability.

Also Smoking is only allowed in certain areas outdoors. Two-night minimum stay at weekends.

IN THE KNOW

Our favourite rooms Room 4 is the most romantic, with vintage loungers on an ample shaded terrace overlooking the pool. Room 8 has a big sunny terrace, leather club chairs and a roll-top bath. Ask for a room with a pool view, rather than one at the front of the hotel.

Hotel bar There's an appropriately good stock of Ricard and other aniseedy liquor, served at the elegant zinc bar, open late during summer months. You can also order from a cocktail menu of popular classics.

Hotel restaurant None as such. Breakfast is served on the poolside terrace from 8.15am until noon, or indoors by the bar. Then it's straight into lunch: a choice of light, cold dishes, served between noon and 4pm.

Dress code Although the hotel operates a strict no-dress-code policy, we suggest you think yachtie: crisp linens with deck shoes or espadrilles.

Local knowledge If you're looking to improve your jet-skiing, water-skiing, parascending or dinghy sailing, all manner of watery excitement is on offer at Pampelonne beach.

LOCAL EATING AND DRINKING

Small, intimate and locally approved, Au Caprice des Deux at 40 rue du Portail Neuf (+33 (0)4 94 97 76 78; www. aucapricedesdeux.com) does a fixed-price three-course menu for €57 a person. For a taste of traditional Provençal cuisine, book a table at the popular Fuchs (pronounced 'foosh') at 7 rue des Commerçants (+33 (0)4 94 97 01 25). Great for a light bite, with no pretentions, Le Café on Place des Lices (+33 (0)4 94 97 44 69; www.lecafe.fr) is one of St Tropez's oldest brasseries, attracting locals and visitors alike. Tropezian movers and shakers lunch at on-the-beach Club 55 (+33 (0)4 94 55 55 55). Legendary discotheque Les Caves du Roy, in the Hôtel Byblos (+33 (0)4 94 56 68 00), is popular among the tanned and the scantily clad. A-listy VIP Room at the Résidence du Nouveau Port (+33 (0)4 94 97 14 70; www.viproom.fr) is open from midnight until dawn.

GET A ROOM!

For more information, or to book this hotel, go to www.mrandmrssmith.com. Register your Smith membership card (see pages 4–5) to enjoy exclusive offers and privileges.

 SMITH MEMBER OFFER A bottle of Provençal rosé.

Hotel Pastis 61 avenue du Général Leclerc, 83990 St Tropez (+33 (0)4 98 12 56 50; www.pastis-st-tropez.com)

Ramatuelle

La Réserve Ramatuelle

STYLE Polished and prestigious
SETTING Exclusive Riviera

'Not a generic painting in sight. No need –
the design, our private lawned terrace and the
view of the Med and Cap Taillat was enough'

La Réserve in Ramatuelle, over the cusp weekend of September/October. Good. The St Tropez peninsula will be awash with the party crowd from Les Voiles de St Tropez for the season's last laugh. Very good. Glitch in the works: Météo-France forecasts BIG rain. Bad. Then again, and to paraphrase Woody Allen: 'Boy-meets-girl in the sunshine – could be platonic. Boy-meets-girl in the rain – could be serious.'

Luckily for Mr and Mrs Smith, Météo-France's Monsieur Poisson had got it wrong. But the Franco-Swiss owners of La Réserve have got it right, very right, creating a remarkable, modern-aesthetic hotel of 23 rooms and 11 villas in a private domain of 14 acres.

If you thought the Swiss only made cuckoo clocks and played *cache-cache* with money, you'd be off the mark. They also possess an incomparable eye for a site: we get jaw-stretching views of a wine-dark Mediterranean, parasol pines and olive trees of near-Biblical age. This isn't hyperbole – the setting of La Réserve is spectacular.

La Réserve has turned the clocks back where it matters (setting, service, calm, space) and forward to where it matters, too (comfort, design, decor, privacy, grasping when less really is more). And there's a spa, as well – the

size of Leamington – with an in-house doctor to advise on body-streamlining treatments, in serious French style. However, our arrival on a sleepy *fin de saison* Sunday didn't augur too well. The carpark told its own predictable story: Geneva plates and Monaco's dinky sky-blue ones. I shuddered. The plastic was melting already, and we hadn't even crossed the sleek threshold. We were ushered into the CinemaScope lobby, and swept along by the panorama of the Baie de Bonporteau to suite 21. Mr Smith immediately spied the bar's long balcony looming above, which rendered the 60-square-metre private terrace not so, er, private.

'Thank you for the upgrade to this suite, mademoiselle, but could you please downgrade us?' Mrs Smith had never heard *those* words before. A perplexed smile, perhaps, but we were ushered straight out; the Swiss management have napalmed the infamous St Tropez arrogance. So, off we trotted to a junior suite, a snip at €840. Smaller, yes, but perfect. For traditionalists like this Mr and Mrs Smith, it had an instant calming effect, clutter-free in cream and neutral tones, with expanses of dark wood. No print curtains, and not a generic painting in sight. No need – the design, our private 30-square-metre lawned terrace, the view of the Mediterranean and Cap Taillat was enough, and more. We both flopped onto the bed with contented grins.

Given the choice of lunch or dinner, we prefer 'long lunch'. Invigorated by the sea air, we mooched up to the bar. Freshly made Rossinis (juice from strawberries, not cartons) in hand, we impolitely peered down into the gardens of suites 20–23, grateful for our downgrade. (This 'private but not really' dottiness, we are assured, will be rectified before long.)

Lunch: suffice to say, nouvelle cuisine is alive and well here, at nouveau-riche prices. Our sea-bass for two was an eye-popping €112, and a bottle of Château Pampelonne rosé (which you can guzzle for a fraction of the price at the eponymous winery, 10 minutes away), was €50. Even by St Tropez standards, that kind of mark-up could feel like *trop*-to-pay, if you weren't feeling flush. The service at every meal was slick, polite and bilingual. However, were you here for much more than a long weekend, the almost curt lunch and dinner menu might prove challenging.

The toss of a coin determined our next move: Mr Smith to the spa and Mrs Smith to the pool. Hewn from the living rock, the spa is quite extraordinary. Here are the stats: 1,000 square metres, 13 treatment rooms, 24 different treatments, indoor heated pool, hammam and a gleaming gym full of contraptions and wizardry. The massage itself: sublime. I even slept the sleep of the innocent. Mrs Smith was equally laudatory about life poolside. She had ensconced herself at the eastern end, overlooking the grounds and the sea. No white plastic furniture here – rather soft, industrial-sized beanbags, and fabric-and-wood loungers with plump towels. Pool boys are on hand to provide free (yes!) bottles of Evian, and the pool itself is long and shallow and ideal for relaxing.

La Réserve Ramatuelle is magnificent. At their peril, fine hotels forget detail, detail, detail. It's the dinosaurs who cling to location, location, location. Here's a tale: we returned from supper (don't skip sunset cocktails, whatever you do) to find the perennial cat's cradle of Mr Smith's headphones painstakingly untangled. As neat as fresh snow trails, they'd been placed on the desk. From any hotel, anywhere, that's impressive. Then, they went one step further. They did not deposit any platitude and/or chocolate on the Siberian goose pillows. Sometimes, it's what a hotel doesn't do that makes it *really* impressive.

Reviewed by Simon Gaul

NEED TO KNOW

Rooms 23, including 16 suites. There are also 12 villas.
Rates Low season, €400–€2,200; high season, €650–€3,500, including buffet breakfast and tax.
Check-out 12 noon. Check-in, 3pm.
Facilities Outdoor and indoor heated pools, very big spa with 13 cabins, gardens and terrace plus Crème de la Mer products, free WiFi throughout, book and DVD libraries. In rooms: flatscreen TV, DVD, pre-loaded iPod, bottled water and free soft drinks, pillow menu in suites.
Children Calm and quiet prevail here, but kids are welcome. Cots are provided free; extra beds for older children cost €210 a night. Babysitting can be arranged with a local nanny for €20 an hour.
Also Two rooms have wheelchair access. The spa offers personalised seven-day programs for fitness and/or relaxation.

IN THE KNOW

Our favourite rooms All the bedrooms are done out in muted taupes and crisp whites, with private terrace or garden, complete with sea-as-far-as-you-can-see views. Suite Camarat is one of the biggest and, as well as the Mediterranean panorama, has floor-to-ceiling windows, two bedrooms and a lounge area.
Hotel bar Relaxation is on tap in the elegantly understated bar, open every day until 2am. Drinks can be ordered any time in the lobby or poolside, for that top-up of St Tropez pleasure.
Hotel restaurant Dining here is a laid-back experience, with food served either in the softly lit lounge or on the terrace, under breeze-rippled canopies. The kitchen liaises with the spa to create bespoke healthy menus.
Top table The majestic Mediterranean views are the star attraction, so nab a table by the glass doors.
Room service A selection of dishes from the restaurant menu is available 24 hours a day.
Dress code Keep it pure and simple with post-beach chic: crisp linens and minimal make-up.
Local knowledge Give your tastebuds a treat with a visit to a local *cave* to sample wines of the region: Château de Pampelonne (+33 (0)4 94 56 32 04) and Château Minuty (+33 (0)4 94 56 12 09; www.chateauminuty.com), both in Gassin, 13km away, produce excellent rosé.

LOCAL EATING AND DRINKING

The restaurants, bars and cafés of St Tropez are only 13km away but – be warned – in high season, the road can get clogged with traffic. Drive the 13km to Pampelonne beach to find the area's most acclaimed eateries. Chez Camille on Quartier Bonne Terrasse (+33 (0)4 98 12 68 98) dishes up fantastic traditional bouillabaisse. For platefuls of unadulterated glam, join the celebrities at La Voile Rouge on Pampelonne beach (+33 (0)4 94 79 84 34), but book well ahead to snag a table. People-watch in the velvety intimacy of Café de Paris, overlooking St Tropez port (+33 (0)4 94 97 00 56), or escape from the crowds in Octave Café in Place de la Garonne (+33 (0)4 94 97 22 56), a low-key piano bar that channels Fifties film-star fabulousness.

GET A ROOM!

For more information, or to book this hotel, go to www.mrandmrssmith.com. Register your Smith membership card (see pages 4–5) to enjoy exclusive offers and privileges.

 SMITH MEMBER OFFER A 30-minute spa treatment each.

La Réserve Ramatuelle Chemin de la Quessine, 83350 Ramatuelle (+33 (0)4 94 44 94 44; www.lareserve.ch)

Smith & Friends
Stylish self-catering

OUR ONLINE COLLECTION OF HIP HOUSES, CHIC COTTAGES, SERVICED APARTMENTS AND ROCK-STAR VILLAS

The Smith & Friends self-catering collection features more than 100 places to stay in Europe, Australasia and the Americas, all perfect for a party of friends, a family break, or a secluded escape for two. Fluffy towels, crisp linens, inspired interior design – Smith & Friends stays offer the same style, character and luxury that you would expect from a Mr & Mrs Smith hotel: self-indulgent 21st-century self-catering at its finest. New properties join the cherry-picked portfolio every month, from cottages and townhouses to serviced apartments and stately homes.

COAST
Med-side mansions, Barrier Reef retreats, beautiful Balearic villas with private pools...

COUNTRY
Cosy Cotswolds cottages, hip French châteaux, ravishing homesteads in the fields of Tuscany...

CITY
Sleek, concierge-serviced designer apartments in London, Paris, Barcelona, Edinburgh, Manchester and beyond...

SKI
Chalets and lodges, high in chic and laced in luxury, in Chamonix, Courcheval and Verbier...

Smith's expert Travel Team can match the perfect boutique hideaway to specific dates, budgets and occasions. There is no booking fee, and Smith members receive free gifts and loyalty points (www.smithandfriends.com).

(on track)

A smooth, scenic train journey makes travelling a pleasure. And in France, it's easy, efficient and, frequently, excellent value. Most of the hotels in this book are easily reached by rail. This map is your at-a-glance guide to getting there.

Most towns are linked by the French railway's comprehensive coverage. With Paris as its hub, the network casts its web wide over the country and out into Europe. High-speed lines provide swift links to Belgium, Spain, Italy, Switzerland and – thanks to Eurostar's undersea swoop – the UK, in just a few hours.

For help with journey-planning or to book tickets, visit:
eurostar.com – for travel to/from the UK and SNCF tickets
seat61.com – an insider's guide to European travel

sncf.com – online home of France's national railways
raileurope.com – for Continental ticket sales

FIVE REASONS TO TRAVEL BY TRAIN

End up exactly where you want to be Flying can leave you kilometres from your intended destination facing a transfer headache; most trains go from city centre to city centre

Reduce your carbon footprint Rail travel causes a fraction of the CO_2 emissions of flying, and is more energy-efficient than driving

Room to manoeuvre You're not strapped to your seat – stroll around, stretch your legs with your family, visit the buffet carriage or have a first-class supper delivered straight to you

Watch the world go by Soak up the scenery. Green fields and forests, pretty villages and mountains – enjoy that impressionistic blur of passing landscapes

Easy going No check-in queues, stress-free security scans, no lost baggage, no traffic jams, no hidden costs

KEY

Eurostar
Eurostar direct ski train (winter)
Eurostar direct Avignon train (summer)
TGV
Other SNCF services

EUROSTAR™ STATIONS
Paris Hôtel Daniel, Hotel Keppler, Hôtel Particulier
Montmartre Hôtel Récamier, La Réserve Paris

SNCF STATIONS
Aix-en-Provence La Villa Gallici, La Bastide de Moustiers, Le Couvent des Minimes Hôtel & Spa
Alençon Château de Saint Paterne
Angoulême Château de la Couronne, Le Logis de Puygâty

Auray Le Lodge Kerisper
Antibes Cap d'Antibes Beach Hotel, Les Rosées
Autun Moulin Renaudiots
Avignon Hôtel Crillon le Brave
Bédarieux Le Couvent d'Hérépian
Biarritz Arguibel
Cavaillon La Maison sur la Sorgue, Le Mas de la Rose
Grasse Bastide Saint Mathieu
Lyon Château de Bagnols
Montpellier Baudon de Mauny, Domaine de Verchant
Nice Cap Estel
Nîmes Jardins Secrets
Sedan Chez Odette
Saint-Gervais-Le-Fayet Alpaga, Les Servages d'Armelle
Saint-Raphaël Hotel Pastis, La Réserve Ramatuelle

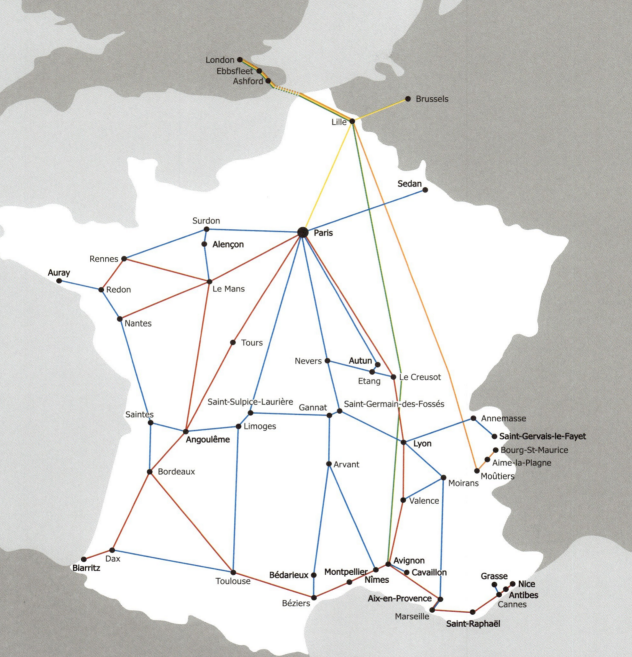

(something on the house)

 Look out for this Smith member offer icon at the end of each hotel review.

As a BlackSmith member, you're automatically entitled to exclusive added extras: it's our way of saying thank you, and ensuring your stay is as enjoyable as possible. Activate your free membership now (see pages 4–5) to take advantage of the offers listed below when you book one of these hotels with us. For more information, or to make a reservation, visit www.mrandmrssmith.com or talk to our expert Travel Team on 0845 034 0700.

ALPAGA Rhône-Alpes
A bottle of champagne.

ARGUIBEL Aquitaine
A drink on the house (wine or champagne); a pass each (worth €30) to the Loreamar Thalasso Spa at Grand Hôtel Saint-Jean-de-Luz; and tickets for the Basque Eco-Museum in Saint-Jean-de-Luz.

LA BASTIDE DE MOUSTIERS Provence
A basket of seasonal fruits and flowers in your room, and a complimentary after-dinner drink of Génépi, an Alpine liqueur.

BASTIDE SAINT MATHIEU Côte d'Azur
A bottle of Valcolombe Cuvée Baroque or champagne. Stay three to four days and make your own fragrance at Galimard perfumery in Grasse. For bookings of five days or more, you'll also be treated to dinner (not including wine) at a local gastronomic restaurant.

BAUDON DE MAUNY Languedoc-Roussillon
A bottle of local wine.

CAP D'ANTIBES BEACH HOTEL Côte d'Azur
A bottle of rosé and a 30-minute Omnisens massage.

CAP ESTEL Côte d'Azur
A bottle of champagne and, if your stay is three nights or longer, a 30-minute massage each.

CHATEAU DE BAGNOLS Rhône–Alpes
Wine tasting at a local vineyard or, when the *vendange* intervenes, two bottles of Beaujolais red or white.

CHATEAU DE LA COURONNE
Poitou-Charentes
A bottle of champagne.

CHATEAU DE SAINT PATERNE Normandy
A bottle of the Norman apple liqueur known as pommeau.

CHEZ ODETTE Champagne-Ardenne
A bottle of champagne.

LE COUVENT D'HEREPIAN
Languedoc-Roussillon
A bottle of Château de Raissac.

LE COUVENT DES MINIMES HOTEL & SPA
Provence
Free use of the L'Occitane spa throughout
your stay, plus home-made macaroons or
other treats in your room on arrival.

DOMAINE DE VERCHANT
Languedoc-Roussillon
A bottle of red or white from the hotel
vineyard, and a 10 per cent discount on spa
treatments and massages.

HOTEL CRILLON LE BRAVE Provence
One champagne breakfast for two.

HOTEL DANIEL Paris
Mariage Frères tea, served with Ladurée
macaroons or other sweet treats.

HOTEL KEPPLER Paris
Drinks on arrival, and river-cruise tickets.

HOTEL PARTICULIER MONTMARTRE Paris
A bottle of fine wine.

HOTEL PASTIS St Tropez
A bottle of Provençal rosé.

HOTEL RECAMIER Paris
Two tickets to the Louvre or Musée d'Orsay.

JARDINS SECRETS Languedoc-Roussillon
A bottle of rosé.

LE LODGE KERISPER Brittany
A glass of champagne each and a box of
Breton salted caramels.

LE LOGIS DE PUYGATY Poitou-Charentes
A bottle of sparkling Charlemagne wine.

LA MAISON SUR LA SORGUE Provence
Drinks every night of your stay, and
10 per cent off in the hotel boutique.

LE MAS DE LA ROSE Provence
Wine tasting at a neighbouring vineyard.

MOULIN RENAUDIOTS Burgundy
A pair of tickets to the Musée Rolin in Autun.

LA RESERVE PARIS Paris
Two half-day passes for a nearby spa, usually
€100 each; members staying three nights or
more also get a free treatment each.

LA RESERVE RAMATUELLE St Tropez
A 30-minute spa treatment each.

LES ROSEES Côte d'Azur
A bottle of champagne on arrival.

LES SERVAGES D'ARMELLE Rhône-Alpes
A bottle of Savoie wine.

LA VILLA GALLICI Provence
A bottle of Provençal rosé.

(useful numbers)

DIALLING CODES
France: +33
Drop the 0 from the following area codes when ringing from abroad:
Paris: 01
Northwest: 02
Northeast: 03
Southeast: 04
Southwest: 05

AIRLINES (DOMESTIC)
Airlinair (France: 08 10 47 84 78; www.airlinair.com).
Brit Air (France: 36 54; www.britair.com).
Air France (France: 36 54; www.airfrance.com).

AIRLINES (INTERNATIONAL)
Air France (Australia: 1300 390 190; France: 36 54; UK: 0871 663 3777; US: 1 800 237 2747; www.airfrance.com).
BMI (UK: 0844 848 4888; rest of the world: +44 (0)1332 648181; www.flybmi.com).
BMI Baby (UK: 0905 828 2828; rest of the world: +44 845 810 1100; www.bmibaby.com).
British Airways (Australia: 1300 767 177; France: 08 25 82 54 00; UK: 0844 493 0787; US: 1 800 247 9297; www.ba.com).
EasyJet (France: 08 26 10 33 20; UK: 0905 821 0905; www.easyjet.com).
Ryanair (France: 08 92 78 02 10; UK: 0871 246 0000; www.ryanair.com).

AIRPORTS
Angoulême (+33 (0)5 45 69 88 09; www.aeroport-angouleme-cognac.com).
Biarritz (+33 (0)5 59 43 83 83; www.biarritz.aeroport.fr).
Bordeaux (+33 (0)5 56 34 50 50; www.bordeaux.aeroport.fr).
Brest (+33 (0)2 98 32 01 00; www.airport.cci-brest.fr).
Brussels (+32 (0)2 753 7753; www.brusselsairport.be).
Dinard Saint-Malo (+33 (0)2 99 46 18 46; www.saint-malo.cci.fr).
Geneva (+41 (0)2 27 17 71 11; www.gva.ch).
Lorient (+33 (0)2 97 87 21 50; www.lorient.aeroport.fr).

Lyon Saint-Exupéry (+33 (0)4 26 00 70 07; www.lyon.aeroport.fr).
Marseille (+33 (0)4 42 14 14 14; www.marseille.aeroport.fr).
Montpellier (+33 (0)4 67 20 85 00; www.montpellier.aeroport.fr).
Nantes (+33 (0)2 40 84 80 00; www.nantes.aeroport.fr).
Nice (+33 (0)4 89 88 98 28; www.nice.aeroport.fr).
Paris (+33 (0)1 70 36 39 50; www.aeroportsdeparis.fr).
Rouen (+33 (0)2 35 79 41 00; www.rouen.aeroport.fr).
Toulon-Hyères (France: 08 25 01 83 87; www.toulon-hyeres.aeroport.fr).

FERRY OPERATORS
Brittany Ferries (UK: 0871 244 0744; France: 08 25 82 88 28; www.brittanyferries.com).
Condor Ferries (+44 (0)1305 761551; www.condorferries.co.uk).
LD Lines (UK: 0800 917 1201; France: 08 25 30 43 04; rest of the world: +33 (0)2 32 14 52 09; www.ldlines.com).
P&O Ferries (France: 08 25 12 01 56; UK: 0871 664 5645; rest of the world: +352 34 20 80 82 94; www.poferries.com).
Sea France (UK: 0871 423 7119; rest of the world: +44 845 458 0666; www.seafrance.com).

TRAINS
Eurostar (UK: 0870 518 6186; rest of the world: +44 1233 617575; www.eurostar.com) runs passenger trains through the Channel tunnel.
Eurotunnel (France: 0810 63 03 04; UK: 0844 335 3535; rest of the world: +33 (0)3 21 00 20 61; www.eurotunnel.com). Train services that take you and your car through the Channel tunnel between Folkestone and Calais.
Rail Europe (UK: 0844 848 4064; US: 1 800 622 8600; rest of the world: +44 1732 526700; www.raileurope.com) sells tickets online for pan-European rail journeys, including Auto Train car-by-rail routes.
SNCF (France: 36 35; www.voyages-sncf.com) sells French rail tickets, including TGV services.

MAPS, MOTORING AND MORE
Automobile Association (UK: 0800 085 2721; rest of the world: +44 161 333 0004; www.theaa.com). European

route planning and breakdown cover (for UK residents).
Grande Randonnée (www.grande-randonnee.fr). The
official website for France's network of walking trails.
ViaMichelin (www.viamichelin.com). Continental
route planning.

TAXIS AND TRANSFERS

Cham-Van (France: +33 (0)6 32 24 03 94; rest of the
world: +44 (0)20 8144 6347; www.cham-van.com). Book
transfers from Geneva airport to Megève.
Holiday Taxis (+44 (0)1444 257041; www.holidaytaxis.
com). Book transfers from rail stations and airports.
ResortHoppa (UK: 0871 855 0350; rest of the world: +44
(0)1342 305677; www.resorthoppa.com). This transfers
portal covers Paris, Lyon and Geneva airports.
Taxis de France (www.taxis-de-france.com). Cab firms
can upload their business details to this listings site.

AUTOMOBILES

Avis (France: 08 21 23 07 60; UK: 0844 581 0147;
US: 1 800 331 1212; www.avis.com) offers standard car
and van hire from train stations and airports nationwide.
Elite Rent (Côte d'Azur: +33 (0)4 93 94 61 00; Paris:
+33 (0)1 40 24 24 24; www.eliterent.com) has a fleet of
luxury and sports cars, including 4x4s, available for hire
in Paris and on the Côte d'Azur.
Europcar (France: 08 25 35 83 58; UK: 0871 384 9847;
US: 1 877 940 6900; www.europcar.com) has desks in
most French train stations and airports.
Hertz (France: 08 25 80 09 00; UK: 0870 844 8844; US:
1 800 654 3001; www.hertz.com) operates nationwide,
serving most French airports and train stations.
Platinium Rent (+33 (0)4 93 99 90 63;
www.platinium-ca.com/rent) leases luxury and sports
cars, as well as super cars, on the French Riviera.

BALLOON TOURS

Air Escargot (+33 (0)3 85 87 12 30; www.air-escargot.
com) flies over the Burgundy countryside.
Air Pegasus Montgolfières (+33 (0)2 37 31 01 96;
www.air-pegasus.com) is based south-west of Paris,
organising flights mainly out of châteaux.
Alpes-Montgolfière (+33 (0)3 85 87 12 30; www.
alpes-montgolfiere.fr) offers flights over the Alpine peaks.
Hot Air Balloon Provence (+33 (0)4 90 05 76 77;
www.montgolfiere-provence-ballooning.com) flies over
the Luberon countryside.

HELICOPTER TRANSFERS

Groupe SAF (Dec–Apr: +33 (0)4 79 08 00 91; summer:
+33 (0)4 79 38 48 29; www.saf-helico.com) has a fleet of
34 helicopters in the Alps and on the Riviera.
Jet Systems (France: 08 20 82 06 98; rest of the world:
+33 (0)5 46 43 82 87; www.jet-systems.fr) flies out of
Brittany, the Loire, Poitou-Charentes and Aquitaine.
Whitetracks Helicopters (+44 (0)7796 640841; www.
whitetracks.co.uk) organises transfers, shared or private,
to resorts in the French Alps, Paris, and on the Riviera.

TOURIST BOARDS

Aquitaine (+33 (0)5 56 01 70 00;
www.tourisme-aquitaine.fr).
Brittany (+33 (0)2 99 28 44 30;
www.tourismebretagne.com).
Burgundy (+33 (0)3 80 28 02 80;
www.bourgogne-tourisme.com).
Champagne-Ardenne (+33 (0)3 26 21 85 80;
www.tourisme-champagne-ardenne.com).
Languedoc-Roussillon (+33 (0)4 67 20 02 20;
www.sunfrance.com).
Normandy (+33 (0)2 32 33 79 00;
www.normandie-tourisme.fr).
Paris (www.parisinfo.com).
Poitou-Charentes (+33 (0)5 49 50 10 50;
www.poitou-charentes-vacances.com).
Provence (+33 (0)4 91 13 84 13; www.visitprovence.com).
Rhône-Alpes (+33 (0)4 72 59 21 59;
www.rhonealpes-tourisme.com).
Riviera Côte d'Azur (www.cotedazur-tourisme.com).
St Tropez (www.ot-saint-tropez.com).

LINGERIE AND EROTICA

Agent Provocateur (+44 (0)870 600 0229; www.
agentprovocateur.com). Cutting-edge purveyors of
naughty night attire and burlesque-style basques.
Coco de Mer (UK: +44 (0)20 7836 8882; US: 1 310 652
0311; www.coco-de-mer.co.uk). Luxury massage oils and
grown-up toys crafted from jade and pearls.
Figleaves (UK: 0844 493 2932; US: 1 866 751 2589; rest
of the world: +44 (0)20 3170 0169; www.figleaves.com).
Labels such as Freya and Damaris, delivered to your door.
Myla (+44 (0)870 745 5003; www.myla.com) has a seductive
collection of slinky lingerie and bedtime playthings.
Princesse Tam Tam (+33 (0)1 49 59 21 00; www.
princessetamtam.com). Delectable French lingerie.

(who are Mr & Mrs Smith?)

Our reviewers are a hand-picked panel of people we admire and respect, all of whom have impeccable taste, of course, and can be trusted to report back to us on Smith hotels with total honesty. The only thing we ask of them is that they visit each hotel anonymously with a partner, and on their return, give us the kind of insider lowdown you'd expect from a close friend.

REVIEWERS WHO'S WHO

Valérie Abecassis STYLE SPOTTER
A self-described 'pure Parisienne', Valérie recently celebrated 10 years as a fashion writer for French *Elle*, previously working in radio at major French stations RTL and Europe 1. She travels and socialises constantly and has become adept at sorting fashion gold from dross. She believes there is a distinction, with hotels as with fashion, between cheap flashy copies and the real thing – discreet, well-crafted and authentic. By nature, she is a Mediterranophile but also follows her husband to the Atlantic destinations he prefers.

Lisa Allardice ARTS REPORTER
A press trip to review the six-star hotels of the Seychelles for *Harpers & Queen* spoiled Lisa early in her career. When she isn't being a good *Guardian* journalist, washing out old milk bottles and discussing the state of the NHS, she still loves jetting off to review Mr & Mrs Smith hotels. For her day job as editor of the *Guardian Review*, the only time she leaves her desk in King's Cross is to make the annual pilgrimage to a wet field in Wales for the Hay Festival. She does also get out sometimes to interview the odd writer, such as Martin Amis and Margaret Atwood.

Réda Amalou BOUTIQUE BUILDER
As a partner in AW2, the architectural practice he founded, French architect Réda knows a thing or two about high-end hotel design. His first project, the Nam Hai in Vietnam, has landed him awards and acclaim worldwide, and his work has taken from one end of the globe to the other, experiencing both the heights of luxury and the depths of design hell. Despite journeying far and wide to work on some of the world's most mind-blowing resorts, Réda's favourite place is still his Paris home.

Frédérique Andreani EX-PAT EXTOLLER
As creator of online lifestyle magazine Chic Londres (www.chiclondres.com), Frédérique has fun interviewing people such as Nicole Farhi, Ron Arad, Vincent Cassel, Hélène Darroze and Alastair Campbell, and writes about all things cool in London. She is also UK correspondent for *Le Point*, one of France's leading current affairs magazines, and has recently become a contributor to the relaunched *The Lady*. She was born in Paris, where she studied history and politics, moving to London in 1999.

David Annand MODEL REVIEWER
10 years of writing assignments and seven years of fashion modelling have taken *GQ Style* associate editor David on a pretty comprehensive tour of the world's hotels. In marble-floored palaces in the Arabian desert, and Milanese dives, David, who has modelled for Prada and Rolex, has whiled away many hours watching films dubbed into languages he does not speak, and getting drunk on his own. So it's a welcome change to finally be allowed to take Mrs Smith along for the ride.

Barry Ashworth BEAT POET
Touring with his band (Dub Pistols) and DJing, Barry has circumnavigated the globe multiple times; the highs of his career have taken him to hotel heaven, the lows to rock 'n' roll Babylon. Living out of a suitcase as he plays at top clubs and festivals in exotic locations, he naturally appreciates the finer things, and the small details that make a big difference to where you stay. He has a suitable Mrs Smith, Siobhan Murphy, who also travels the world, executive producing commercials and music videos and searching for unusual locations for her clients.

Oona Bannon CHAIR PERSON
Back in 2002, Oona made her first contribution to Mr & Mrs Smith when, as account director at Bloom, she ran the design project behind the Mr & Mrs Smith brand and our first books. She then turned her attentions to her furniture brand Pinch (www.pinchdesign.com), which she runs with her husband, Russell Pinch. Together, they design and manufacture award-winning contemporary furniture and lighting, which appears on the pages of the international style press, from *Wallpaper** to *Elle Decoration*. Oona's time as an undercover Smith agent has allowed her to fantasise about her own dream brief: a Pinch-designed hotel room.

Jess Cartner-Morley FASHION EDITOR
Although she's been fashion editor of *The Guardian* for a decade, Jess has kept a soft spot for travel writing ever since her first assignment, a week spent 'reviewing' strawberry daiquiris and lobster in the Caribbean. As well as being a regular on the New York/Milan/Paris run, Jess has been to Rome to dine with Valentino, to Shanghai to toast Ferragamo and to Liverpool to shop with the WAGs. The first thing she checks out on checking in is always, always the room-service menu.

Ilse Crawford DESIGN DOYENNE

Alongside her brand consultancy, Ilse heads the design company Studioilse (www.studioilse.com), creating charismatic and long-lasting brands, and designing buildings, furniture and products with positivity. Past projects include the award-winning Inn brand and the Soho House Group. Studioilse is currently working on a guesthouse in Stockholm, a new breed of wellbeing hotels in France and an event space in Hungary, in collaboration with Tadao Ando.

Charlotte Crisp MAGAZINE MAVEN

Having worked for *Cosmopolitan*, *Loaded*, *More*, *Bliss* and *New Woman*, Charlotte has partied with celebs in hotel rooms across the globe in the name of journalism and filed features everywhere from a bed of ice in the Arctic Circle to a yacht moored in Monte Carlo. Charlotte was assistant editor of a women's glossy when she began moonlighting as a Mr & Mrs Smith reviewer; having never gone camping in her life and freely admitting to an obsession with fancy-pants hotels, she says these days her hotel-lust dial remains set firmly to maximum.

Anthony Demetre CHAMPION CHEF

After many years of grind and toil in restaurant and hotel kitchens, Anthony took the plunge in 2006 and, with his business partner Will Smith, opened his own restaurants: Arbutus and, in 2007, Wild Honey, which are among London's most talked-about bistros. As a chef with a passion for quality, Anthony has a keen eye for detail and a great sense of what feels right. And, he says, escaping from the four walls of a kitchen for well-earned rest and recreation with his family is a priority.

Ligia Dias JEWELLER EXTRAORDINAIRE

Owner and designer of the Ligia Dias Colliers jewellery collection (www.ligiadias.com), Ligia specialises in edgy necklaces, stocked at Dover Street Market, whose buyers call her work 'ethereal but very contemporary'. She says she aims to combine raw, almost industrial materials with luxury values. Currently living in Paris, Ligia was born in Switzerland and holds a Portuguese passport.

Simon Gaul GALLIVANTING GENTLEMAN

Born nomadic and brought up sailing the Mediterranean, Simon finally settled in sunny Monaco 17 years ago. Owner of the Travel Bookshop in Notting Hill (www. thetravelbookshop.com), he has written travel guides, and freelances for publications ranging from *The Daily Telegraph* to *Brides*. He has driven from London to Peking, made it through South, Central and North America, and sailed most oceans, stopping in charming fleapits and charmless five-starrers from Micronesia to the Taklimakan Desert, so he has a gimlet eye for a good hotel.

Ian Griffiths JAUNTING JOURNO

Cutting short a promising career at McDonald's, where he was glowingly described as 'average', Ian entered the murky world of journalism. He has since travelled widely, penning pieces on Serbia, Peru, Lebanon, Germany and his beloved home city of Liverpool for *The Guardian* newspaper. Ian has worked for guardian.co.uk for the last six years.

Raphael Ibanez TEAM CAPTAIN

The former France rugby captain began his career in his home town of Dax, made his international debut against Wales in 1996 and went on to win 98 caps for his country. He is the world's most capped player in his position, and has played in three World Cups. He won two Grand Slams with France and two Six Nations tournaments; in the UK, he played for Saracens and then London Wasps. As a broadcaster, he has been a member of the BBC's Six Nations team since 2007. His interest in hotels and interior decoration is well documented – since he visited his native region for Mr & Mrs Smith.

Sarah Maber MEDIA MARVEL

The Times Weekend's assistant editor Sarah Maber began her career as a junior reporter on the *Dorset Evening Echo*, before moving to London and losing her country burr working on *Company*, *Cosmopolitan*, *Marie Claire*, *Red* and *Psychologies*. There she discovered the delights of the press trip and, now, only a bed the size of Liechtenstein and a walk-in wet room will do. She became a mother in 2009, and now intends to introduce young Martha Mae to the world of five-star boutique hotels.

Christine Manfield CULINARY AMBASSADOR

Drawing on the tastes and flavours of many cultures, Christine is a highly regarded chef, food writer, presenter, teacher and gastronomic traveller. She owns the highly acclaimed Sydney's Universal restaurant, previously running East@West in London and Paramount in Sydney.

Her books have spiced up the lives of keen cooks from Melbourne and Mumbai to Manhattan and New Malden. (www.christinemanfield.com).

Mourad Mazouz RESTLESS RESTAURATEUR

Mourad caught the travel bug early on, leaving his native Algeria at 16 and heading for Paris. After a stint in music PR, he spent the next six years on the move, between south-east Asia, the Caribbean and Los Angeles. Back in Paris, in 1998, he launched his first restaurant, Au Bascou, followed by 404, his first authentic North African restaurant, today part of a hip enclave that includes pop-art bar Andy Wahloo and eaterie Derrière. Mourad's London restaurants are the celebrated Momo, and ground-breaking Sketch. He also created Almaz by Momo in Dubai and Momo at the Souk in Beirut, opening September 2010. He still has the travel bug!

Rasmus Michau SOCIAL ENTREPRENEUR

One-time L'Oréal marketing executive Rasmus heads up Hmm!, a creative design company specialising in luxury goods (Cartier, Uniqlo, Diesel) and masterminds some of the most stylish soirées in Paris. Tapping into the trend for cocktail culture, he spearheaded the launch of Blitz Tequila, and is the brains behind bars in Paris and (soon) London and Berlin. With a vast social network, both online and off, Rasmus is a master at creating a buzz, and knows a hotel worth tweeting about when he sees one.

Patricia Michelson CHEESE CHOOSER

In 1991, Patricia started her business in her north London garden shed, when she brought back a wheel of Beaufort from a ski trip. Today she runs La Fromagerie from Highbury, where the original shop is located, and Marylebone's shop and café, with a busy kitchen turning out seasonal food and produce for both (www. lafromagerie.co.uk). Patricia sources all her cheeses from small independent makers, visiting farms and finding new producers herself. She is married to Danny, also her business partner, lives in London, and has two daughters.

Victoria Moore OENOPHILE WRITER

The Guardian wine scribe Victoria says one of the most romantic nights of her life was spent in a hotel less than half a mile from her house, but she does venture further afield, too, investigating wine regions around the world. Her expertise has made her a tricky customer on occasion, sending back room-service tea in Manhattan, and getting behind the bar in Cornwall because the martinis weren't up to scratch. Her book, *How to Drink,* is a guide to everyday enjoyment of the grape and the grain.

Tom Morton CRAFTY CURATOR

A curator at the Hayward Gallery and contributing editor at *Frieze* magazine, Tom's movements in the contemporary-art world have taken him from the seedy glamour of New York's Chelsea Hotel and a converted cinema in Tel Aviv to stately pleasure domes in Sharjah, a former refugee centre in Amsterdam, and what may very well once have been a rabbit hutch in Tokyo.

Kate Pettifer MISS ADVENTURE

Spells as a campsite rep, ski guide, and crew on a tall ship mean that Kate knows the travel industry inside as well as out. These days she prefers to write about it, indulging a hankering for adventure (skiing, diving, bobsleighing), with recovery time in hip hotels. She has penned for the good (*The Sunday Times Travel Magazine*, *The Daily Telegraph*, *Reader's Digest*), the bad (*International Tanker Review*) and the healthy (*Zest, Health & Fitness*). Loves: freshly cooked breakfast. Hates: lifts with wall carpet. Always packs: a swimsuit, because you should never let a good pool pass you by.

Ruth Phillips HARMONIOUS WORDSMITH

As an oft-touring cellist, Ruth has complained about the noise in self-catering cottages, pubs and palaces. As a writer, she has searched for the Parmesan grater in city apartments and châteaux. As a walker, she has slept in tents, tea-houses and spas. She lives in a semi-restored, half-ruined hamlet in Provence with her husband, the painter Julian Merrow-Smith, their three cats and, soon, an adopted baby from Mali. Ruth is currently finishing a memoir and thinking about family-friendly retreats (www. meanwhilehereinfrance.blogspot.com).

Linda Pilkington SCENT SEEKER

As the founder of Ormonde Jayne fine perfumery (www. ormondejayne.com), Linda has an unrivalled nose for beauty and rarity. And, having lived in the bushveld of South Africa, run a soya farm on the Argentine sierras and opened a boutique hotel in Rio de Janeiro, she knows a thing or two about the power of consoling weary travellers with the finest comforts. Between flower-finding missions to Madagascar and Tahiti, she lives in leafy Primrose Hill with her husband and two young sons.

Rufus Purdy WORD WIZARD
A former editor at Mr & Mrs Smith, Rufus began his career dressed as a giant banana, handing out flyers at Covent Garden Tube station. Following a stint as junior sub-editor at *Harper's Bazaar*, he was pigeonholed for life by working at *Condé Nast Traveller*, and has since claimed free holidays as travel editor at *Psychologies* and on jaunts for *The Observer* and *The Sunday Times Travel Magazine*. Highlights of his post-Smith career include learning how to butcher a pig and penning erotic fiction for *The Times*. He is currently working on a novel.

Nigel Tisdall GLOSSY GLOBETROTTER
One wet Monday morning in 1985, Nigel's world-spanning career began when he went to London's Liverpool Street station and caught a train to Hong Kong. Since then, he's been roaming all over the globe, writing principally for *The Daily Telegraph* and its luxury supplement, *Ultratravel*. Currently travel editor of *Marie Claire*, he is constantly checking into hotels. The best? 'A tent in Antarctica – until it blew away.' The worst? 'A candlelit lodge in the Peruvian Amazon, where I just happened to spot a cockroach on my toothbrush…'

Philippe Trétiack SERIOUS SCRIBE
Special correspondent for French *Elle* and regular columnist in *Beaux Arts* magazine and *Elle Décoration*, Philippe is a writer, architect and sometime agitator. His confrontational journalistic style has taken him from zones of construction to territories of destruction, from Bombay to Caracas, from investigating the Antimafia in Italy to covering the legacies of Chernobyl and Hiroshima. For Mr & Mrs Smith, he braved the cobbled squares and streets of Nîmes.

MR & MRS SMITH TEAM

CEO **James Lohan** is one half of the couple behind Mr & Mrs Smith. James' first company, Atomic, created the infamous Come Dancing parties and club promotions. He built on this success by designing and producing events for clients such as Finlandia vodka and Wonderbra, then went on to co-found the White House bar, restaurant and members' club in London. Since publishing Mr & Mrs Smith's first book, James has visited almost 1,000 hotels and, now a father of two, he's become a keen advocate of our child-friendly hotel collection, Smith & Kids.

Chief technical officer **Tamara Heber-Percy**, co-founder of Mr & Mrs Smith, graduated from Oxford with a degree in languages, then left the UK for Brazil, where she launched an energy drink. She went on to work at one of the UK's top marketing agencies as a consultant for brands such as Ericsson and Honda and in business development for Europe, the Middle East and Africa. She left in 2002 to run her own company, the County Register – an exclusive introductions agency – and to launch Mr & Mrs Smith.

Asia Pacific co-founder and managing director **Simon Westcott** grew up in London, but has called Melbourne home for more than 10 years. A graduate of Oxford and Indiana universities, he is a former global publisher and director of Lonely Planet, and has been a contributing editor for *Travel + Leisure Australia/New Zealand*. He has travelled extensively in Australia, NZ, Asia, Europe and North America, always and only with a single soft leather holdall from Gurkha.

Chief financial officer **Edward Orr** has worked in investment banking and managed companies in their early stages for more than a decade. As a result, he has stayed in hotels on every continent – and, generally, he doesn't like them. This makes him qualified not only to look after Mr & Mrs Smith's finances, but also to have penned the odd review. He can confirm that Smith hotels really are special enough to be a treat, even for the most jaded corporate traveller.

Publishing director **Andrew Grahame** launched the UK's first corporate-fashion magazine in 1990. After moving into catwalk shows and events, he transferred his talents from fashion to finance, launching *Small Company Investor* magazine. He started a promotions company in 1993 and, after a spell as a restaurant/bar owner in Chelsea, turned his hand to tourism in 1997, creating the award-winning London Pass and New York Pass, which give visitors access to the cities' attractions. With Juliet, Andrew co-produced and co-presented our TV series *The Smiths' Hotels for 2* for the Discovery network.

MR & MRS SMITH IN LONDON

Associate director **Laura Mizon** spent her younger years in Spain and, after graduating from Manchester University, returned to her childhood home to work for four years at an independent record label in Madrid, promoting the emerging Spanish hip-hop movement. When she joined Mr & Mrs Smith as a freelancer in 2004, it soon became clear that Laura was to play a key role. She is now responsible for building relationships with like-minded brands, and all things operational.

Editor-in-chief **Juliet Kinsman**, part of the original team, helped create Mr & Mrs Smith's distinctive voice and can be caught leaking travel secrets in numerous publications, from *The Observer* to *The New York Times*, as well as on TV and radio. Juliet's woken up in more stylish bedrooms than a high-class harlot, and reviewed more hip hotels and holiday houses than most people have sent postcards. Born in Canada, she's had stints in Africa, America, Greece and India, but her heart belongs to Kensal Green, and she celebrates her West London neighbourhood on her blog, park-life.org.

Managing editor **Anthony Leyton** joined Smith in 2007 to provide short-term help launching a handful of hotels in Asia, and has been an editorial fixture ever since. Before being embraced by the Smith family, he worked for *The Independent* and has penned pieces for publications both top-drawer (*The Daily Telegraph*) and top-shelf (*Fiesta*). He has had a love of travel ever since he found bullet holes in the walls of a hotel room in New Orleans.

Contributing editor **Sophie Dening** was one of Mr & Mrs Smith's founder editors, co-piloting the first two hotel collections with Juliet and recently returning to edit this very book. As a freelance journalist, she specialises in UK travel and restaurants, contributing to *High Life*, *Square Meal*, *Country & Town House* and *The Daily Telegraph*, for whom she seeks out the best new restaurants, food pubs, beach cafés and hotel dining rooms. When she isn't asking chefs for their foraging secrets or ordering another half of bitter shandy somewhere off the A49, Sophie likes eating figs in the South of France and rambling in East London, where she lives and works.

Associate editor **Lucy Fennings** cut her travel teeth early; as daughter of a hotel PR, she visited far-flung flophouses from French châteaux to Ethiopian *tukuls*. After a year in Dubai (working on *Emirates Woman* magazine and enjoying the kind of dives that require a wetsuit), Lucy honed her production skills at Legalease in London, before exploring Asia. Mr & Mrs Smith found her at *Harper's Bazaar*, keeping her finger on fashion's pulse and sharpening her editorial knife on hapless hotel PR copy. She has been a driving force in making the Smith Travel Blog an award-winner.

Production executive **Jasmine Darby** has been with Smith since she graduated from Manchester University with an art history degree in 2006. Our reviewers know her as the reassuring voice on the end of the phone in a crisis (whether it's lost passports or unexpected stomach bugs), but her areas of expertise are far more wide-ranging. Jasmine ensures that the process of introducing new hotels into the Smith collection runs smoothly, dispatching our reviewers across the world, and helping with every aspect of book production.

Editorial assistant **Sarah Jappy** made her writing debut penning city guides for virginmedia.com, reviews for *Itchy,* fashion and beauty features at *Closer* and accounts of crime and punishment for the *South London Press*. Along with expert opinions on topics including the marzipan-to-pastry ratio of the perfect almond croissant, and where to source the best moules marinières, Sarah has brought Smith 12 years of Irish-dancing prowess.

Editorial assistant **Caroline Lewis** joined the Mr & Mrs Smith team from World Travel Guide, where she wrote about some of the world's most exotic and glamorous destinations, based in perhaps the ugliest suburb off the M25. Her love of travel began when she disappeared into South America's jungles at the age of 19, much to the (financial and spiritual) displeasure of her father. Now 'her thing' can be described as baking, and she arguably makes the best cupcakes this side of Greenwich Village.

Designer **Gareth Thomas** joined Mr & Mrs Smith in 2009 to become the visual mastermind behind all things Smith-branded. Previously, he worked at London design agency Boston Studio, bringing his graphical flair to luxury brands such as Daylesford Organic, Bamford and Soane. Today, he alternates between creating beautiful layouts for Smith's books and website, and hanging out in the kitchen creating freshly baked surprises for the team.

Head of hotel collections **Katy McCann** grew up in the south of Spain and later became editor of *In Madrid*, the largest English-language publication in the city. She was tracked down by Mr & Mrs Smith in 2004 to develop and expand our hotel collections, which fitted in perfectly with her love of travel and her multilingual skills. Having seen more than 2,000 hotels in the past six years, Katy is probably the world's most qualified person to ensure each property is the perfect addition to the Smith collection.

Hotel collections manager **Mary Garvin**'s earliest travel memory is the 22-hour drive from her native Brooklyn to Florida, packed in sardine-tight among a month's worth of luggage, her parents and five siblings – imagine her delight when she one day flew first class. After graduating from McGill University in Montreal, Mary moved to London where she's lived since, first pulling pints, then organising company travel at interior design firm, Studio Reed and, most recently, scoping out stylish Smith properties across the globe.

Head of hotel relations **Peggy Picano-Nacci** was born in Indonesia and grew up in France. The past 15 years have seen her earn an unrivalled understanding of what makes a great boutique hotel tick. A former sales manager at the Dorchester and an alumnus of Small Luxury Hotels of the World, where she was responsible for the French, Spanish and Portuguese territories, she also makes use of an alarming array of languages when working closely with our member hotels.

Hotel relations manager **Maggie Stack** was born in Chicago but considers Atlanta – where she lived from the age of 10 – her home. She caught the travel bug in 2005 while backpacking around Southeast Asia, and the one year she planned on spending in London swiftly became five. Before joining Smith in 2008, Maggie donned the mantle of head of reservations at Travel Intelligence, and now makes the most of her time exploring Europe and juggling an ever-growing stream of correspondence with the 650+ hotels in the Smith collection.

Head of PR and marketing **Aline Keuroghlian** has worked in travel for 15 years. Stints at Armani and London's quirky Sir John Soane's Museum helped cultivate her love of stylish things. After university came several years of guiding professionals across Italy for niche tour operator ATG Oxford, which made use of her maternal heritage. Nowadays, she puts both her sense and sensibility to work by dealing with some of the most beautiful hotels in the world, as featured in Mr & Mrs Smith's collections.

PR and marketing executive **Sabine Zetteler**, having been born to Finnish and Dutch parents, was always destined to work in a cosmopolitan setting. Her first job was international sales manager at London fashion house Belle & Bunty, jetting between fashion weeks in Milan, Paris, London and Los Angeles. She then worked for the BBC, before emailing her CV to us while on a trip around India. A few days after her return, she found herself sitting at a new desk contemplating her next adventure: promoting Mr & Mrs Smith around the world.

Head of relationship marketing **Amber Spencer-Holmes** may be a Londoner, but she has cosmopolitan credentials, having lived in Sydney and Paris before reading French and English at King's College London. Before joining Mr & Mrs Smith, Amber made waves in the music industry, running a number of well-respected record labels. She is married to our TuneSmith columnist Rob Wood.

Membership and marketing executive **Emma Graves** fell in love with travelling long before graduating in history of art from UEA. She came to Mr & Mrs Smith from a background of managing fundraising, looking after the cultured (at the Tate and the British Museum) and the creative (University of the Arts London alumni). When not seeking out the best shopping and travel offers for Smith members, she can be found checking out exhibitions or listening to her favourite bands – usually in a muddy field.

Smith & Friends manager **Natasha Shafi** acquired an encyclopaedic travel knowledge working at Notting Hill's famed Travel Bookshop and a disarming charm from her role as marketing manager for a Middle Eastern publishing house. Although she came to Mr & Mrs Smith to take charge of office management, she quickly showed she was capable of much more, and now looks after our collection of stylish self-catering properties (see page 290).

US operations executive **Chloe Smith** developed a hunger for travel long before she finished her law degree. Having explored various corners of the world – highlights include living and working in Phnom Penh, discovering the jungles of Sabah and beach-hopping down Mexico's Pacific surf coast – she is now concentrating her efforts on bringing Smith's boutique-hotel expertise to North and South America. During her downtime, she plots her dream trip: conquering the Silk Road overland from Istanbul to Beijing.

Online manager **Patsie Muan-ngiew** left academia with a postgrad marketing diploma under her arm and went straight into the world of advertising and media buying. When she's not maintaining and improving the Smith website, she can be found in front of a sewing machine creating her latest fashion masterpiece. However, we still think that Patsie's greatest achievement is her turn as a Thai jailbird in *Bridget Jones: The Edge of Reason*.

Analyst, PPC and affiliate manager **Andrew Leung** was born in the cosmopolitan city of Hong Kong. Early exposure to varied cultures inspired his interest in travel, leading him to Switzerland where he studied international hospitality management at the Ecole Hôtelière de Lausanne. Working with Mandarin Oriental, Design Hotels and the ilk gave Andrew a taste of boutique hotel life, making him perfect to work on Smith's US expansion. The team quickly realised Andrew had become indispensable, et voilà: he now plays an essential part in shaping the Smith's web strategy.

Head of the Smith Travel Team, **Rebecca Martin** has worked in travel for more than a decade, and now uses skills she learned from her psychology degree to motivate Smith's 20-strong team of consultants. Rebecca has worked as head of global account management for Small Luxury Hotels of the World, and spent eight years at Kuoni, managing the luxury World Class department, where she became a bona fide globetrotter, road-testing luxurious holidays ranging from idyllic Indian Ocean beach retreats to action-packed African safaris.

MR & MRS SMITH IN MELBOURNE

Associate director **Rodrigo Calvo** grew up in Bolivia and hit the road days after his 18th birthday to study marketing in Austin, work as an ad man in Boston, and enjoy island seclusion in Elba, before heading back to South America to launch a marketing consultancy. Rodrigo crossed paths with Mr & Mrs Smith while doing an MBA in London, and set to work expanding the brand in the US. Luckily for Smith, his next attack of wanderlust coincided with the opening of our Melbourne office, and he hotfooted it over to Australia to be part of the Asia-Pacific launch team.

VP of hotel relations **Debra McKenzie** has lived and breathed hospitality throughout her working life, with time spent in front-of-house and managerial roles at the Ritz-Carlton and Hayman Island Resort. After refining her palate in the Sydney restaurant world, Debra went on to globetrot for Kiwi Collection from Australia to Europe – perfect training for her role as head hotel-hunter in Mr & Mrs Smith's Asia-Pacific office. She also flexes her muscles as a photographer and stylist, working in Vancouver and Sydney with blue-chip clients.

Editorial manager **Sophie Davies** grew up in Turkey, Indonesia and Iran, exiting stage left during the revolution. After studying at Oxford, she worked as a researcher for Japanese TV, before swapping bento for boy bands with a features gig at *Just Seventeen*. Having freelanced for *Time Out* and *The Telegraph*, she went on to a six-year stint at *Elle Decoration*, where, as assistant editor, Sophie learned how to spot a good table at 20 paces, and honed her hotel-appreciation skills. When Smith's Melbourne office beckoned, it was time to leave London (and her beloved Arsenal) for pastures new.

Asia-Pacific hotel relations manager **Samantha Anderson** can spot a stylish stay from a country mile. Her career has taken her from Sheraton Hotels to Atomic Events, where she organised parties under the guidance of James Lohan, making her one of the original few present at the birth of Mr & Mrs Smith. After a stretch as a chef at a hotel restaurant in Tuscany, Sam was lured back to Smith to research hotels down under for our Australia/New Zealand collection and to join the new team in her home town of Melbourne.

(where in the world)

THE GLOBAL MR & MRS SMITH HOTEL COLLECTION

ICELAND
UNITED KINGDOM
SWEDEN
ESTONIA
CANADA
DENMARK
IRELAND
NETHERLANDS
GERMANY
CZECH REPUBLIC
BELGIUM AUSTRIA
SWITZERLAND
UNITED STATES
FRANCE
MONACO
SPAIN
ITALY
GREECE
PORTUGAL
TURKEY
CYPRUS
MOROCCO
BHUTAN
CHINA
MEXICO
INDIA
LAOS
THAILAND
UNITED ARAB EMIRATES
CAMBODIA
GUATEMALA
VIETNAM
CARIBBEAN
SINGAPORE
BELIZE
MALAYSIA
BRAZIL
INDONESIA
ZAMBIA
SOUTH AFRICA
INDIAN OCEAN
AUSTRALIA
URUGUAY
ARGENTINA
NEW ZEA

www.mrandmrssmith.com

ASIA

Bhutan Paro, Thimphu
Cambodia Siem Reap
China Beijing, Hong Kong, Shanghai, Yangshuo
India Karnataka, Kerala
Indian Ocean Maldives, Mauritius, Seychelles
Indonesia Bali, Jakarta, Lombok, Sumba, Yogyakarta
Laos Luang Prabang
Malaysia Langkawi
Singapore Singapore
Thailand Bangkok, Chiang Mai, Chiang Rai, Hua Hin, Khao Lak, Khao Yai, Koh Phi Phi, Koh Samui, Krabi, Phuket
Vietnam Nha Trang

AUSTRALASIA

Australia Adelaide, Barossa Valley, Blue Mountains, Brisbane, Byron Bay, Canberra, Central Coast, Central Highlands, Clare Valley, Daylesford, Grampians, Great Barrier Reef, Great Ocean Road, Hobart, Hunter Valley, Kangaroo Island, Kimberley, Launceston, Lord Howe Island, Margaret River, Melbourne, Ningaloo Reef, Northern Beaches, Port Douglas, Red Centre, Southern Forests, Sydney, Top End
New Zealand Auckland, Bay of Islands, Hawke's Bay, Kaikoura, Lake Taupo, Queenstown, Wairarapa, Wellington

EUROPE

Austria Vienna, Zell Am See
Belgium Antwerp, Brussels
Cyprus Limassol
Czech Republic Prague, Tábor
Denmark Copenhagen
Estonia Tallinn
France Beaujolais, Bordeaux, Brittany, Burgundy, Côte d'Azur, Chamonix, Champagne-Ardenne, Courchevel, Dordogne, Languedoc-Roussillon, Normandy, Paris, Pays Basque, Poitou-Charentes, Provence, Rhône-Alpes, St Tropez, Tignes Les Brévières, Vaucluse
Germany Berlin, Munich
Greece Athens, Kefalonia, Ithaca, Mykonos, Santorini
Iceland Reykjavík
Ireland County Carlow, County Meath, Dublin
Italy Aeolian Islands, Amalfi Coast, Capri, Florence, Milan, Piedmont, Puglia, Rome, Sardinia, Sicily, Sorrento, South Tyrol, Tuscany, Umbria, Venice
Monaco Monte Carlo
Netherlands Amsterdam
Portugal Cascais, Douro Valley, Lisbon
Spain Barcelona, Basque Country, Cadiz Province, Córdoba, Costa de la Luz, Empordà, Extremadura, Granada, Ibiza, Madrid, Mallorca, Marbella, Ronda, San Sebastián, Seville Province, Tarifa, Valencia
Sweden Stockholm
Switzerland Adelboden, Verbier
Turkey Istanbul
United Kingdom Argyll, Bath, Belfast, Berkshire, Birmingham, Brecon Beacons, Brighton, Cardigan Bay, Carmarthen Bay, Chilterns, Cornwall, Cotswolds, County Durham, Devon, Dorset, East Sussex, Edinburgh, Gloucestershire, Hampshire, Harrogate, Inverness, Kent, Lake District, Liverpool, London, Manchester, Norfolk, Northamptonshire, North Yorkshire, Somerset, Oxfordshire, Peak District, Pembrokeshire, Powys, Snowdonia, Suffolk, Trossachs, Vale of Glamorgan, West Sussex, Wester Ross, Wiltshire, Worcestershire

REST OF THE WORLD

Argentina Buenos Aires, Córdoba, Mendoza, Salta
Belize Ambergris Caye, Cayo, Placencia
Brazil Bahia, Rio de Janeiro, Santa Catarina
Canada Montreal, Toronto
Caribbean Antigua & Barbuda, Barbados, Grenada, Jamaica, Mustique, St Barths, St Lucia, Turks & Caicos
Guatemala Flores
Mexico Colima, Jalisco, Mexico City, Puebla, Riviera Maya, Yucatán
Morocco Atlas Mountains, Essaouira, Marrakech, Ouarzazate
South Africa Cape Town, Garden Route & Winelands, Hermanus, Johannesburg, Kruger, Madikwe, Western Limpopo
United Arab Emirates Dubai
United States Austin, Berkshires, Big Sur, Boston, Hamptons, Litchfield Hills, Los Angeles, Miami, Napa Valley, New York, Palm Springs, Portland, San Diego, San Francisco, Smoky Mountains, Sonoma County, Washington DC
Uruguay Punta del Este
Zambia Lower Zambezi

(bit on the side)

Visit our online shop and you'll find all you need to complete your escapes – or remember them by. We don't just create boutique-hotel bibles: our sexy music compilations will soundtrack your weekends; a little black-leather luxury will enhance your passports and luggage. At Mr & Mrs Smith, we're all about making the very most of your time away...

JOIN THE CLUB

With this book, you're already a BlackSmith member for six months, and entitled to all sorts of benefits (see pages 4–5 for details). Treat yourself to even more with an upgrade: SilverSmith gets you four per cent back from each booking towards your next hotel stay. You also get half-price deals at new Smith hotels, and Last-Minute Club discounts of over 40 per cent. Become a GoldSmith, and we'll handle hotel, flight, theatre and restaurant bookings – we'll even arrange someone to feed your pets while you're away. You'll get automatic room upgrades at Smith hotels whenever available, free airport lounge access, exclusive Eurostar fares, as well as five per cent back in loyalty credit. And much more, including – ahem – essential black leather extras...

NOT JUST ABOUT PRETTY PLACES

Browse our online boutique and discover elegant travel essentials for globetrotting sybarites:

• How's about a heavyweight black brushed-cotton bathrobe embroidered in gold? Hugh Hefner, we're standing by for your order; £85

• Whet your wanderlust with an oversized, sleekly bound, special Smith edition of the prestigious and authoritative *The Times Reference Atlas of the World*; £49

• A pair of leather luggage tags or a passport holder, designed exclusively for Mr & Mrs Smith by Bill Amberg, ensures your packing has panache; £49

FIVE BOOKS, HUNDREDS OF STYLISH HOTELS, ENDLESS INSPIRATION

Whether you're looking for a romantic spa retreat, a cosy inn or a blow-out beach hideaway, Smith's hotel guides signpost you to the most ravishing stays around the world. Each is, as ever, a capsule kit for an effortless escape, beginning with that all-important BlackSmith membership card. Other guidebooks, as pictured from left to right, include:

- *European Cities*
- *European Coast & Country*
- *UK/Ireland Volume 2*
- *Australia/New Zealand*

TUNE IN AND SWITCH OFF

Essential when you're lounging in a sumptuous suite or hitting the road, Smith CDs make the ideal aural aphrodisiac. Our four *Something for the Weekend* albums move from jazz-funk to soul via sexy rock riffs. The brand-new *In Bed With…* is an inspired romp through a genre-hopping array of the classic and the contemporary, with 16 tracks personally picked by art, fashion, media and music luminaries. This album also supports housing and homelessness charity, Shelter.

THE GIFT THAT KEEPS ON GIVING

Gift vouchers have never been more seductive: treat someone to a stay at any hotel in our collection, with a Mr & Mrs Smith *Get a Room!* gift card. Sleekly packaged in a slim black box, it's perfect for surprising your partner, family or friends – they might even invite you along.

shop.mrandmrssmith.com

BlackSmith, SilverSmith and GoldSmith members get exclusive discounts when purchasing anything from the Mr & Mrs Smith shop. Retail therapy, indeed.

(applause)

thank you

Adrian Houston and Luke White for their inspiring interior shots and landscape photography, William Scott, Adrian's assistant, Susi Coben, his PA, and Hasselblad cameras; Bloom for creating the brand, and for making this book fit to grace the most stylish of coffee tables, with special thanks to Ben White; Ed Bussey, Peter Clements, Paul Portz and Ian Taylor for their strategic insight; Peter Osborne and Sam Millar of Osborne & Little for the beautiful wallpaper prints; Christopher Collier; Frédérique Sarfati, Didier Férat and all at Place des Editeurs; Clive, George, John, Keith and Mark at EMC Ltd; Ian Johnson and his colleagues at Advanced Card Bureau Ltd; Getty Images and iStockphoto for supplementing our destination guide photography; Frédéric Comtet, and the team at Hôtel Particulier Montmartre for their help with the cover; Eurostar, especially Laure Devos; Portfolio Books and Hallmark for getting this book to you; all our stockists; Lynton and his team at D3R for their web wizardry; and the Mr & Mrs Smith Travel Team for taking all your calls. Last, and far from least, everyone who has helped make this France collection a reality: Mary Garvin and Katy McCann for tireless hotel-hunting; all our featured hotels; our reviewers for telling their tales; our wordsmiths Lucy Fennings, Sarah Jappy, Caroline Lewis and Kate Pettifer; David Annand, Jess Cartner-Morley, Patricia Michelson and Victoria Moore for sharing their expertise; Gareth Thomas for his dedication and inspiration designing this book; Jasmine Darby for bringing it all together; and, of course, all the 'other halves' who accompanied reviewers, or provided support and encouragement.

Mr & Mrs Smith

(index)

To book any of the hotels featured, visit www.mrandmrssmith.com

(the small print)

Editor-in-chief Juliet Kinsman
Managing editor Anthony Leyton
Editor Sophie Dening
Contributing editors Lucy Fennings, Sarah Jappy,
Caroline Lewis, Kate Pettifer
Design Gareth Thomas
Art direction Bloom (www.bloom-design.com)
Production Jasmine Darby
Project management Laura Mizon
Font designer Charles Stewart and Co
Wallpaper Osborne & Little
Reprographics EMC Ltd
Printed and bound by C and C Printing. This book is printed on paper
from a sustainable source.
ISBN 978-0-9544964-9-4

Photography Cover (Hôtel Particulier Montmartre), destination images
on pages 130–132, 145, 205 and 247, double page 62–63, and all
hotel images shot by Adrian Houston (www.adrianhouston.co.uk),
except: Bastide Saint Mathieu 72–74, Cap Estel, Les Rosées 88, 90,
91 stairs image, Hotel Pastis 278–280, Les Servages d'Armelle – all
by Luke White; Bastide Saint Mathieu 70–71, Cap d'Antibes Beach
Hotel, Hôtel Crillon le Brave 218–219, 221–222, Jardins Secrets 121
spa image and 122 bottom left, Hotel Pastis 276–277, Les Rosées 89,
91 bathroom image, 92 pool image, La Réserve Ramatuelle – all
courtesy of the hotels. Additional photography provided by Getty
Images and iStockphoto.

First published in 2010 by Spy Publishing Ltd, 2nd floor,
334 Chiswick High Road, London W4 5TA.

British Library Cataloguing-In-Publication data. A catalogue record
of this book is available from the British Library.

Mr & Mrs Smith
2nd floor, 334 Chiswick High Road
London W4 5TA
Telephone: +44 (0)20 8987 6970
Fax: +44 (0)20 8987 4300
Email: info@mrandmrssmith.com

Disclaimer
Please be advised that opening times and room availability of hotels
will vary from time to time; users of this book are advised to reserve
accommodation well in advance. All rates given are inclusive of tax
and do not include breakfast, unless specified. Contact details are
liable to change. Opinions expressed in this book are those of
the individual reviewers and do not represent the opinions of the
publishers. The publishers shall not be liable for deficiencies in
service, quality or health and safety at any particular hotel. All other
complaints or claims for redress must be made directly to the hotel
concerned. Although the publishers have made all reasonable
endeavours to ensure that the information contained in this guide is
accurate at the time of going to press, they shall not be liable for any
loss, expense, damage, disappointment or other inconvenience caused,
in whole or in part, by reliance on such information. If accidental
errors appear in print, the publishers will apply the corrections in
the following edition of this publication. The user of the information
does so at his or her own risk. The publishers are not in any way
responsible for the conditions of the hotels, venues or services, or
third-party acts or omissions at any hotel, venue or service.

Hotels
The hotels featured in Mr & Mrs Smith have paid a fee towards
the management of the membership and marketing programme
conducted by Spy Publishing Ltd. Inclusion is by invitation only;
hotels cannot buy their way into the collection. Mr & Mrs Smith is
funded by private investment.

Membership terms and conditions
Member offers for Mr & Mrs Smith cardholders are subject to
availability and may be changed at any time. The publishers cannot
accept responsibility in cases where a hotel changes ownership and
discontinues offers promised to cardholders by previous hotel
owners. Cardholder offers are valid once per booking made. If
two cardholders share a room in a hotel, they are entitled to
one instance of the offer only. The Smith membership card is
non-transferable and may be used only by the card's signatory.
Holders of the membership card recognise and accept that they
visit any hotel voluntarily and entirely at their own risk.

Mr & Mrs Smith (Asia-Pacific)
Suite 1-C, 205–207 Johnston Street, Fitzroy
Melbourne, VIC 3065, Australia
Telephone: +61 (0)3 9419 6671
Fax: +61 (0)3 9419 6673
Email: info@mrandmrssmith.com.au